D0892041

*oral communication
in the secondary school
classroom*

oral communication in the secondary school classroom

OLIVER W. NELSON
University of Washington

DOMINIC A. LARUSSO
University of Oregon

Prentice-Hall, Inc.
Englewood Cliffs, New Jersey

The frontispiece is by courtesy of Seattle Public Schools,
Shoreline Public Schools, and Blanchet High School, Seattle.

PRENTICE-HALL INTERNATIONAL, INC., *London*
PRENTICE-HALL OF AUSTRALIA, PTY. LTD., *Sydney*
PRENTICE-HALL OF CANADA, LTD., *Toronto*
PRENTICE-HALL OF INDIA PRIVATE LIMITED, *New Delhi*
PRENTICE-HALL OF JAPAN, INC., *Tokyo*

©1970 by

PRENTICE-HALL, INC.
Englewood Cliffs, N.J.

Library of Congress Catalog Card No.: 70-87263

13-638403-X

Current printing (last digit)
10 9 8 7 6 5 4 3 2 1

Printed in the United States of America

ERRATA

ORAL COMMUNICATION IN THE SECONDARY SCHOOL CLASSROOM
Nelson and LaRusso
First Printing

PAGE

39   line three should read:

following five variables, included in a widely used listening test,[6]

168   line twelve should read:

Because of their flexibility, they are most likely to yield direct,

This book is dedicated to teachers
and students whose interactions help
create the marvelous world of learning.

preface

This textbook is concerned with the basic and related problems of teaching and learning. *It views communication as central to the teaching-learning experience, both a means and an end of learning.*

Miller tells us, "Perceiving, learning, and remembering are all modified by the associative habits built up through communication."[1] Mead states, "We must regard mind . . . as arising and developing within the social process, within the empirical matrix of social interaction."[2] Lindgren asserts, "The extent to which a teacher can help students develop insight and understanding regarding their own behavior as individuals and as a group depends to a great degree on the effectiveness of classroom communication. Good communication is needed if students are to understand what they are doing."[3]

Our major premise, therefore, is that *the quality of teaching and learning in the classroom is fundamentally affected by the extent and*

---

[1]George A. Miller, *Language and Communication* (New York: McGraw-Hill Book Company, Inc., 1951), p. 221.

[2]George H. Mead, *Mind, Self and Society* (Chicago: University of Chicago Press, 1934), p. 133.

[3]Henry C. Lindgren, *Educational Psychology in the Classroom* (3rd. ed.) (New York: John Wiley & Sons, Inc., 1967), p. 153.

nature of communication which takes place there. Indeed, as Lindgren points out: "The education process can be viewed as a vast and complex sequence of problem-solving experience. In such problem-solving, more communication is desired, not less."[4]

This work, moreover, views oral-aural processes as basic and strategic modes of comunication; it recognizes speaking and listening not only as the principal mediators of information, but as primary agents for formulating thought, organizing and intergrating knowledge, and building desirable self-regarding concepts and mature social attitudes. In short, it recognizes oral-aural communication as central to most teaching-learning processes. And from this major postulate the textbook derives its central thesis: namely, that, *regardless of subject matter being taught, whatever is done to improve the quality of oral communication in the classroom is likely to produce corresponding improvement in the amount and calibre of learning which ensues.* This view in no way minimizes the importance of reading, writing, observing, and direct experience as modes of learning. It suggests, however, that, in addition to being basic, oral-aural procedures may supplement and expedite such modes of learning.

Let it be understood that *this work is not a plea for more speech in the classroom.* As a matter of fact, in some instances what is needed is less, not more speech. What is sought is *better* communication, more careful attention to the strategies of oral-aural communication in the classroom. In short, this textbook calls for the guidance of the oral processes in teaching and learning in ways that promote optimal communication. Let it also be noted that stressing improvement of oral-aural communication in the general classroom as an object, as well as a medium of learning, should by no means be regarded as a substitute for basic speech instruction provided in classes designated for that purpose, but rather as an opportunity for reinforcing speech learning initiated in such classes. Both approaches are needed in today's schools in which a basic objective is the improvement of communication.

Reflecting an awareness of the important role oral communication plays in the learning process, current textbooks on teaching methods provide some helpful guidelines for using speech activities in the classroom. Of necessity, perhaps, much of their coverage of this subject is quite general and little more than suggestive in nature. To secure treatment in depth of this important aspect and means of education, one

---

[4]*Ibid.,* p. 337.

must turn to specific sources in the field of speech. This field, however, like many others, has become extremely broad, increasingly specialized, and, in some aspects, highly technical. These trends have tended to complicate the task of the classroom teacher who seeks meaningful and practicable answers to a host of questions regarding the use of speech in the classroom. It is the purpose of this textbook, therefore, to deal directly with this problem by presenting, in a non-technical fashion, concepts, principles, and methods concerning oral communication and its application to teaching and learning.

Although it makes reference to teacher speech standards, this textbook is not concerned specifically with the teacher's personal speech skills. Rather, as indicated above, its chief interest lies in the improvement of teaching and learning by focusing attention on *speaking and listening as means of pupil development and instruments of learning.* Therefore, while the content deals with oral communication, its orientation is essentially pedagogical. It is intended to be used as a basic textbook for speech, English, or communication service courses having to do with teacher preparation, or as a supplementary textbook for certain professional education courses. And although the book is designed primarily for use in preparing secondary school teachers, its basic principles and many of its suggested activities may be readily adapted to the needs of intermediate classroom teachers.

Methodologically, the approaches to teaching-learning stressed in this work are largely student-centered, with primary emphasis upon securing student involvement through problem-solving and discovery procedures. It recognizes the importance of sensing and meeting individual needs of pupils and creating an environment wherein pupils may grow toward becoming self-respecting, socially mature individuals.

ACKNOWLEDGMENTS

Much of the substance of this textbook has evolved from the authors' many years of teaching experience at the University of Washington. However, both its conception and development reflect the influence of many persons: some whose works are herein cited. Grateful acknowledgment is given to numerous school administrators, classroom teachers, and colleagues for their invaluable contributions to many sections of this book. The authors, however, are especially grateful to the following persons for valued counsel and materials: Laura Crowell, Horace G. Rahskopf, Robert Post, Jody Nyquist and John Palmer of the Speech Department, University of Washington; Geraldine Brain Siks, School of Drama, University of Washington; John R. Miles, Snohomish Public Schools; Elmon Ousley, Bellevue Public Schools; J. Norman Cromarty and Ellen McComb Smith, Seattle Public Schools; Charles Blondino, Kent-Meridian Public Schools; William Fredericks and Lana Rae Tussing, Shoreline Public Schools, State of Washington; Mark W. Lee, Whitworth College, Spokane; and Maury Sheridan, Blanchet High School, Seattle.

OLIVER W. NELSON
DOMINIC A. LaRUSSO

table of contents

ORIENTATION

part I   *a teacher's view of communication*

1   the shadow and substance of learning   3
2   speaking and listening   14
3   barriers   33

APPROACH

part II   *toward better communication*

4   observing student characteristics   45
5   providing an optimum climate   56
6   selecting and guiding activities   70
7   evaluating the speaking-listening act   82

METHOD

part III   *key speech forms*

8   discussion   93
9   dramatization   122
10   the short talk   152
11   oral interpretation of literature   174

APPLICATION

part IV   *oral communication in the classroom*

12   english   203
13   social studies   230
14   mathematics and science   253
15   the fine and applied arts   270

APPENDICES

A   securing optimum interest and skill   287
B   cooperating in speech and hearing therapy   313
C   speech resources: anthologies, films, and recordings   317

index   320

ORIENTATION

PART **I** *a teacher's
view of
communication*

1 the shadow and substance of learning

The mysteries of learning, like teaching, have long been the object of man's curiosity and confusion. The learner has been thought to be a sponge, an immovable object, a semi-permeable substance; the teacher has been referred to as a catalyst, an inquisitor, an occasional enemy, a friend and leader. Neither is generally thought to be motivated by a genuine desire to improve himself and, as a consequence, the society in which he lives—from which he draws and to which he contributes. Yet, without such motivation, the trials and tribulations sometimes associated with learning-teaching experiences would hardly be endured. The individual would soon become infected with the attitudes and habits of despair and defeat. No machines, no books, no collection of rules will substitute for the proper mixture of advice and direction, of *theory* and *practice,* which makes every successful learning-teaching situation. Good pedagogy is, in fact, the legitimate offspring of a bona fide marriage between theory and practice. Improperly wed, practice can emerge as a dominant, narrow, and crippling force which brings forth the sting of monotony and meaningless activity; theory shows itself as untested, misunderstood, and misapplied when the student is made to feel inept and continuously uncomfortable. In short, the effective pedagogical situation includes one who *communicates* supportive attitudes and habit patterns (relevant theory and practice) to those who have a self-recognized need for learning. The essentials of experiences of this sort include an understanding of the *importance* as well as the nature of the process which is basic to any situation of leadership, be it social, religious, or intellectual.

Most leaders in education, religion, business, or industry would acknowledge the fact that some role is played by the process of communication in their daily attempts to administer their organizations. Few, however, would agree with the statement that *"leadership is communication"*; few would accept the thoughts of Woodrow Wilson who noted that:

> The instructed few may not be safe leaders except insofar as they have communicated their instruction to the many, except insofar as they have transmitted their thoughts into a common, a popular thought.... The dynamics of leadership lie in persuasion.[1]

The importance of communication for teachers can hardly be overstated since, without it, their work would cease to exist. Without it teachers would never hope to make their ideas, moods, desires, and attitudes known; they could never hope to understand the fears, doubts, or inhibitions of those with whom or for whom they work. Only teachers who operate with this understanding can be effective.

But a knowledge of the *importance* of communication in learning functions is only one of the requirements for effectiveness. Perhaps a more definitive discussion of the actual relationship between learning and communication will help to explain why.

Learning, its process and philosophy, has fascinated man since earliest times. Primitives inevitably assumed the role of teaching their progeny what they knew about life as a simple expedient for survival. Civilized man, convinced of the importance of continuing this practice, systematized what he knew of the process and made it the charge of a specialized few among his fellows. Each society added its peculiar experiences serving its own major needs. The Assyrians and Egyptians emphasized numerical relationships; the Hebrews stressed a knowledge of oral-aural symbols; the Greeks practiced rote for all things; and the Romans drew from their predecessors to offer a wide combination of subjects and methods to their children.

Within the modern period, since the advent of psychology as a

---

[1] Woodrow Wilson, *Leaders of Men*, ed. T. H. Vail Motter (Princeton: Princeton University Press, 1952), pp. 41–42.

discipline, various theories of learning have been vying for supremacy among the many schools of psychology and education. A broad classification would include theories which have been labeled philosophical, psychological, and eclectic.

Philosophical theories, including those of Barzizza, Vittorino da Feltre, Juan Luis Vives, the Port Royalists of France, the Jesuits of the Renaissance, Jean-Jacques Rousseau, Pestalozzi, Maria Montessori, John Dewey, and many others appear to place greatest emphasis upon the creation of a proper *atmosphere* for learning. Content, its understanding and use, dominates the concern of these theorists regardless of their era. The thought is that the proper "spiritual" environment enhances the learner's ability to create a meaningful and lasting bond between himself and the thing to be learned. It invites the learner to become *involved* with the thing to be learned; it helps to prevent the interjection of the learner's self-image between himself and the object of learning; it motivates the learner to assume a flexible, selfless, but active posture toward the learning experience.

The psychological theories, including conditioning and gestalt or field concepts, appear to coalesce in a concern for motivation. From the Pavlovian school of primary need fulfillment, through the period of emphasis upon instincts, to the more current concern for primary and secondary levels of motives, thought in this area has been directed toward the learner. A systematic study has been made of his internal environment and the various methods of constructing rewarding bonds between it and his external environment. Statistical approaches, as a separate methodology, have fostered the development of programmed instruction. Typified by B. F. Skinner's belief that anything which can be verbalized can be taught in a teaching machine, the proponents of this school strive to devise a course book for every conceivable subject. The ultimate success of the various programs depends heavily upon the accumulation of noncontroversial, unambiguous, uniform, and serially related material. All learning must be in bits that can only be totally accepted or rejected by the learner and, at the moment, cannot be involved with concepts of value or processes of criticism. In a word, the programmed instruction approach depends upon the auto-manipulation of the learner's internal environments of mood, understanding, and appreciation by forced choices made from a very precisely interrelated series of informational bits.

The eclectic school of learning draws the essentials from existing theories and offers a composite as its own theory. Thus, when the

proper atmosphere surrounds a careful and sensitively dynamic relation between stimulus, need, and reinforcement, purposeful behavior
changes will follow. And these behavior changes may be of a concrete
physical nature (swimming, dancing, driving a car, or typing) or of a
more symbolic type (reasoning, imagining, or speaking). But irrespective of the type, goes the eclectic argument, the key to behavioral
change is the maintenance of a viable relationship between the
organism and his environments—internal and external.

The one constant in each of these schools of learning is the role
played by environments inside and outside the learner. Whether
internal or external, the individual's environment acts as the limitless
repository of his learning experiences and awaits only the proper
combination of elements—time, place, spirit, and circumstance—to
reveal its treasures. Behavior in a man can be influenced in large part
by the nature of his environments. A sense of well-being can help to
create and shape certain activity while a sense of discomfort, depression, or fear can account for another. Modifications in one's external
environs can also lead to modifications in his regular activity.
Obviously, a stalled elevator will lead most individuals to climb the
stairs in order to get to an office on the third floor. Faced with a
friend experiencing depression, one's ordinary relationship with him
alters so that cooperative, compassionate deeds and words dominate.
In this way, human behavior is influenced and directed.[2]

But many times the environment is not or cannot be altered. One
cannot always remove delinquent boys from a slum to a mountain
camp in order to encourage less delinquent behavior. Nor can one
alter many of the common physical deformities of the body through
surgery or drug therapy. However, it is rare that an individual's
concept of his environments cannot be altered. The delinquent boys
can be persuaded that their immediate external environment does not
exercise complete control over their behavior. The blind or deaf person
can be made to focus upon the positive elements of his environments
to overcome his difficulty. The child who is afraid of the dark can
reconstruct his image of dark places, although the dark places remain.
The world of the mentally ill person, while occasionally altered in a
physical way (substitution of spacious, green surroundings for a
crowded and noisy city) is most generally altered by altering that

---

[2] Karl W. Deutsch, *Nationalism and Social Communication* (Boston: M. I. T. Press,
1953) posits this thesis on a national scale.

person's view of the world. This is precisely what most psychiatrists find to be the bulk of their labors, and this remains the most important aspect of a teacher's endeavors. In our present world of infinite sociophysical complexities, more and more emphasis must be placed on this phase of directing human behavior since the individual becomes less and less able to cope directly with his environment.

Paradoxical though it may appear, the gadgetry of this century helps to minimize man's contacts with himself and his physical environment. He now has successfully created a permanent mediator through which his contacts are made.[3] Thus, he is put into a position of continuous interpretation much as a commander of a submerged submarine who must depend upon various gauges and dials. And, as with the commander, the individual of the twentieth century fashions his actions almost exclusively in terms of his perception or interpretation of a *meta*world created by him—the concepts, images, and symbols. Few things are as thoroughly accepted as the fact that people react to their impressions of the world rather than to the world itself; as a consequence, uniformity in behavior is virtually impossible unless attention is directed more toward modifying these perceptions than toward altering the physical sources of the stimuli impinging upon people. The persistent hope of mankind has been rooted in the assumption that one *does* have the capacity to overcome his environmental limitations—from the paucity of his internal (intellectual) environs during his youth to the difficulties of his external surroundings during his adult years. The problems of mankind are not so much technological or physical as they are conceptual or "imaginary"; they are not so much a part of the real world as they are a part of our image of the real world.

A key, if not the *only* key, to the process of altering human behavior by altering the individual's *concept* of his environment—thereby effecting learning—is *communication*. Unable to walk about and physically manipulate his environment, the average individual utilizes the system of symbolization which his society provides for him and "talks himself" into an evaluation of that environment which will help him solve any immediate problem caused by it. Daydreaming, of course, is the most dramatic example of this ability to manipulate

---

[3] See David Riesman, *The Lonely Crowd* (New Haven: Yale University Press, 1950) for an excellent description of the metamorphosis involved in constructing these motivators of behavior.

images and perceptions of the immediate environment. Folklore, myths, various social rituals, and the like are also examples of this phenomenon at work. Rationalization, a purely symbolic activity, is another.

The essence of human learning resides in man's ability to alter the images and concepts *with* which he works and *to* which he is inevitably tied. These images and concepts are purely symbolic and, as such, must be shaped and handled only through the process of communication. In the overwhelming majority of instances, this has been done through the written—and even more—the oral modes. Without this essential process, the mind of one individual can rarely be contacted, probed, and, when necessary, shaped by himself or by another. As the body concerns itself with processing the ingredients of physical life—food, water, and air, so the mind attends to processing the ingredients of intellectual and spiritual life—perceptions and images of experience. Throughout his long history, man has always realized that the forces of cooperation and control depended upon the control of images and concepts to which his fellows were exposed. For this reason, teachers and dictators, priests and witchdoctors have ever sought to manipulate the systems and procedures needed to construct, energize, and express the images which direct man. Through these systems, authoritarians have long recognized, are shaped the bridges or tunnels connecting private motivation and public order. In short, control of man's communication systems insures control of much of man's behavior; in brief, when one can determine the nature and function of the images ingested by another, he can predict and manipulate the behavior which follows.

The complexity of man's various systems of communication has, thus far, prevented any great flood of models attempting to represent them. Yet, partially in response to technological dominance, there has been a resurgence of visual representations of many abstract concepts. Models have been constructed for Marxian interpretations of dialectic, Dante's concept of morality, and Thomas Aquinas' view of being and essence. In communication, the Bell Telephone films and models are well known.

Models of human communication—man speaking with man—must necessarily remain symbolic. Simple one-dimensional diagrams have been used most frequently to portray the myriad subtle psycho-physical adjustments which constantly attend the simplest act of human speech. And, perhaps this is as close as man will ever come to constructing a physical representation of the oral-aural process at the center of his existence. The judgments, value systems, specific experiences, changing interpretations, and the like which are brought to bear by just *one* of the communicants during just *one phase* of a dialogue would, if charted, confuse rather than clarify this immensely fluid and complex process. Yet, some attempt can and should be made to clarify and deepen the understanding of various parts of this process. Certainly, various charts, diagrams, and tables can let us know what oral communication *is not*. If various popular misconceptions ("communication is a two-way process") can be removed and new ideas introduced for consideration ("feedback") through the use of models, then they should form a part of any serious study of this miraculous phenomenon.

Any single-dimension sketch or diagram should be read as though it were three dimensional, and should include the fundamentals of any act of oral communion. Most obviously, there is a speaker-listener immersed in an atmosphere of time-space and certain fairly stable physical phenomena. The speaker-listener may well be the same person alternating roles or it may be two or more persons alternating roles. In either event, it must be remembered that the act of alternation is not a simple switch-on of one phase of the process while the other phase is switched off; indeed, the two phases of speaking-listening are actually dove-tailed at any given moment of conversation. The most effective speaker is the one who *listens as he speaks*—to himself *and* to the nonverbal messages issuing forth from his silent partner in this act of communion.

To these very fundamental conditions must be added the more complex states of the individual's internal environment. More than the actual physical sounds and lights and objects that impinge upon his senses, the speaker-listener is being constantly bombarded by the changing shapes and patterns of relationships developing in the images drawn from these physical surroundings. Thus, it is actually *not* the physical presence of the other listener which sparks behavioral modifications in a speaker so much as it is that speaker's *image* of the listener; the speaker reacts to his own concept of what the listener is, what he believes, what he is doing, and why. When a student responds to a teacher's question, more often than not, he responds not to what the teacher actually said, but to what he *thought* (the image) the teacher said. This image is created as much by the actual physical sounds emanating from the teacher and affecting his eardrum as by the student's related images of school, his role as student, the teacher's role, the teacher as a person, his fellow students, his image of their image of him, etc. Thus, it would be inefficient, unreasonable, and even cruel for a teacher to assume that his question was the sole stimulus to which the students react. Conversely, it would be naive, short-sighted, and dangerous for the student to presume the same thing. As partners in the common experience of learning, it is imperative that each brings a realization of the iceberg-like structure of communication. The greater part of these encounters is concealed from casual observation and he who assumes that surface aspects constitute the whole of learning or communication is destined to suffer the same fate as the sailor steering between icebergs, guided by the identical philosophy.

The accompanying sketch (Figure 1) attempts to portray something of the complexity involved in any act of oral communication and, there-

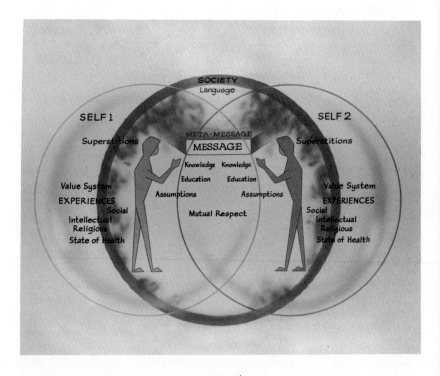

FIGURE 1

fore, in any act of learning. Both figures are enclosed in three circles : society, language, and self. The largest circle, and that which contains at least a portion of each of the others, is *society*. Within it exists the next largest circle, language, whose circumference is perforated as it enters the sphere of the self. Here, because of the action of the self, language and society have greater intercourse. The most efficient communication occurs where the four circles overlap (society, language, self 1, and self 2), precisely because of shared aspects such as knowledge, education, assumptions, mutual respect, etc. One should note, however, that *complete* unity is not possible since many (if not most) of the other ingredients which constitute the self are generally partially or completely outside the overlap area. Moreover, some of these same ingredients are outside the circles of language and society. Many experiences in the life of a growing individual are well without the bounds of his particular society, as are some of his fears, values, or superstitions. Because of these exclusive aspects of one's life, any message one seeks to share with another must, perforce, carry the possibilities and the realities of confusion; simple confusion if the ingredients are shared in some ways but not in others. The more *obvious* message of any communicative act usually falls within the overlap area. Yet, even part of that message often falls outside this section of efficient communication. Take the simple declaration: *"We have a nice place by the shore."* On the surface, the message appears clear, distinct, and free from misunderstanding. However, if one charted the possible images which could be constructed by a listener who shared *everything* in common with the speaker *save* general experience in living, the following could happen:

WE	HAVE A	NICE	PLACE	BY THE	SHORE
Family	Own	Large	Cabin	On	Ocean
Friends	Rent	Cozy	Shack	Near	River
Buddies	Use	Plush	Lodge	Close	Lake
Company		Modest	Hotel	View	Bay
Club			Land		Puddle
Society					

More so would be the case with statements such as :

> Democracy is the best form of government.
> Get more will power into your life.
> Joy, you must try harder.

Each of the possible images conjured up by the listener (let alone those produced by the speaker) serves to create a metamessage over and above the obvious message. Because of the peculiarities of backgrounds, the metamessages of speaker and listener are seldom, if ever, in accord with one another. Yet, more often than not, it is to this message that the subsequent response of the listener is directed. It is for this reason that supervisors, teachers, and parents are often amazed at the response of employees, students, or children who apparently insist on doing exactly the opposite of what was intended by remarks directed to them.

SUMMARY

Communication is at once the tool and the end of learning. More than a simple acquisition of information, learning is the process of placing the information in dynamic relationship with other knowledge. In the last analysis, only through the alchemy of oral communication (personal or public) do informational bits become motivational patterns. What one is and what he becomes are clearly the result of the complex interplay between inner and outer compulsions made manifest in the images he communicates to himself and to others.

SELECTED READINGS

Benezet, Louis T. "The Trouble with Excellence." *Saturday Review* (October 21, 1961), 44–45, 63–64.

Brown, Marcus. "Knowing and Learning." *Harvard Educational Review,* XXXI (Winter, 1961), 1–20.

Bruner, J. *Essays for the Left Hand: On Knowing.* Cambridge: Harvard University Press, 1962.

Cassirer, Ernst. *Essay on Man.* New Haven: Yale University Press, 1945.

Deese, S. E. *The Psychology of Learning.* New York: McGraw-Hill Book Company, 1967.

Emig, J. A., and others. *Language and Learning.* New York: Harcourt, Brace & World, Inc., 1966.

Ericson, E. H. *Insight and Responsibility.* New York: W. W. Norton & Company, Inc., 1964.

Gagné, R. M. *The Conditions of Learning.* New York: Holt, Rinehart & Winston, Inc., 1966.

Highet, Gilbert. *The Art of Teaching.* New York : Alfred A. Knopf, Inc., 1950.

Hilgard, E. R. "The Human Dimension in Teaching." *Association of Higher Education College and University Bulletin,* XVII (March 15, 1965), 1–3, 4.

Jones, M. R., ed. *Human Motivation: A Symposium.* Lincoln : University of Nebraska Press, 1965.

Skinner, B. F. "The Science of Learning and the Art of Teaching." *Harvard Education Review,* XXIV (Spring, 1954), 86–97.

2 *speaking and listening*

Chapter One called attention to the philosophy that communication was at once the tool and the end of learning. Oral communication, in turn, was presented as that type of communication which serves most effectively in the acquisition, development, evaluation, and expression of learning—regardless of the subject matter. At this point in our discussion, we shall focus more specifically on the role of speaking-listening behavior, the components of this important activity, and some of the basic principles involved in its efficient use.

THE ROLE OF SPEAKING-LISTENING

Any attempt to examine the role of speaking-listening behavior must begin with the matter of learning. Although it has been implied in earlier parts of this discussion, it should be definitely stated that any concern with learning has to do with the attempt to reduce trial and error activity in each situation faced by the individual. As he progresses, the learner moves more and more quickly to his intended solution without overt loss of time and energy. This does not mean that he engages in *no* trial and error; it means that energy is conserved by a shift from *actual* trial and error activity to a more *symbolic* mode. The progress of this shift is best seen in children. First exposures to situations usually elicit gross and random bodily action: pegs are

14

lifted, forced into each hole, turned and twisted until they are "made to fit." As the child advances, he does less of the actual lifting, forcing, turning, and twisting; he pauses and makes most of these moves symbolically—usually by talking to himself about the possibilities. He now reduces the process of *real* action to two or three possibilities. And so it goes with even the most complicated situations. Words are hurled instead of fists when aggression seems to be the only way of resolving some dispute. Even in this substitution of words for more gross physical action, there is a hierarchy. As the move is made away from punishing force, the substitute words first chosen are threatening and forceful. These become less so as the learner senses the value of going through this solution internally (cursing under his breath, "mentally" reprimanding the other person, etc.); thus he can move to a less aggressive symbolic activity in the hope of finding a more permanent solution to his problem. Eventually, of course, the individual reaches the peak of all effective learning: a single, effective response which goes beyond the obvious and immediate. At this stage, the learner gives evidence of covert trial and error which has been complex, timeless, and self-evaluative; at this stage, he moves to symbolic activity which is as threatening as the situation which provoked it, to symbolic action which substitutes love and under-

THE EBB AND FLOW OF COMMUNICATION IS INEVITABLE.
(*Courtesy Shoreline Public Schools.*)

standing; at this stage, he moves from a narrow and selfish response to a broader and more civilized activity.

In all of this, the person must make regular use of the speaking-listening act because it is the only activity capable of handling *most,* if not all, of the experiences of life. But even more important, not only is it the singular act basic to *cognition* as well as *re-cognition,* it remains the *only* act able to provide new information *and the relationships surrounding this new knowledge.* Since mere acquisition of new knowledge is useless, the speaking-listening activity turns neutral experiences into learning situations by providing the only immediate and flexible means of defining relationships in the form of interpretations, insights, and interests. A youngster venturing into the woods alone does not automatically return a more learned individual. His exposures and interactions are not necessarily distilled, catalogued, and filed away for future use in similar or related situations. By looking at a bush, the young learner has no way of knowing whether it is poisonous or not. Even with prior vicarious experience in the form of reading about various plants, the youngster must "talk to himself" as he decides whether or not to touch it. He must compare the shape and color of the leaves with those described or shown in his reading; he must articulate his conclusion, even to himself, as he moves to an internal discussion involving the possible consequences of his conclusion. All this, and he still remains a captive of himself; he is still confined within the borders of his own effectiveness in the use of this symbolic activity. He still operates as the originator, developer, and evaluator of the images used in the complicated process of learning. Yet, in the company of another, he can engage in the speaking-listening transactions which *will* help him to sift, examine, distill, apply, and retain salient information, insights, and appreciations. By voicing his comparisons (between his prior reading knowledge and his current observations), he exposes his train of thought to the evaluation of his companion. In turn, the companion exposes his acceptance, rejection, and doubts by his spoken reaction. Further, he may benefit the young woodsman by calling attention to information not provided by the earlier reading experience; he may describe uses for the bush or its fruits unknown to the novice; and, finally, he might well insure the worth of his young friend's solution by increasing his list of possible consequences. Thus, the learning experiences of every individual are hastened and improved through the use of the speaking-listening process. What he learns about his personal world, the world about him and, more to the point, the *relationships* between these two worlds is rooted in his speaking-listening transactions. "For a reason hard to understand," says Professor Harold Martin of Harvard University, "we do not seem to have a full grasp on experience itself until we have symbolized it in some fashion; we do not *know* until we have been *told*."[1] And especialy is this the case when that experience involves the personal self. Without the understanding of that self *as communicated by another,* an individual cannot even know himself adequately.[2] This is especially crucial since, in effect, it means that most people know themselves *only* through the images communicated to them by others. For the average teacher of young persons, this dramatic fact expands the influence of classroom encounters. What is learned by the youngster is not necessarily restricted to the subject matter. Often, too often, an important concomitant learning bit is acquired about the self. "John, you still do not have the correct answer," furnishes information which helps the youngster pinpoint his progress toward the correct solution of a problem in math, but it also could be interpreted by him as a definition of inner image. "I *still* don't have it (*after many fruitless tries, after long and worthless activity, after others have long since got it*). Therefore, I will *never* get it." Examples of this sort, and extensions of it, are legion. They occur daily in the lives of everyone and furnish the ingredients which form the core of being.

Oral communication—the activities of speaking and listening—plays an important role in the deportment of the individual as he applies the fruits of his learning. Used as a tool, as discussed above, the speaking-listening act is instrumental in the acquisition, development, evaluation, and retention of information, interpretations, insights, and interests throughout the life of any human being. Used as an index, it provides a reliable means of measuring the inner growth of everyone. As Overstreet contends :

> . . . Speech defects not caused by actual organic malformation are understood, most often, as character defects, as an expression of some basic failure to work out a right relation-

---

[1] Harold C. Martin, *The Logic and Rhetoric of Exposition* (New York: Holt, Rinehart & Winston, Inc., 1958), p. 1. See also Dorothy L. Sayers, "The Lost Tools of Learning," *The Hibbert Journal*, XLVI (1947), 1–12.

[2] See Thomas Hora, "Tao, Zen and Existential Psychotherapy," *Psychologia*, II (1959), 236–242. Also pertinent is George Mead, *Mind, Self and Society* (Chicago: University of Chicago Press, 1934), especially pp. 135 ff.

ship with life. Stammerings, stutterings ... are widely recognized as having their roots in emotional disturbances. ... But habitual dullness, pomposity, sarcasm, lack of tact, platitudinizing, pedantry, indiscriminate stressing of details—these too should properly be regarded ... as evidence that the individual has ... failed to continue his psychological growth.[3]

Overstreet continues, with the following paradox,

In no area of our maturing ... is arrested development more common than in the area of communication. It is so common that it is not even noticed; it is taken for granted as natural. The person who is mature in his communicative powers is noted as an exception to the rule. The person who is immature—halting, clumsy, obscure, rambling, dull, platitudinous, insensitive—is the rule. ...[4]

It has long been recognized by psychiatrists and the most proficient educators that the health of the inner world is maintained through good oral communication. Only through effective speaking and listening can that inaccessible of all worlds be revitalized, stirred, touched, transfused, confronted, and tested. Because of the importance of oral communication in the development of the personality, much money and energy is spent for the *restoration* of these abilities. Oddly, relatively little time or money or effort is expended to insure the proper instillation of these abilities.

Another important phase of human activity heavily dependent upon the effective use of speaking-listening efforts is that of *creation* and *recreation*. Unfortunately, most individuals go from cradle to grave without the realization of their creative powers. More is the pity, since they have actually been involved in creative performances almost daily but have been denied the exhilaration by the lack of a sense of creativity. Few teachers and even fewer friends have the ability, *or take the time* if they do have such ability, to help develop such a sense in others. Such a sense involves an awareness of creative acts and a characteristic pattern of judgments about the value of them. Thus, the mud pies of most children go unheralded as creative

---

[3] Harry Overstreet, *The Mature Mind* (New York: W. W. Norton & Company, Inc., 1949), p. 57.

[4] *Ibid.*, pp. 54–55.

products in much the same way as do their efforts at dance, song, coloring, and the like. They "know how" to take part in such activities but have little of the rationale which would enable them to evaluate them; and without this evaluation, a creative sense is rarely born. With it, however, the individual can begin to look for and select more and more opportunities for creative experiences and, *in the process, insure a flexible posture toward himself and his environment.* This extremely important sense of creativity is developed early and thoroughly when consciously enacted through the speaking-listening activities of the young learners. When the child is made to realize that, through the proper use of these activities, he *can* and *does* create, more creative performances will follow. When he realizes that speaking and listening afford him the opportunity to enlarge, shorten, mix, color, divide, multiply, continue, enrich, and preserve his various worlds, an interest in creativity will have been born.

Whether the focus of his concern be mathematics or biology or music, the enlightened teacher can encourage student growth by calling attention to the creative aspects of the speaking-listening activity. This is done most easily by the teachers of language, of course. Until called to their attention and demonstrated, few students realize the creative aspects of even the simplest speaking-listening behavior. They have to be led (directly or indirectly) to the revelation that, by giving substance to their internal worlds in the simple act of choosing a certain word, they create as truly as when they give form to clay. Their own individual patterns of word choice, sentence structure, and rhythm could provide as much value to the world as any more easily recognized object of art. Coining new words and phrases, constructing new metaphors and similes can produce as much joy as will ever be experienced by the average person. New horizons are created as much by James Joyce's product of creativity, *panaroma,* as they are by an oil painting of a landscape or a flower. To speak of "probing and fluffing an idea" produces as valuable a pattern of new experiences as does the construction of a new song. The listener to such an act of creation, unlike the reader, can observe the artist in the process of creating his work of art. He witnesses (and is affected by) the various stages of the physical and spiritual efforts of his fellow communicant. But more, he *can share directly* in the process of creation. Through his verbal and nonverbal actions, the listener can encourage, delay, modify, or destroy the delicate progress of his counterpart's creative moments.

The worth of speaking-listening in the personal progress of the individual is revealed, finally, in its role of *catharsis*. Not unrelated to the other roles mentioned previously, this function also occupies a niche of its own. Free, easy, and continuing "discharge" of inner images and feelings is the prime ingredient in a person's learning. It also is involved in an important way in the individual's creative and performing actions. But, most directly, it is a part of the continuing inner health of every man, woman, and child.

Carl Rogers, noted psychologist-psychoanalyst, has long maintained that psychotics are those persons who have lost the ability to communicate with themselves and with other people.[5] More explicitly, he writes that

> The task of psychotherapy is to help the person achieve, through a special relationship with a therapist, good communication within himself. Once this is achieved, he can communicate more freely and more effectively with others. *We may say then that psychotherapy is good communication, within and between men.* We may also turn that statement around and it will still be true. *Good communication, free communication, within or between men, is always therapeutic.*[6]

Any effort to communicate orally is actually a movement designed to escape from the loneliness, depression, exhaustion, fear, and doubt bottled within our skin-enclosed world. By "unburdening" these states, by giving them body and shape the speaker brings them within the area of control. In effect, the speaker releases to conquer, whether this release is experienced in the classroom, in church, in the home, or on the sandlot. The revolt of minority groups and student populations appears to have been triggered by burning and mushrooming inner frustrations over "the establishment's" inability to "tell it like it is." Unfortunate though many of the consequences may be, solutions are more possible now than ever before.

But the cathartic role of speaking and listening activities is not restricted to the task of releasing diseased states of mind. It serves

---

[5] Carl R. Rogers, "Communication: Its Blocking and its Facilitation," *Northwestern University Information*, XX (April 21, 1952), 1–15 especially.

[6] Carl R. Rogers and F. J. Roethlisberger, "Barriers and Gateways to Communication," *Harvard Business Review*, XXX (July–August, 1952), 46.

also to *reward* the speaker on occasion. Every so often, each of us feels the need to "release the inner man" just to let him demonstrate our presence. Children are wont to do this more often than adults since they have yet to feel the strictures of society's rules in this regard. Nevertheless, it is a rare adult who has never succumbed to singing in the shower, whistling in the woods, humming in the seclusion of his own office. It is this same desire which leads to the oral applause characteristic of many evangelical religious services, fraternal meetings, sports contests, and other similar gatherings. By giving his wispy thoughts an audible form, the speaker often seeks to exhibit and to shine. In many instances, he seeks the exhilaration of "joining" with himself and with others. In their oral-physical nature, many adolescent songs and dances are extreme examples of this same desire and, in truth, are not as novel as they are made out to be. In each new song are the echoes of the historic oral-aural forces converging to elicit communion and reward the inner man. In each new speaking-listening activity is contained the means and the opportunity for a healthful catharsis. For the average adult, proper use of this opportunity means a chance of mending and repair; for the average young person, it means a way of insuring a strong foundation; for society, it means hope.

This hope was recognized by most societies throughout man's long history. The Oriental cultures rewarded and punished acts of speech as they did acts of deed. The Greek championed speakers as they applauded warriors and later civilizations preserved the words of their key historical moments even more than the events of those moments. In the middle of the seventeenth century, Thomas Hobbes, involved and concerned with the turmoils of English society, declared, "The most notable and profitable invention of all others was that of speech ... without which there had been amongst men neither Commonwealth, nor Society, nor Contract, nor Peace, no more than amongst Lyons, Bears, and Wolves."[7] Almost three hundred years later, John Dewey pronounced that

> There is more than a verbal tie between the words *common, community* and *communication*. Men live in a community by virtue of the things which they have in common; and communication is the way in which they come

---

[7] Thomas Hobbes, *Leviathan* (London: Everyman's Library, 1934), p. 12.

to possess things in common. . . . Not only is social life
identical with communication, but all communication
(hence all genuine social life) is educative.[8]

The role of speaking and listening behavior, then, has long been
recognized as inseparable from the health and welfare of society. At
no time in history has there been stronger appreciation for the role of
communication in the communal actions of men. At no time previously
have as many groups of individuals been so concerned for more and
better communication to preserve social welfare. Children are
clamoring to be heard, racial and religious minorities are demanding
their moments on the podium, and nations are insisting more and
more on summit conferences to solve differences in everything from
political disputes to economic standards. And all because of the
universal regard for the flexible nature and real power of this unique
human transaction.

Whatever the society, man has always depended upon oral communication as the basis of his educational system. He has used it as
the major mode of informing, persuading, controlling, and cooperating
with his fellow men. In moments of crisis, he has made use of its various
roles to preserve tradition or create innovation.

Inevitably, the numerous societies of man have also relied upon
speaking-listening conduct to serve their religious needs. This activity
forms the base of religious ritual; it has a necessary part in liturgy,
communion, prayer, petition, repentence, and ultimate salvation as
defined by these societies. And, in consequence of this universal
involvement of the oral mode in all things religious, silence took on
new proportions as an *active* force. No longer considered the mere
absence of sound, silence came to be thought of as the manifestation
of doubt and insecurity. To this day, although many religions have
gone beyond this thought to develop a positive image of deep communion, most still cling to the belief that: "he who does not sing the
praises of his creed, believes not." To some extent, of course, this
same philosophy is embraced by educators, politicians, friends, and
family members who feel threatened by regular and extended
moments of silence during acts of oral communication.

Even the legal systems of man founded themselves on the oral-

---

[8] John Dewey, *Democracy and Education* (New York: The Macmillan Company,
1923), pp. 3–6; quote from p. 5.

aural conduct. Noting that such conduct occurred as an obligatory part of Everyman's social encounters, it seemed obvious and necessary for the leaders of society to make use of this conduct in controlling behavior. Questions of fact, definition, or motivation which surround all legal disputes find their resolution in the speaking-listening activity of which we have been speaking. Charges are made, explained, and defended against by speakers to a selected audience. In the course of each of these subactions, oaths are taken, witnesses called, and evidence related—again, in oral form. Finally, the select audience retires to deliberate (speaking-listening with each other), returns its judgment, and the sentence of the judge is conveyed to the defendant— again, through the mode of oral communication.

Perhaps the most eloquent testimony of society's evaluation of the worth of the speaking-listening activity is its insistent faith in the existence of a one-to-one relationship between a man's word and his deed. Contracts are issued, money and time expended, lives created, directed, and terminated all on the basis of a belief that what a civilized being said in the presence of another civilized being cemented a bond which transcended time, space, form and material.

COMPONENTS OF THE SPEAKING-LISTENING ACT

The complex nature of oral communication has been discussed at some length in Chapter One. Here, it should suffice to detail such aspects of this phenomenon as will increase the teacher's understanding and appreciation.

As the tool and the end of learning, oral communication has been shown to be involved in all phases of the learning process, from the acquisition of material to the expression of it. But the most engrossing observation to be made is that, as a dynamic process, oral communication (the speaking-listening act) provides the all-important sense of relationship. Informational bits, gathered for their own sakes, insure no learning; they are not marks of intelligence. The truly educated man is one who has the ability to create and describe relationships among whatever informational bits he has in his possession. In the important process of interaction we have referred to as oral communication, the essential ingredient is not the speaker or the listener or the subject or the occasion; *it is,* rather, *the relationship* which exists among them. Quite beyond the content of any speaking-listening transaction, there is always a concomitant message of relationships being expressed. More often than not, this message supersedes and overshadows the content or subject matter and, if these relationships are not optimum, the content of the message is of no avail. A poor, tense relationship between student and teacher will prevent the simplest message of content from being understood and learned. A child closely bound to another teacher by strands of love and respect will easily learn the most complicated concept. The essential components of *any* speaking-listening activity, those which spark and feed the all-important atmosphere of relationships include: *attitudes, thoughts, language, bodily action,* and *voice.* Carried to every encounter by both speaker and listener, these components interact with each other to determine the success or failure of the attempt to communicate.

Attitudes, those learned and characteristic tendencies which predetermine the response to various worlds, are generally socially induced. Earlier the point was made that our image of "self" is essentially that which has been mirrored back to us through the oral actions of our fellows. We consider ourselves good or bad, intelligent or stupid, friendly or unfriendly, charming or boorish by virtue of having had these labels attached through a series of speaking-listening experiences. What can be done, what will even be attempted by many students is all too frequently determined by the incidental remarks of their teachers. If the tendency of teachers is to define every student endeavor in terms of "you are" instead of "you did" then the self-image of these students will be shaped quickly and will play a prominent role in all of their future encounters with the world. Unfortunately, there are teachers who habitually speak in terms of "John is" to their colleagues. They are inclined to relate that: "Johnny is dull" rather than "Johnny does not do well in my class," or "Mary is a boor" rather than "Mary hasn't managed to interest me yet," or "Pete is a liar" rather than "Pete lied to me on one occasion." Enough comments of this first order, which generalize and crystallize character instead of defining deeds and instances, and the youngster will begin to believe such labels. He cannot do otherwise since his reservoir of experiences about himself and the world is very limited. And it is this attitude toward self which governs the nature, direction, success, or failure of the individual's attempts at social interaction through oral communication.

Similarly, the individual's attitude toward others will operate to influence his pattern of speaking-listening behavior; it will affect the frequency of such activity as it will determine the nature, tone, scope, and direction. Since oral communication is actually a manifestation of cultural tradition modified by personal interpretation, at once the listener can judge (though not always infallibly) how well the speaker is involved with his worlds. The language used (slang, poor grammar, profanity, or their opposites), the examples employed (exclusively personal incidents, cliché observations, meaningless and exaggerated statistics, or their opposites), the length and manner of presentation (interminable harangues, monologue, inflexible vocal tone, or their counterparts) and the choice of time and place define pretty clearly just where the individual speaker stands in relation to his worlds.[9] One who truly recognizes and respects the "human-ness" in others will reveal it in his speaking-listening habit patterns. He will be recognized by his tendency to speak carefully and listen well, by his flexibility of patterns, and by the sophisticated ease with which he moves from subject to subject and mood to mood. His willingness to adapt style, rhythm, and thoughts to those best suited to his listener reflects a deep and abiding faith in the value of his fellow man. He has, simple enough, a love for humanity and a belief that when the "light of this love dies down, the shadow of the beast in each of us grows larger." Such a speaker-listener would ask:

> Come, share my thoughts with me
> That we may both be free
> Where the craggy meets the bluing
> And the song of life is—*We* !

> Come help me probe and fluff
> The deep internal stuff
> With a word that wraps the feeling
> And a belief reworks a bluff.

> Come join my mind and soul
> Which lose the common goal
> In their stride toward civil being
> And a need to guard a role.

---

[9] Note again the observations of Mead, Rogers, Overstreet, and others in this regard. See also Jay D. Haley, "An Interactional Description of Schizophrenia," *Psychiatry*, IV (1959), 48–65.

Come hold my heart with care
And stroke my troubles bare
As your tongue defines the vagueness
And kindly ears help my repair

—Dominic A. LaRusso

Thoughts, as a factor in the success or failure of the ordinary speaking-listening experience, have rarely been considered in any way other than as statements of subject matter. Our point here is that this part of the oral communication transactions includes everything from reflex contributions to considered evaluations. Whatever the level of the encounter—informal conversation or formal disputation—the speaker-listener must involve himself in selecting, joining, evaluating, and employing the material from the reservoir of his private world. And more: the *relationships* mentioned at the beginning of this chapter must be discerned and developed. Judgments of word choice, speaking rate, supporting material, length of the presentation are all made *and* continued according to the changing states of the listener, the influence of time, the affect of the place, and the nature of the subject. Instantaneous inferences, insightful imagination, and relevant recall are required as regular contributions in any meaningful speaking-listening experience. The ordering and arranging process which lies at the heart of the dynamic relationships constituting learning must be applied to all facets of the experience. Thus, in addition to a concern for the proper sequence and extension of ideas, the successful speaker-listener is continuously involved in ordering and arranging the optimum conditions of time, place, and circumstance. The teacher, as a successful communicant, worries as much about the influence of the *form* of his communication (monologue-dialogue, written-oral) as he does about his choice of language or the examples and illustrations used. Even more vital to the success or failure of the endeavor is his willingness to enlarge the role of *listening* in his teaching procedures. Thought by many to be little more than the passive counterpart to speaking, listening has not been widely conceived as an educational imperative. Yet it has invariably been associated with the teaching prowess of all the great educators of history. For them, it served to encourage self-discovery in their students' learning efforts while it also provided a channel through which flowed information and insights defining possible barriers of effective learning. As psychotherapists have discovered, one helps another to learn by listening more than by speaking, for without the release of the hidden doubts, fears, and misconceptions neither the learner nor the teacher can direct the journey or gauge the progress.

Inextricably intertwined with the attitudes and thought patterns of the speaker-listener is the matter of *language*. Surely the thought that every human being is at once confined and liberated by his system of symbolization (language) is not novel. The thoughts of da Vinci were as much defined by the fact that he was an Italian as by the fact that he was an exceptional human being. To learn about himself and his world, da Vinci used those symbols already in existence, those used with regularity by his parents, teachers, and friends. To express his reactions he employed the same symbols he used in acquiring the experiences which now make up his reactions; the circle is now complete. A man speaks, therefore, with the force of his entire history. His past as well as his present perceptions guide his selection of symbols (verbal or nonverbal) as they do the time and place of their expression. To a degree, he dresses his ideas and feelings as he dresses his body—according to the fashion of his time but interpreted by his choice of size, color, and material. While the body of linguistic symbols is pretty much described for most participants in the speaking-listening experience, the specific word choice, sentence construction, rhythm, and time-place of expression remains an individual matter. For this reason, a concerned speaker-listener will remember to consider the *several* meanings attached to oral messages before action is taken to accept, reject, modify, reprimand, or reward. When doubt exists over which meaning is to prevail, the only justified reaction is a question designed to discover the relation between speaker *intent,* message *content,* and listener *retent.* The following example should serve to demonstrate the need for such a reaction:

SPEAKER INTENT	MESSAGE CONTENT	LISTENER RETENT
1. I'm suffering because I was not careful about storing my work.		1. He's sharing an observation.
	Confound it,	2. He's sharing a feeling.
2. Sympathize with me.	*I can't find my*	
3. Help me.	*assignment!!*	3. He's blaming himself.
4. What did you do with my assignment?		4. He's blaming me.
		5. He's asking for help.
		6. He's asking for sympathy.

When these possibilities exist in virtually every single speaking-listening occurrence, no matter how trivial, who dares to rest on the *literal* message offered? Who in the teaching profession would be so insensitive as to rest upon a knowledge of language gathered years ago? Who fails to see the need for a continuously creative approach to his linguistic habits? Language, although not the sole factor directing the success or failure of oral communication acts, exerts strong pressure on word choice, sentence arrangement (including wise use of transitions), and linguistic devices such as metaphors, similes, and parallel construction. The true liberal, therefore, is one who has the benefits and flexibility given to him as a result of his familiarity with many languages.

The fourth component of effective oral communication is *bodily action*. Posture, gesture, and movement are as much a part of the universal concept of speaking as the language itself. Without these aspects, oral communication could not exist. These are basic to the production of voice, the shaping of thoughts, and the manifestation of many attitudes. Man is said to think with his whole body; he also communicates with his whole body. Unfortunately, because of poor training or, worse yet, active opposition to training in this area, most speaker-listeners are truly handicapped. As a consequence, many fail to realize that success is precluded in many instances by a conflict between the verbal and the nonverbal messages they issue simultaneously. The message which is heard often conflicts with the message which is seen. One who avoids looking at the listener, who seats himself at quite a distance from the listener, and whose body is flaccid and unresponsive should not wonder if the listener fails to believe the linguistic message "I am terribly anxious to hear your views on this." Contrary to the advice of some charlatans operating in the field of "persuasion" or "communication," there is no one correct posture, gesture, or movement which serves all activities and all persons. For the sake of efficiency, it is enough to remember that the posture, gesture, or movement employed during speaker-listener encounters should contribute rather than detract from the linguistic message of the speaker. In moments of doubt, one ought to avoid using any action which he must plan. Patterns of *any* kind lose their effectiveness in proportion as they become standard or universal. As with the verbal symbols, one ought to maintain a spirit of continuous creativity toward his use of the nonverbal.

The final component involved in oral communication is the most obvious — *voice*. The universal practice of judging one's personality through the index of voice is well known. Lack of special training and recurring misjudgments do not appear strong enough to interfere with this practice. The wise communicator, aware of this tendency, does everything necessary to produce a voice which is responsive, audible, intelligible, and pleasant. Responsiveness includes such simple factors as variable pitch and loudness. The dull monotony of a teacher's voice at two in the afternoon is too difficult for any adolescent to fight successfully. A variable rate is also conducive to success. Any rate which is consistently above the normal range of 150 to 185 words per minute will discourage attention more often than it will encourage it. Similarly, any rate habitually below the normal will elicit irritation and rejection rather than comfort and acceptance. The optimum vocal pattern manifests, above all, a purposeful rhythm. In the movement from silence to sound, sound to sound, one level of loudness to another, the listener is drawn by a force as basic as his heart beat and as old as the sun. He sees it in his life, in the seasons of the year, and in the patterns of his activities and when he does not, he is disturbed. Conversely, anything directed toward his attention and acceptance cannot afford to violate this deep-rooted sense of rhythm.

PRINCIPLES OF ORAL COMMUNICATION

At one point in this discussion, mention was made of the importance of a *sense* of creativity. There is a fine distinction between the *sense* and the "know how" of creativity. That same distinction exists between the sense of communication and the "know how" associated with it. Here, we wish to note that this entire work has been organized with the belief that *all* teachers share in the responsibility for the *sense* of communication in their students even though some are more directly concerned with the "know how" than others. This *sense* of communication is made up of a feeling and a characteristic pattern of judgments regarding the value of the process and the relationships which exist among its components. Adolescents are usually in the process of forming a sense of communication, but they must be helped. They "know how" to take part in oral interactions, but have little of the rationale which develops the flexibility and control, the proportion and detail marking the sensitive communicant. The development of this sense is spurred by a knowledge of certain universals:[10]

1. *Effective oral communication is organized, meaningful, and selectively particular.* Simply stated, this principle recognizes the impossibility of "universal" speeches, arguments, or language. It stresses the role of *immediacy* as a quality of effectiveness. Unless the tone, mood, material, and presentation of *any* message are adapted to the needs of the involved speakers and listeners, success becomes a matter of happenstance. More to the point, this principle underscores the thought that order and meaning are determined by the communicants operating at the time.

2. *Effective oral communication is in tune with the dynamics of the immediate environment.* An extension of the first principle, this concept directs attention to the need for flexibility. As the essential components of any speaking-listening situation are dynamic and ever-changing, so the entire process must be. It must be realized that:

> Unlike its written counterpart, oral communication can only be revealed in an "unfolding" process which is within the control of the individual speaker. No one can ascertain with certainty precisely what direction and color the speaker's thoughts will take until he releases them—and this includes the speaker himself, in most instances. This very act of unfolding contains within it the privilege and the *responsibility of modification of adaptation to the changing needs of the speaker, listener, or occasion.* And it is this very flexibility which makes the speech adventure unique and wonderful.[11]

3. *Effective communication is socially responsible.* As noted earlier, this unique and wonderful process acts as a tool and an end in the lives of the individual and the society in which he lives. Times occur, therefore, when a conflict develops over the priority to be accorded to individual needs or to social requirements. In other instances, a shifting order has to be fashioned to serve the equally pressing needs of the person and social worlds. In moments of doubt, however, it should be remembered that the individual's first

---

[10] See Dominic A. LaRusso, *Basic Skills in Oral Communication* (Dubuque: William C. Brown Company, Publishers, 1967), Chapter 2.

[11] *Ibid.*, p. 22.

responsibility as a social organism is the proper development of the *self;* without this, he cannot exercise his social responsibilities. For all that, the sensitive communicant is constantly aware of the *intimate* and *controlling* nature of the process. He guards against indiscriminate use of his speaking-listening abilities since the innermost aspects of another human being are involved. He treasures the thought that, by his actions as speaker-listener, he can heal or wound another; he can clarify a point or deepen a confusion; he can inspire to hope or doom to despair; in short, he shares in directing the life of his fellow men.

SUMMARY

As both tool and end in the social life of a human being, oral communication ramifies throughout the whole of his experiences from birth to death. He needs it to learn and to use the fruits of his learning. Creative activity is enhanced through its use and the health of his internal world is maintained by it. It is an imperative part of his education, needful in his religion, and indispensable to his legal systems. And it is each of these things because, in its effective state, it is (1) organized, meaningful, and particular, (2) dynamically suited to the immediate environment, and (3) socially responsible.

SELECTED READINGS

Bateson, G., and J. Ruesch. *Communication: The Social Matrix of Psychiatry.* New York : W. W. Norton & Company, Inc., 1951.

Broadbent, D. E. *Perception and Communication.* New York : Pergamon Press, 1958.

Buber, Martin. *Between Man and Man.* New York : The Macmillan Company, 1948.

Davis, R. "The Human Operator as a Single Channel Information System." *Quarterly Journal of Experimental Psychology,* IX (August, 1957), 119–129.

Dittman, A. D., and L. C. Wynne. "Linguistic Techniques and the Analysis of Emotionality in Interviews." *Journal of Abnormal and Social Psychology*, LXVIII (1961), 201–204.

Huxley, A. *The Art of Seeing*. New York : Harper & Row, Publishers, 1942.

Laird, C. *The Miracle of Language*. Greenwich, Conn. : Fawcett Publications, Premier Books, 1963.

Lewis, T. F., and R. G. Nichols. *Speaking and Listening*. Dubuque, Iowa, William C. Brown Company, Publishers, 1965.

Morris, Charles. *Signs, Language and Behavior*. Englewood Cliffs, N.J.: Prentice-Hall, Inc., 1946.

Rioch, D. McK. "The Sense and the Noise." *Psychiatry*, XXIV, Suppl. to No. 2 (1961), 7–18.

Taylor, Gordon. *Creative English*. Leeds, England : E. J. Arnold and Son, Ltd., 1958.

Watzlawick, P. *An Anthology of Human Communication*. Palo Alto, Calif. : Science and Behavior Books, 1963.

3 *barriers*

When one considers the intricate nature of communication and notes the many points at which something may go awry in conveying a simple statement of fact, one is amazed that human beings understand each other as well as they do. I. A. Richards pointedly declares that "Misunderstanding is the rule; understanding a happy accident." If only communicating an idea, concept, or feeling were as simple and as dependable as delivering a bag of groceries; if only we could but deliver our concepts intact to others, how many misunderstandings, how much pain might be avoided, how much time saved. Perhaps. Perhaps with such exactness, the game of communication would lose much of its mystery, its challenge, its excitement, its charm. Such speculation, however, is purely academic, since we cannot transfer a thought intact from one mind to another. We can only represent our thoughts by encoding them into speech symbols which, through sound and light waves, we direct toward a receiver (listener) who in turn, we trust, will decode our symbols in a fashion that will approximate the message as we conceived it. This is the aim of all communication. Such remarks as "I have a perfect understanding with Joe," "I understand you, Mary," "We see eye to eye," or "I agree with Senator Doolittle" are actually either figures of speech or examples of wishful thinking. On the other hand, such observations as: "We seem to understand one another," and "I think what Senator Doolittle is saying . . ." and "I think what he means is . . ." are probably more consistent with what is actually possible in an act of communication.

Place two or more persons in some type of social relationship, communication of a sort is bound to ensue, if only on a nonverbal level. The question is not whether any communication is taking place in a classroom, but rather *what is being communicated?* How much of what we want our pupils "to get" actually comes through to whom? What "by-product messages" are students getting, i.e., something called to a student's mind, related or unrelated to the topic in question: In general science—INERTIA: "I must remember to fasten my seat belt"; in English—THE STAG AT EVE HAD DRUNK HIS FILL: "I like stag parties."

This work is concerned with oral communication as a medium of learning and as a basic function of human behavior. Improving communication includes, among other measures, recognizing and analysing the causes of communication failure or distortion. By such recognition and analysis we take an important step toward eliminating many of the barriers to good communication. Of course, communication failures and distortions are rarely due to single causes but rather to a complex of origins. For purposes of identification, it may be helpful to classify major causes as to general type or point of origin. The following categories provide us with such a classification: (1) problems arising from semantic or linguistic origins, (2) factors associated with the speaker, (3) factors associated with the listener, and (4) factors associated with time and place of the communication event.

COMMUNICATION DIFFICULTIES: LINGUISTIC ORIGINS

Possibly the most common source of communication difficulties can be found in the failure to understand the nature of language and to appreciate the elusiveness of words. If not the most common, surely this source is most frequently overlooked or ignored in day to day human relations.

Oral language includes both the language symbol (the word, sentence, paragraph) and the manner of utterance (the speaker's particular techniques for revealing his intended meanings through voice and action). However, for the moment we shall confine our discussion to those aspects of *the nature of words* which may lead to communication difficulties.

Most of us know fully well that *the word is not the thing:* we know that words are but symbols used to *represent* things not to *be* things. Yet we frequently behave as if we believed the word were the thing:

that through some magic when we use a particular word in reference to a thing our listeners will, presto, visualize the thing or experience the thing as we do. To keep our thinking straight we remind ourselves of the existence of the parallel worlds: the real world and the verbal world, as emphasized in Chapter One.

And we do our best to remember that the verbal world can never be a facsimile of the real world; and since it cannot, the verbal world is subject to errors of representation. It is essential that we continually remind ourselves of the limitations of language to represent our experiences with the real world. Words used in direct relation to things are likely to be most reliable; words used with reference to other words—particularly when we deal with high level abstractions, such as *loyalty, patriotism, love*—are likely to be most unreliable. In such cases the possibilities of losing one's self and one's listeners are considerable.

Another language pitfall is concealed by our failure to recognize that *words may have a variety of meanings.* Take the word *range* for example: (1) Home, home on the *range!* (2) The animals might *range* far from camp. (3) Check the *range* of this gun. (4) The Wasach *Range* lies east of Salt Lake City. (5) The scores *range* from 72 to 98. (6) Stay clear of the firing *range.* (7) She prepared dinner on her new kitchen *range.* Here contextual cues are necessary to deduce the intended meanings. Hayakawa reminds us that "dictionaries are helpful in providing us with a record of what various words have meant to authors in the distant and immediate past."[1] Dictionary meanings may be helpful in resolving disputes of definition, but they do not alter the fact that words have a way of becoming one's personal property : most words in a very real sense are products of one's personal experience. *Home, family, mother* denote different things to different people. Words also have a way of taking on new meanings, additional meanings, even though in some cases only temporarily, as the language of adolescents eloquently testifies.

Still another linguistic source of communication difficulty is the lack of understanding of the abstraction process.[2] For instance, the failure in either speaking or listening to sense where one *is* on the "abstraction ladder" at a given point in discourse can lead to con-

---

[1] S. I. Hayakawa, *Language In Thought and Action*, 2nd ed. (New York: Harcourt, Brace & World, Inc., 1964), p. 55.

[2] *Ibid.*, Chapter 10 "How We Know What We Know."

fusion. Failure to distinguish between the language which describes, specifies, particularizes and the language which generalizes, infers, interprets can be troublesome. Both "languages" are needed; but confusions arise when one "language" is used either unknowingly or deliberately as a substitute for the other. Similarly, confusions can develop from failures to distinguish among statements of fact, judgment, and opinion. Note, for instance: "As a matter of fact, he ought to be suspended from school"; or "The truth of the matter is, he is a fool." In these instances the speaker either is not aware of his inconsistencies or he is deliberately posing judgment and opinion as facts. Similarly, it is well to remember that the linguistic behaviors of children in a given classroom situation are bound to differ; home backgrounds and socio-economic strata have been shown to affect the verbal-cognitive development of children.[3]

Language is not a perfect instrument of communication, and we should remember this. However, it is also important to remember that most communication problems of the type we have been discussing are not due to the inherent nature of language but to our lack of understanding of how language works (including knowing its potentials and limitations), and to our lack of skill, wisdom, and responsibility in using words. Hayakawa puts it directly: "When the use of language results, as it often does, in the creation of aggravations or disagreements and conflicts, there is something linguistically wrong with the speaker, the listener, or both."[4] Let us therefore review some of the factors specifically associated with speaker and listener which might give rise to such communication difficulties.

FACTORS ASSOCIATED WITH THE SPEAKER

As noted in the previous chapter, communication may be intrapersonal: we may talk to ourselves; we may react to our own speech; we may talk out our thoughts to help clarify our understandings. For the moment, however, we are concerned with interpersonal communication and its related problems. And while we grant that the

---

[3] *Ibid.*, p. 18. See, for example, Basil Bernstein, "Social Structure, Language and Learning," *Educational Research*, III (June, 1961), 163–76.

[4] Hayakawa, p. 18.

listener stands watchman at his own linguistic portal in determining what gets in and what happens to whatever is let in, it is the speaker of the moment who must accept prime responsibility for the communication event. At what points is he particularly vulnerable to communication failure?

The speaker may lack credibility. A speaker must know what he is talking about. He must have a reputation for accuracy, for truthfulness, for thoughtfulness. When these qualities are lacking in the speaker, listeners are likely to turn him off; or they "misread" him when he actually has something worthwhile to say.

The speaker may fail to meet listeners on an appropriate plane. He may overestimate their knowledge of his subject and thus he may "talk over their heads." Or, what is worse, he may underestimate their understanding of the subject and thus offend his listeners with seeming condescension.

The speaker's purpose and motives may be obscure and his line of thought confused. The "map" ought to represent the "territory" as faithfully as possible. When it fails to do so, the listener has a good chance of becoming lost. Likewise, the person who fails to distinguish the important from the trivial invites boredom—a communicative failure.

The speaker's manner may be obstructive. Intentionally or not, the speaker may give the impression of being egotistical, insecure, or indifferent: impressions which may nullify or destroy desired communication. Bodily actions may distract the listener's attention from the verbal message, may even contradict what is said vocally. For example, the speaker's language may convey potentially interesting information, but his manner suggest boredom and that, rather than information, may be communicated.

Similarly, *the speaker's voice and articulation may be sources of communication distortion.* If the speaker cannot be heard or easily understood, or if his voice is dull, and his pronunciation inaccurate, communication may suffer.

The speaker may fail to observe and appropriately adjust to his listener's response. Feedback failures are considered a major cause of faulty communication. Failure to note listener inattention, signs of disagreement, bewilderment, fatigue, etc., can perpetuate poor communication.

Although student audiences are likely to be quite charitable toward peer member speaking, they are also quite discerning and can and will tell one another quite frankly what they like and do not like about a presentation. Pupils can be helped to discover and to eradicate causes of faulty communication due to speaker errors of commission and omission.

FACTORS ASSOCIATED WITH THE LISTENER

Ultimately it is the receiver-listener who determines what is communicated in a given situation: the amount of information received and the interpretation given to this information. Oddly enough, the full significance of this fact has only recently been appreciated. The increased recognition of the need for effective communication in all areas of life has motivated much interest in listening research, which in turn has been instrumental in developing listening improvement procedures and programs at all levels of education.

Studies by Nichols, Bird, Russell, Finkbeiner, and others have confirmed some of our commonly held views on listening, and at the same time dispelled many of our misconceptions regarding its nature. Particularly relevant to the present work, however, are findings that have helped identify some of the factors which may interfere with effective communication. We shall limit our attention to: (1) factors associated with verbal ability, (2) those associated with attitudes and verbal habits, and (3) those associated with mental and physical states.

Verbal ability

Listening, like reading, is a verbal skill. Both are receptive, interpretative processes. But they are not identical verbal processes. Studies[5] have found correlations between reading and listening comprehensions ranging from .44 to .67. The comparative low correlation is explained by the fact that reading is a visual-verbal behavior, while listening is an audio-visual-verbal process which involves somewhat different neural pathways within the central nervous system. The fact that the reader sets his own pace while the listener must accommodate his response to the rate of the speaker also serves to distinguish the

---

[5] See, for example: Dana Still, "Relationship between Listening Ability and High School Grades" (Doctoral Dissertation, University of Pittsburg, 1955).

Correction in front of book

verbal behavior of reading from that of listening. Although there is much that is unknown concerning the verbal nature of listening, the ~~following directions, (3) test for recognizing transitions, (4) test of~~ are considered important: (1) test of immediate recall, (2) test of following directions, (3) test for recognizing transitions, (4) test of oral vocabulary, and (5) test of recall of factual information and ability to draw inferences. To the extent that the receiver lacks the capacity to recognize, assimilate, and recall the essential elements of a speaker's message, communication obviously will suffer.

Motivation

Listening research[7] has confirmed what many teachers have suspected: that there is a low correlation between student scores on listening comprehension tests and their scores on unannounced tests of routine classroom listening. The low correlation is attributed to differences in motivation in the two situations.

Thinking-listening habits

From research carried out at the University of Minnesota, Nichols and Stevens[8] report six bad listening habits, each a rationalization for not listening. They are: (1) faking attention, (2) listening for facts instead of meanings, (3) avoiding difficult listening, (4) prematurely dismissing a subject as uninteresting, (5) criticizing speaker's delivery and physical appearance instead of paying attention to the message, and (6) yielding easily to distractions. In another report, Nichols and Lewis[9] cite *wasting the advantage of thought speed* as an additional cause of poor listening. The advantage referred to occurs as a result of our being able to think (talk to ourselves) four or five times as fast

---

[6] *Brown-Carlsen Listening Comprehension Test* (New York: Harcourt, Brace & World, Inc., 1965).

[7] Joy D. Finkbeiner, "A Study of the Relationship between Listening Ability and Listening Performance of Ninth Grade Pupils" (Master's Thesis, University of Washington, Seattle, 1962).

[8] Ralph G. Nichols and Leonard A. Stevens, *Are You Listening?* (New York: McGraw Hill Book Company, 1957), pp. 104–112.

[9] Ralph G. Nichols and Thomas R. Lewis, *Listening and Speaking* (Dubuque, Iowa: William C. Brown Company, Publishers, 1954), pp. 23–25.

as anyone can talk to us. What we do with this available time as we listen to others is critical to effective communication. If we use it to think about what is being said, to note relationships to ideas already expressed, and to weigh the logic of assertions, communication will prosper. If, on the other hand, we allow ourselves to daydream, to debate subvocally, or to take mental detours, the advantage of thought speed will be largely lost and communication will suffer.

Carl Rogers[10] calls our attention to another all-too-common communication deterrent: the tendency to prejudge, condemn, and "turn off" those who disagree with us. Most of us attend to messages we like to hear, to views that reinforce our beliefs. It is the exceptional person who has the courage and the will to withhold judgment until he has made a reasonable effort to understand the other person's view on a controversial point.

Mental and physical states

Listening efficiency may also be reduced by disruptive physical and mental states. Physical discomfort, anxiety, preoccupation with personal problems may interfere with communication, especially when the incentives to listen are not particularly compelling.

FACTORS ASSOCIATED WITH
TIME AND PLACE

Our third category of potentially disruptive influences includes a host of physical and social factors, peculiar to a particular school, classroom, or group of students. Time of day, size, shape, illumination, temperature, color scheme, and arrangement of the room affect communication, as do number of pupils in the room, pupil-pupil and pupil-teacher compatibility. There is evidence, for example, that seating arrangement influences group dynamics and, consequently, communication in discussion situations. Bales and Borgatta[11] report that communication

---

[10] Carl Rogers, "Barriers and Gateways to Communication," *Harvard Business Review*, XXX (July–August, 1952), 19.

[11] Robert F. Bales and Edgar F. Borgatta, "Size of Group as a Factor in the Interaction Profile," in *Small Groups: Studies in Social Interaction*, eds. A. Paul Hare and others (New York: Alfred A. Knopf, Inc., 1955), pp. 396–413.

varies inversely with size of the participating group. Crowell[12] suggests that optimum size of group has been found to vary with nature or purpose of the discussion. For example, five to seven appears to be an optimal number of participants for problem-solving discussion. On the other hand, study groups may profitably be extended to eleven or twelve, and exploratory groups to twenty-five participants with good results.

Within limits, of course, many of the foregoing factors constitute interferences only to the extent that participants allow themselves to be disrupted. Some sources of distraction can and should be eliminated: temperature, seating, lighting, many intraclass noises can be adjusted. Student-created distractions certainly should not be tolerated. However, their causes should not be ignored. Whispering, shuffling, and other disruptive behavior may not always be due to cussedness: the class assignment may have been unwisely chosen; there is a basketball game that night; the speaker is unmercifully dull; perhaps pupils have not been made to feel responsible as an audience. Alert teachers will help their pupils to recognize, analyze, and when possible, remedy disruptive influences. Pupils may have to learn to live with some sources of disruption. One cannot change the time of day, eliminate all coincidental noises, or provide a seating arrangement that is ideal for every pupil in the room.

SUMMARY

We have reviewed some of the principal sources of communication disruption and distortion in the classroom. We have noted those associated with the nature of language, and those identified with the speaker, listener, and the situation. The competent teacher develops a sensitivity to the causes of communication failure and with the help of his pupils takes the necessary steps to reduce such causes and to create an environment that fosters optimal communication. In Part Two of this volume we shall indicate some preliminary steps for accomplishing these objectives. Parts Three and Four develop in greater detail methods for strengthening oral communication as an effective medium and worthy object of learning.

[12] Laura Crowell, *Discussion: Method of Democracy* (New York: Scott, Foresman & Company, 1963), pp. 31–35.

SELECTED READINGS

Berlo, David K. *The Process of Communication.* New York : Holt, Rinehart & Winston, Inc., 1960.

Brown, Charles T., and C. W. Van Riper. *Speech and Man.* Englewood Cliffs, New Jersey: Prentice-Hall, Inc., 1966.

Hayakawa, S. I. *Language in Thought and Action,* 2nd ed. New York : Harcourt, Brace & World, Inc., 1964.

Johnson, Wendell. *Your Most Enchanted Listener.* New York : Harper & Row, Publishers, 1956.

Lee, Irving. *How to Talk With People.* New York : Harper & Row, Publishers, 1952.

————. *Handling Barriers in Communication.* New York : Harper & Row, Publishers, 1957.

Nichols, Ralph and Leonard A. Stevens. *Are You Listening?* New York : McGraw-Hill Book Company, 1957.

Overstreet, H. A. *The Mature Mind.* New York : W. W. Norton & Company, Inc., 1949.

Rogers, Carl. "Barriers and Gateways to Communication." *Harvard Business Review,* XXX (July–August, 1952), 19.

Ruesch, Jurgen and Welden Kees. *Non-Verbal Communication.* Berkeley: University of California Press, 1956.

APPROACH

PART **II** *toward better communication*

4 *observing student characteristics*

In preceding chapters we have considered the nature of communication, reviewed the fundamentals of speaking and listening, and noted some of the conditions which affect communication efficiency. We come now, as we must, to an essential first step in preparation for improving oral communication in the classroom, whether viewed as a medium of learning or as a personal skill. This first step takes us directly to the central figure of secondary education: the high school pupil.

Knowing one's pupils has long been recognized as one of the essentials of successful teaching. The alert teacher can learn much about the nature of his pupils through observing their speech behavior. It should be borne in mind, however, that such observations constitute only one of many mechanisms for "reading" one's pupils. Even more important, however, is to realize that such observations must be made in light of knowledge of the behavior tendencies of high school pupils in general. In this chapter, therefore, we shall be talking about some of these tendencies. We shall dwell briefly on the general characteristics of adolescents, note some of their language manifestations, and identify some of the means for discovering individual differences in their behavior.

GENERAL CHARACTERISTICS OF ADOLESCENCE

As prospective or practicing high school teachers, our readers are doubtless quite familiar with the general characteristics and behavior tendencies associated with adolescence. We recall some of these tendencies chiefly because of their potential influence upon pupil communication and their implications for prescribing classroom speech activities.

Adolescent characteristics of particular significance include: (1) marked growth of the body, with its attendant problems of muscular coordination and unpredictable vocal response; (2) the development of sex functions and sexual awareness, with their effects upon socialization; (3) tendencies toward erratic emotional behavior, with its obvious effects on adjustments in speaking situations; (4) increased social awareness and sensitivity to peer esteem, with the accompanying effects upon pupils' self-images and their mechanisms for forming such images; (5) strong self-interests and growing independence and assertiveness: argumentativeness, impulsiveness, tendencies to rebel; and (6) growth of idealism and the propensity for hero worship. The ability to recognize these and other adolescent characteristics and to react to them understandingly is crucial to successful teaching; crucial because they impinge upon the processes of communication. They affect the child's attitude toward speech in general, particularly his own speech, thereby determining when and how he speaks and listens. The wise teacher will make an effort to remember that many of the so-called "disciplinary problems" which occur in the high school classroom are virtually preordained: built-in tendencies, as it were. The beginning teacher may derive some consolation from the thought that specific acts of student rebellion may not be directed toward him personally, but toward teachers or adults in general.

What we have been saying about the adolescent population is pretty much the standard description of the high school pupil as we have known him in past generations.[1] Is this description applicable to today's adolescent? Is there any evidence that today's teen-ager differs in any important respects from his counterpart of earlier periods? We have ample reason to believe that the knowledge

---

[1] For comprehensive treatment of the subject, see, for example, A. A. Schneiders, *Personality Development and Adjustment in Adolescence* (Milwaukee: The Bruce Publishing Co., 1960).

explosion, the speed of social change, the turbulence of a world at war and near-war have had profound effects upon youth along with the general population. In his timely book, *Adolescents and the Schools,* James Coleman[2] lists five factors (paraphrased below) which he asserts have influenced the social organization of adolescence, thereby affecting the behavior of youth in significant and recognizable ways:

1. *Increased social sophistication of teen-agers.* For a variety of reasons, teen-agers are becoming socially sophisticated earlier than ever before. Exposure to radio, TV, movies, and books is making children wiser in the ways of the world than youth of an earlier age. While it may not have made them more serious or more responsible, it has made them less in awe of adults, less willing to listen to a teacher just because he is a teacher.
2. *The school's encompassment of the total community of adolescents.* Most adolescents are now attending high school. The adolescent's social sphere has become the social system of the high school.
3. *The gradual diminution of the need for the adolescent in the adult world.* Labor-saving devices and other changes in the economy have tended to isolate youth, relieve them of any responsibility in the adult world.
4. *Emergence of commercial entertainment designed specifically for adolescents.* The popular music field and dance motifs are best examples.
5. *Compulsory school attendance.* For many pupils the motivational challenge accompanying compulsory attendance is quite different from that of voluntary attendance.

Coleman contends that the five aforementioned influences have been instrumental in producing a "peculiar set of circumstances," circumstances which in effect have to some extent isolated the adolescent from the rest of society. Coleman summarizes the "circumstances" thus:

> Adolescents have their own little society, with special symbols and language, special interests and activities. It is a society composed of people who are wordly-wise in many ways, of people who are more adult than child, yet a society of people without responsibilities, a society subject to the demands placed upon it by others—that is, by adults. To

---

[2] James S. Coleman, *Adolescents and the Schools* (New York: Basic Books, Inc., Publishers, 1965), pp. 10–11. Used by permission of the publisher.

be sure, adults are doing this for their "own good," but it is
the adult who decides what is good and what is not. Such a
situation invites trouble. It encourages leadership that
asserts itself against the adult demands. It encourages a
disdain for those who exert extra effort to meet adult
demands. It encourages a status system among adolescents
based on such extra-school activities as dating and sports.
In sum, it effectively impedes education, keeping the effort
expended on learning at a minimum.[3]

We believe it safe to assert that today's adolescent is not physio-
logically or emotionally different from his counterpart of the 1870's or
even the 1770's. However, greater sophistication has endowed today's
adolescent with a type of maturity not commonly found in the high
school population of former generations. High school teaching which
ignores this fact of life is likely to experience serious disappointments.
It is conceivable that isolating the adolescent from the adult world
has increased the communication barrier between adult and youth:
between teacher and pupil, and in so doing has further complicated
the problems of teaching.

LANGUAGE CHARACTERISTICS OF
HIGH SCHOOL PUPILS

In our review of some of the general characteristics of adolescents, we
have alluded briefly to teen-age jargon and the language of adolescent
society. Enigmatic as this language may be to most adults, teachers
had better keep abreast of its developments, if only to remain in
contact with their pupils. Fortunately, teen-agers also speak a more
standard type of American-English, albeit not too well at times.
What are some of the language characteristics of teen-agers, other than
their jargon?

The following list of adolescent language characteristics, quoted
from a report of the Commission of the English Curriculum of the
National Council of Teachers of English, provides us with some useful
information regarding this point:

---

[3] *Ibid.*, p. 12.

STUDENTS *(level 12–15 years)*:

1. Desire to have fun, manifesting itself in language expression related to sports, amusements, and humorous situations; develop increased maturity in interests through clubs and teamwork; show interest in reading and talking about animals, adventure, mystery, collections, and explorations, but resist tasks requiring lengthy application; girls show interest in sentiment and romance.

2. Desire to be interesting is manifested in the individual's pursuit of his own welfare, and in human relationships, with increasing social sensitivity to reaction of individuals and the group.

3. Desire to understand and express themselves through dramatization and imaginative thinking; show wide variation in educational attainment; desire to realize their capacities as shown in their attempts to understand personal abilities and to seek interests that will fulfill their recognized language needs.

4. Desire to become informed and to discuss ideals by which men live (manifested in hero worship); and express a challenging attitude toward social problems, and a concern about right and wrong.

5. May display aggressiveness in speech and a tendency toward constant argumentation; show a liking for parliamentary procedures; enjoy hobbies involving use of much technical knowledge and skill and employ a more logical approach to solving problems; read periodicals and books related to interests; experience a need to express a new awakening to beauty.

STUDENTS *(level 15–18 years)*:

1. Reveal great variations in degrees of development in the various language arts; a small percentage have developed the ability to write creatively, but a greater number probably have powers that are undeveloped; often show reluctance in sharing their production; manifest far less difference in reading interests between sexes than between individuals; exhibit a wide range in ability in various aspects of language power; an individual may be skillful in one or more abilities (as reading or speaking) and immature in aspects of others (as skill in spelling or punctuation in writing); range from almost total inadequacy to a successful degree of fluency in oral expression; increase in writing skills as their thinking becomes more clarified; acquire skill in discriminative use of many types of instructional materials.

2. Extend language experiences in the treatment of mature problems, including relationships among persons, sexes, economic classes, races, political parties, nations and periods of history; boys seek fiction and talk about physically vigorous and morally courageous heroes; girls enjoy romantic stories.

3. Increase in power to think together in large groups (whole classes), to share opinions, and to reach a common feeling and understanding; are so preoccupied with radio and television programs popular with the group, and with activities, pleasures, and friends that it is necessary that all reading and expression suggested by the school be meaningful to them in order to compete successfully for their out-of-school time; are willing to use their specific talents for the group (e.g., postermaking, lettering, running machinery, writing verses, planning programs); cooperate because of group loyalty.

4. Make considerable use of slang and swearing in their speech since it serves not only to furnish a form of expression for their emotions, but also to attract attention of adults and to show belongingness in their own group; are interested in dramatics for personal satisfaction and to gain status within the group.

5. Desire intensely to gain information on their special interests, so are easily led toward becoming good readers; appreciate the importance of vocational success and are willing to master necessary language skills and adult standards; many delight in expressing opinions, very often in a critical way; are willing to "sharpen" their powers of discrimination to select from many sources those literary experiences including books, periodicals, music, radio programs, plays, etc., which best fill their needs.

6. Have begun to see remote goals and are willing to go through experiences and practices in language even though tedious, because of the values anticipated in successful accomplishments; develop interest in becoming informed on human relationships and issues; enjoy the beautiful in nature, literature, and human beings; strive to acquire beauty for themselves as a means of securing favorable reaction, as expressed in words, from the group.[4]

The findings cited by the National Council's Commission tend to confirm many of the general conclusions regarding adolescence

---

[4] Reprinted from the Commission on the English Curriculum, *The English Language Arts in the Secondary School*, NCTE Curriculum Series, Vol. III (New York: Appleton-Century-Crofts, 1956), pp. 16–20. By permission of the National Council of Teachers of English.

mentioned earlier in this chapter. More important, perhaps, the findings offer numerous clues for teaching adolescents through wisely selected speech-listening activities, about which more will be said later.

ADOLESCENTS AS INDIVIDUALS

Thus far in the present chapter, we have given major attention to the behavior tendencies of adolescents in general: the teen-age group as a segment of the total population. While it is appropriate to take note of central tendencies of this group, *we must not lose sight of the adolescent as an individual*, teen-ager$_1$, teen-ager$_2$, teen-ager$_3$ and so on who make up our high school classes. As emphasized earlier, it should be every teacher's aim to get to know his pupils as unique individuals as quickly and as thoroughly as possible.

High school teachers are fully aware that teen-agers present a vast array of individual differences, which must be reckoned with if teacher-pupil communication is to occur. Teen-agers differ sexually, socially, intellectually, physically, and scholastically. They differ in their rates of physical, mental, and social maturation. High school classes may include pupils ranging from low-average to superior intelligence. These pupils represent an unbelievable assortment of home backgrounds. They manifest various degrees of physical attractiveness. Their motivations range from those of the potential dropout to those of honor students intent on a career in law, medicine, education. As we have said, the alert teacher studies his pupils: he observes them in a variety of situations. He is cognizant of their speech and listening characteristics: he notes the reticent, the loquacious, the thoughtful, the irresponsible, the drudge, the impulsive, the fluent. Through observation and review of the student's personal file, as well as other means, he learns much that can be of value to him in approaching each learner with some degree of prescription.

In studying the pupil as an individual *it is very important that we consider him as a member of a class,* remembering that his behavior is in various ways influenced by the other members of the class, the teacher, the subject being taught, and physical features of the class-room. Grouping by class, as we know, is a convention, an *administrative arrangement* to facilitate organized instruction. Even with some attention to ability grouping this arrangement offers no way of predicting what the "mix" in classes will be. Recent experimentation with groups of various sizes has yielded some promising results: sufficient at least to assure us that teachers will continue to work with groups of pupils as classes, subgroups of classes, and combinations of classes representing various kinds of "mixes." Successful teaching—effective communication, and, therefore, productive learning—is highly dependent upon how well teachers understand the dynamics of their classes: how pupils relate to one another, how comfortable and how motivated they feel in a particular class environment. We have learned from industry as well as from experience in education that individuals work and learn best when they relate and communicate effectively with those around them.

This facet of our effort to understand the pupils we teach, therefore, has to do with group dynamics, the interpersonal relationships of members of a particular class: Geometry$_1$, English II$_a$, World History II. The teacher is indeed fortunate when, seemingly without extra effort on his part, members of his classes seem to blend into a unified, constructively oriented group with common objectives. For various reasons, at the beginning of a semester most classes are likely to be little more than collections of individuals, albeit loosely bound together as members of adolescent society and identified as *the taught* as distinguished from *those who teach*. Having some knowledge of the dynamics of one's classes can be crucial to intelligent planning, individual and class motivation, productive class activities, and above all, to designing prescriptive guidance and assignments for the individual pupil.

METHODS OF STUDYING CLASS DYNAMICS

Members of a class may be studied informally or through the use of sociometric tests. Through observing their students' reactions in various situations, most teachers are able to gain some helpful information regarding the interpersonal relations of their class members. They note, for example, the different "in-groups," the apparent group leaders, the potential class leaders, the loners, and the rejects. Obviously, the ability to observe accurately, objectively, and analytically is essential.

Another, and, in some respects, a more effective and valid means of providing information regarding intraclass relations is the *socio-*

metric test. This device, actually not a *test* in the usual sense, consists of a stimulus question administered to the members of a class to secure information regarding their attitudes toward and understandings of other pupils in the group. The information thus obtained is plotted on a chart known as a *sociogram.* Though not particularly difficult to administer, the sociometric test needs to be carefully planned and worded and the results thoughtfully interpreted.

In securing information for a sociogram, it is essential that the subject be introduced in a realistic situation. For example, the "situation" may be a need for forming a student work group, a steering committee for a class project, a social committee, a library study group, or the like. It is important that the question be so worded and directed as to require the individual to consider the other members of the group in relation to himself in the performance of a particular task. It is also essential that the question be so phrased as to cause pupils to express themselves spontaneously and honestly. They should be assured that results will be used as suggested in the explanation accompanying the actual question, but will not be seen or used by anyone other than the teacher. After distributing a card or slip of paper to each member of the class and asking pupils to write their names at the top of the page and the names of their choices below, the teacher will explain the situation: e.g., the need for certain committees in connection with class work, and then request pupils to list in order of preference the names of three classmates with whom they would prefer to work on a particular committee.

Responses are tabulated on a chart (sociogram) and the results interpreted. The teacher will first extract the information relevant to the immediate situation: e.g., forming committees. He will then examine the information for clues regarding the dynamics of the class. For example, he will note possible implications for class management, lesson planning, and use of oral activities.

The teacher will attempt to analyze the nature of the class dynamics: discover the motivations and possible reasons for various choices and rejections. As previously suggested, observations, student's permanent files, personal inventories, conferences, all may be helpful in providing some of the answers to this question. In dealing with a low-status pupil, for example, Fessenden, and others,[5] suggest that

---

[5] Seth A. Fessenden and others, *Speech for the Creative Teacher* (Dubuque, Iowa: William C. Brown Company, Publishers, 1968), pp. 180-81.

among other steps, the teacher determine the nature of the person's out-of-class contacts, the home situation; his methods of securing approval or attention, the extent to which he voluntarily isolates himself. Similarly, the teacher needs to discover, if possible, the bases for certain students' popularity. He would try to determine whether the students' motives seemed sincere, whether their attitudes were constructive, what their chief assets were and what liabilities, if any, might need attention. Subsequent "tests" should be given at appropriate intervals, their results compared, and possibly new strategies designed to meet more prescriptively the needs of class members.

Finally, the teacher will endeavor to use the findings of his investigation for developing improved class interpersonal communication. He will try to assist pupils in building favorable self-images and due respect for others. He will strive to create an atmosphere that encourages freedom of expression with responsibility, that respects the youngster as a person, that provides a setting and means whereby students working, thinking together, with teacher as guide, can face and resolve problems cooperatively. Such an atmosphere can convert a collection of individuals into a unified group, a group learning about life by living it. This is the atmosphere that can help individuals toward becoming mature human beings.

The foregoing brief discussion of sociometric testing should by no means be considered an ample guide for using sociometrics in the classroom; it is intended primarily to indicate something of the nature of sociometry and to suggest its potential value as a classroom procedure when properly administered.[6]

SUMMARY

In this chapter we have renewed our acquaintance with the teen-age high school pupil. We have recalled some of the general characteristics commonly associated with adolescence; we have noted in particular certain language manifestations attributed to youth from twelve to eighteen. We have indicated some of the ways today's teen-agers differ from their counterparts of previous generations. We have also remembered that while adolescents possess a number of traits that

---

[6] Helen H. Jennings, *Sociometry in Group Relations,* rev. ed. (Washington, D.C.: American Council on Education, 1959).

serve to identify them as a group, they differ in many significant respects. Finally, we have viewed the adolescent as a member of a high school class.

From this brief stock-taking of student characteristics, perhaps we may more fully appreciate some of the challenges and opportunities the high school teacher faces in his efforts to guide youth toward self-realization. Effective teaching and effective learning depend upon effective communication: both interpersonal and intragroup. Understanding the adolescent as a member of a particular age group, as an individual, and as a member of an instructional group is the first important step in achieving such communication. In the remaining chapters of this section, we shall give attention to three additional steps preparatory to considering in some detail key speech forms and how to use them in the classroom as developed in Parts Three and Four. In these sections every effort has been made to select activities and learning procedures in light of our understanding of the nature and needs of adolescents.

SELECTED READINGS

Alexander, William M., and Paul M. Halverson. *Effective Teaching in Secondary Schools.* New York : Holt, Rinehart & Winston, Inc., 1956.

Crow, Lester D., and Alice Crow. *Adolescent Development and Adjustment,* 2nd ed. New York: McGraw-Hill Book Company, 1965. Chapter 8 "Importance of Interests and Attitudes."

Havighurst, Robert J. *Human Development and Education.* New York : Longmans, Green & Co., Inc., 1953.

Jennings, Helen Hall. *Sociometry in Group Relations,* rev. ed. Washington, D.C. : American Council on Education, 1959.

Lee, James M. *Principles and Methods of Secondary Education.* New York : McGraw-Hill Book Company, 1963. Chapter IV "The Secondary School Student : Person and Learner."

Remmers, H. H., Harry N. Rivlin, David G. Ryans, and Einar R. Ryden, eds. *Growth, Teaching, and Learning.* New York : Harper & Row, Publishers, 1957. A book of readings.

Schneiders, Alexander A. *Personality Development and Adjustment in Adolescence.* Milwaukee : The Bruce Publishing Co., 1960. Part III "The Psychology of Adolescence."

5 *providing an optimum climate*

Perhaps it is semantic quibbling to contend, as some educators do, that teachers do not teach; at best, all they can hope to do is to create an environment in which, with guidance, pupils learn. Certainly all teachers will agree that the psychological and physical climates of a classroom are inseparably related to learning. Climate and educational processes are reciprocal: i.e., certain factors associated with good teaching and effective learning serve to create a stimulating climate. Conversely, good climate helps facilitate effective communication and worthwhile learning.

In the previous chapter, we spoke of the dynamics of classroom interpersonal relations. Such relations help determine the character of classroom climate. But there are other situational or climatic factors which influence communication and learning. In this chapter we shall consider some of them as elements of a *second step* preparatory to using and guiding oral communication in the classroom. We shall give particular attention to (1) the physical setting, (2) the social and psychological climate, and (3) the teacher.

THE PHYSICAL SETTING

First of all, as with geographical climate, the classroom atmosphere is influenced by the location and nature of the physical surroundings. The size, shape, arrangement, lighting, temperature, color scheme of the room may affect its atmosphere. We are aware of man's ingenuity in manipulating so-called natural climates to his advantage. Witness such innovations as irrigation of desert land, air-conditioning, refrigeration, cloud-seeding: all in the interest of providing more abundantly for man's material needs and comforts. Likewise, in recent years educators have manipulated the physical setting of the traditional classroom in numerous ways to facilitate communication associated with learning experiences in today's secondary schools.

Good teaching and effective learning, of course, can occur in the most limited surroundings. A creative teacher can convert an ordinary classroom into an extraordinary center of learning. Nevertheless, good physical surroundings can assist the creative teacher and his pupils in achieving their objectives more efficiently and more effectively. Today's emphasis upon problem-solving and inquiry methods, variable grouping, and shift from teacher- to student-centered learning calls for flexible arrangements and procedures. Let us explore some of the ways in which a semitraditional classroom may be adapted to serve the communication requirements of various classroom procedures.

SUGGESTED SPECIFICATIONS

1. Movable student desks or tables and chairs.
2. Library table(s) and chairs.
3. Book shelves for accommodating classroom library materials.
4. Demonstration table.
5. Portable lectern.
6. Available projection equipment (16mm motion picture, slide or strip, overhead and opaque projectors; screen; provision for darkening the room).
7. Chalkboard, bulletin boards, and display area.
8. Teacher's desk and chair.

Figures 2 through 8 illustrate a number of the most common arrangements for expediting communication in many of the basic classroom activities described in Parts Three and Four of this volume. The following letters designate the equipment illustrated in figures 2

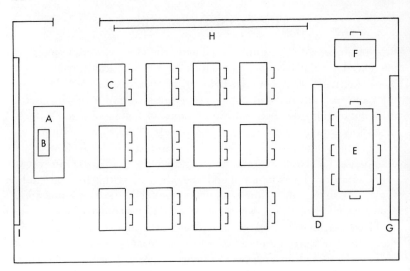

FIGURE 2. ARRANGEMENT FOR LECTURES, REPORTS,
A–V PROJECTIONS.

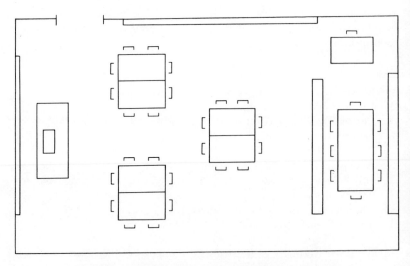

FIGURE 3. ARRANGEMENT FOR SIMULTANEOUS GROUP
DISCUSSIONS, COMMITTEE PROJECTS, SMALL
GROUP ACTIVITIES.

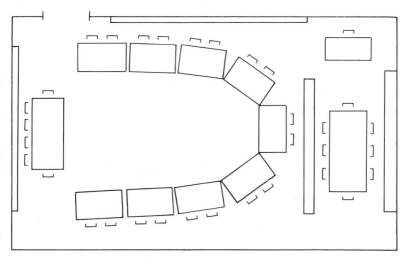

FIGURE 4. ARRANGEMENT FOR PANELS, SYMPOSIUMS,
AND INTERPRETATIVE READING.

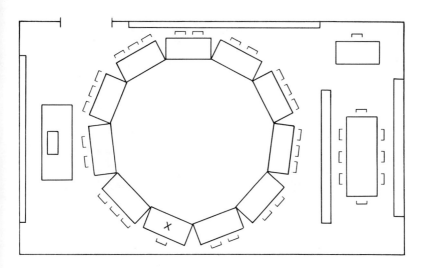

FIGURE 5. ARRANGEMENT FOR TEACHER-LED
DISCUSSION.

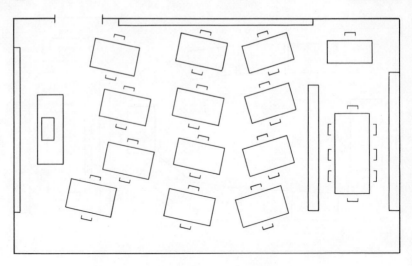

FIGURE 6. ARRANGEMENT FOR REVIEWING, REHEARSING
FOR REPORTS, TESTING, ETC.

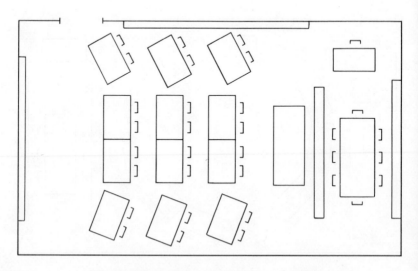

FIGURE 7. ARRANGEMENT FOR DRAMATIZATIONS—
PROSCENIUM STYLE.

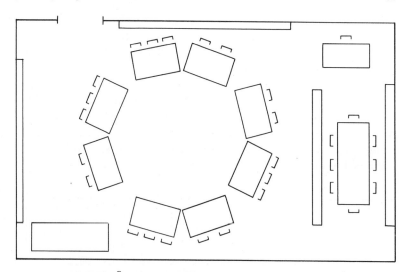

FIGURE 8. ARRANGEMENT FOR DRAMATIZATIONS—
ARENA STYLE.

PHYSICAL CLIMATE CAN BE INTELLECTUALLY
STIMULATING.
(Courtesy of the Seattle Public Schools).

through 8: A, demonstration table; B, lectern; C, student table with chairs; D, low room-divider; E, library table with chairs; F, teacher's desk with chair; G, book shelves; H, bulletin board; I, chalkboard and retractable projection screen.

Current school construction designed with today's teaching-learning needs in mind, not only incorporates much of what we have considered above, but extends the provision for flexibility in additional ways. Figure 9, for example, illustrates one school's[1] physical arrangement for expediting teaching-learning activities involving the combined efforts and talents of four teachers acting as a team.

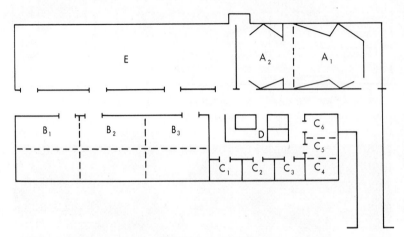

FIGURE 9. FLOOR PLAN OF SPEECH-ENGLISH WING OF
SHORECREST SENIOR HIGH SCHOOL.

(A_1 and A_2, lecture room. Capacity: 100-120; carpeted, inclined floor; small stage; retractable screen and sliding chalkboards; projection equipment housed off-stage. A_1 and A_2 may be separated with divider. B_1, B_2, and B_3 large carpeted classroom : can be used as one or as three separate classrooms or as six separate areas by using room dividers. Capacities : 120, 40, and 20. Movable tables and chairs. C_1 through C_6, small-group centers. Capacity: 6 to 10. Adjustable tables and chairs; carpeted floors. Room dividers may be retracted to combine units. D, bookroom and secretarial office. E, assigned to classes other than speech and English.)

---

[1] Reproduced here by permission of Shoreline Public Schools, suburban Seattle.

This plan provides appropriate spaces for various kinds of instruction. For example, space "A" seats 100 to 120 pupils, a combination of four conventional groups, for general lectures, motion pictures, and dramatics. "B" spaces provide functional areas for medium-size groups (20–30 pupils), where teacher-led discussion, reports, dramatizations may take place. "C" spaces offer areas for small group activities. The total complex makes possible supervision and coordination of the work of several sections of pupils in various combinations of groupings.

PSYCHOLOGICAL CLIMATE

To the extent that they facilitate effective grouping for instruction, increase the chances of good communication, and offer greater promise for pupil (and teacher) motivation, physical surroundings may be expected to contribute also to the psychological climate of a classroom. There are, however, other forces at work in a classroom which help to create a favorable environment for learning. We refer, of course, to such factors as curiosity, good study habits, respect for thoroughness and accuracy, freedom to explore, and the spirit of helpfulness among pupils and between pupils and teacher. We have in mind the kind of atmosphere which pervades the classroom when teacher and pupils enjoy a feeling of mutual respect, when learning seems to be a joint venture with students and teacher sharing in the activities and in the excitement of the quest. There is evidence that such an atmosphere is most likely to develop when the problem-solving or discovery method is wisely and effectively employed, when the procedures are essentially student-centered rather than teacher-directed. It is a permissive atmosphere which encourages objective, creative, and analytical thinking. It is an atmosphere which developes from recognizing the multi-level nature of speech and language as determined by psychological and socio-economic factors.

As any speech teacher will attest, a favorable psychological climate is especially important to effective and efficient oral communication, and, hence, to learning. An atmosphere fraught with tension, whatever the cause, is not conducive to free interplay of minds nor to good speaking and listening. Anything which is likely to disrupt thought processes, negatively affect emotions, and interfere with muscular coordinations is likely to reduce speaking and listening effectiveness. We suggest that good speaking and listening are most likely to thrive in an atmosphere wrought by exercise of good motives, good will, good work, and good humor. To reiterate a statement of the preceding chapter: understanding the dynamics of one's classes and appropriately guiding the "forces" therein constitute important steps for developing a favorable classroom atmosphere.

There are innumerable ways of causing a child to learn a body of information, a skill, or a concept. However, the conditions under which the learning takes place, as well as the methods of learning, help to determine what actually is learned and how thoroughly a thing is learned. More importantly perhaps, such conditions, along with the methods of learning employed, often determine the students' attitudes toward the thing learned as well as the learning experience itself. Even though conditions and methods appear to achieve immediate objectives, if in the process such conditions and procedures serve to alienate pupils' interest in learning, or fail to kindle the desire for continued learning, their seeming effectiveness may be self-defeating.

THE TEACHER: PERSON, COMMUNICATOR, EDUCATOR

We have considered both the physical setting and psychological climate of the classroom. In both, the teacher plays a major role. With his pupils, the teacher plans ways in which his room may be best adapted to learning; he may even have a hand in designing physical facilities when new buildings are being planned. It is the teacher who "reads" the class dynamics and attempts to guide the forces into productive channels. But even more important, it is the teacher who by precept and example sets the educational tone of the class and provides guidance for effective communication, effective learning. This takes some doing. Not all teachers can perform all such functions with expertise. What persons are most likely to succeed? Those who are masters of their subject? Those who are well versed in methodology? Those who understand the ways of their pupils? To some extent, of course, all of these. One is prompted simply to say it takes a *good* teacher. But what are the characteristics of a *good* teacher? Ask anyone: ask parents, ask teachers, ask pupils—all have opinions of what constitutes a good teacher. But what *is* good teaching? What is the relationship between how well a pupil learns and what the teacher is or does? What factors associated with teaching are most likely to influence learning? A good deal of educational research has attempted to provide valid answers to these questions; thus far the results have not been very fruitful. The problem lies chiefly in the relative nature of competent teaching. In his exhaustive teacher characteristics study, Ryans asserts:

> A description of competent or effective teaching must be considered to be relative—relative to perhaps three major sets of conditions: (1) the social or cultural group in which the teacher operates, involving social values which frequently differ from person to person, and time to time; (2) the grade level and subject matter taught; and perhaps (3) intellectual and personal characteristics of the pupils taught.[2]

In spite of the absence of *infallible* criteria for determining the characteristics of good teaching, it is essential that teaching competence be judged, teachers evaluated, and prospective teachers guided toward the competencies believed essential to successful teaching. Professional educators have attempted to provide some direction to such evaluations by developing lists of desirable teacher competencies, behavior traits, and attitudes. Information for such lists has been gathered from observations, interviews, studies of teacher records, pupil opinion polls, experimental studies, and school administrator judgments.[3]

---

[2] David G. Ryans, *Characteristics of Teachers: Their Description, Comparison, and Appraisal* (Washington, D.C.: American Council on Education, 1960), p. 371.

[3] See, for example: A. S. Barr, "The Measurement and Prediction of Teaching Efficiency: A Summary of Investigations," *Journal of Experimental Education*, XVI (June, 1948), 5–9; Paul Witty, "Some Characteristics of the Effective Teacher," *Educational Administration and Supervision*, XXXVI (April, 1950), 193–208; Frank W. Hart, *Teachers and Teaching* (New York: The Macmillan Company, 1934); Ben D. Wood, *Principles and Procedures of Teacher Selection* (Philadelphia: American Association of Examiners and Administrative Personnel, 1952); Russell N. Cassel and W. Lloyd Johns, "The Critical Characteristics of an Effective Teacher," *Bulletin*, NASSP XL (November, 1960), 119–24.

Of particular significance in such lists of teacher characteristics is the frequent mention of factors pertaining to *oral communication competence*. Clark's study (1963)[4] of school administrator opinion regarding teacher speech needs confirms conclusions reached by several earlier investigators that "speech ability in general is positively related to teaching competence," and reaffirms the position taken in this work that effective oral communication is essential to good teaching and learning. On this premise it is possible and we believe profitable to consider the oral communication dimension of teaching in terms of certain rhetorical principles. Drawing from the several sources to which we have alluded in this chapter, as well as our personal experience in teacher education, we offer the following observations regarding the rhetorical character of good teaching :

1. *Obviously, first of all, a teacher must know his subject.* This means knowing it from day to day, keeping abreast of new developments in his field. Some of the teacher-communicator's ethos originates in his credibility. Does his knowledge have depth? Is his information reliable and are his inferences sound? At the same time, does his knowledge show some breadth of interest? Does he sense the relationship of his field with other areas of learning? The behavior of the worthy teacher reflects worthy motives: a genuine love of learning and a strong desire to help others learn. It reflects honesty and fairness.

2. *The successful teacher reaches his pupils through emotional means (pathetic appeals).* He is enthusiastic about his subject, his manner reflects genuine enjoyment of teaching; there is ample evidence that he likes young people. He likes them especially for what they are : active, curious, frank, resourceful, unpredictable, basically fair. He will admit that not all pupils or even whole classes of pupils are altogether likeable. However, because he is genuinely concerned with problems of human growth, he will continue his efforts to discover latent resources in his pupils which if properly tapped may help such pupils develop into self-respecting, productive citizens. With all pupils he tries to link class assignments with incentives that have emotional appeal for youth: physical activity, group identification, and group approvals, dramatics, amusement, problem-solving. The worthy teacher believes in his work and in himself; he is dedicated to serving others. Laura

---

[4] Richard W. Clark, "An Investigation of the Speech Needs of Classroom Teachers and SpeechTraining Programs in Washington State Teacher Training Institutions," (Master's Thesis, University of Washington, Seattle, 1963), p. 86.

Crowell notes the importance of teacher attitude in creating a class-room atmosphere from which students will form worthy attitudes "towards learning, toward responsibility, toward public issues, and toward people." She mentions five attitudes which she believes the teacher should so strongly manifest that the students could not fail to catch them. They are: (1) "enthusiasm for learning; (2) high standards for achievement; (3) considered judgment; (4) respect for others as individuals; and (5) respect for self."[5]

3. *The effective teacher-communicator is logical and intellectually provocative in his approaches to learning.* His general planning is orderly, purposeful, and well conceived in terms of the pupils for whom the instruction is intended. His powers of reflective and analytical thinking enable him to lead class discussions and pose stimulating questions. His responses to pupil efforts are calculated to stimulate the pupils to further active thinking. Such comments as the following are typical: "A good thing to know . . . Aha, there's a new idea . . . Are you satisfied with that statement? . . . Don't be too easily discouraged . . . Give us one concrete example . . . Can you prove the statement? . . . Let's stick to the question."[6]

4. *The effective teacher is a competent speaker and an efficient listener.* We believe he should listen more often than he talks. When he talks and listens he exemplifies those standards he applies in evaluating the speech-listening behavior of his pupils.[7] Although in the study previously mentioned, Clark identifies some nineteen speech abilities as "strongly desirable" for effective teaching, he reports the following six as most closely associated with teaching success:

ABILITY
1. to think critically and orderly.
2. to listen critically.
3. to use the voice effectively with clear articulation and acceptable pronunciation.

---

[5] Laura Crowell, "Attitudes Are Contagious," *The Speech Teacher*, II (November, 1953), 257–60.

[6] A. S. Barr, *Characteristic Differences in the Teaching Performances of Good and Poor Teachers in the Social Studies* (Bloomington, Illinois: Public School Publishing Co., 1929), pp. 42–44.

[7] See Chapter 2, pp. 29–31.

4. to use oral language effectively.[8]
5. to read aloud.
6. to serve as a leader and member of group discussion.

Much of what a teacher *is* as a person and as a teacher is revealed in his actions and in his speech : interest in his subject and his pupils; command of subject matter; confidence, mental and emotional maturity; powers of concentration, and ability to use language as an effective medium of thought and feeling. A good teacher, we believe, is, as Quintilian would have him, "a good man speaking well."

SUMMARY

Thus, we have reviewed some of the salient features of "a climate for effective communication," an atmosphere for learning, with the teacher the over-arching single influence on the nature of this atmosphere. The numerous speaking-listening activities suggested in Parts Three and Four of this work are designed to help the creative teacher capitalize upon and further strengthen *the learning climate* discussed in this chapter.

SELECTED READINGS

Amidon, Edmund, and Elizabeth Hunter. *Improving Teaching: The Analysis of Classroom Verbal Interaction.* New York: Holt, Rinehart & Winston, Inc., 1966.

Burton, William H. *The Guidance of Learning Activities,* 3rd ed. New York : Appleton-Century-Crofts, 1962.

Fessenden, Seth A., Roy I. Johnson, P. Merville Larson, and Kaye M. Good. *Speech for the Creative Teacher.* Dubuque, Iowa : William C. Brown Company, Publishers, 1968. Chapter I "Speech and the Teaching Personality."

Highet, Gilbert. *The Art of Teaching.* New York : Alfred A. Knopf, Inc., 1950. Chapter II "The Teacher."

---

[8] Clark, *op. cit.,* p. 88.

Hearn, Arthur. "Case Studies of Successful Teachers." *Educational Administration and Supervision,* XXXVIII (October, 1952), 376–79.

Overstreet, Harry. *The Mature Mind.* New York : W. W. Norton & Company, Inc., 1954.

Ryans, David G. *Characteristics of Teachers: Their Description, Comparison, and Appraisal.* Washington, D.C.: American Council on Education, 1960.

Trump, J. Lloyd, and Dorsey Baynham. *Guide to Better Schools.* Chicago : Rand McNally & Co., 1961.

6 *selecting and guiding activities*

In turning now to the actual use of speaking-listening activities in the classroom, it is essential that we remember it is only when such activities are wisely selected and competently used that they may be expected to contribute in a positive way to learning effectiveness. In the present chapter we shall first consider some of the bases for selecting speech activities and then outline minimal requirements for their wise use as methods in secondary school teaching.

BASES FOR SELECTING SPEECH ACTIVITIES

One of the special features which make speech so useful to classroom instruction is its versatility and adaptability. With the ever-increasing complexity of his social existence, man, in his ingenuity, has managed to evolve many adaptations of simple talk to meet the diverse communication needs of life. Thus it was that in response to his tendencies for social control, man somehow must have arrived at the beginnings of the solo talk from which developed various forms of public address, including the lecture, sermon, oration, and demonstration speaking. With the advance of the democratic form of government came the growth of forensic speaking—formalized debate and parliamentary procedure. With its roots in Socratic method, discussion, in its several forms, has come to full flower in the twentieth century as a technique of inquiry, evaluation, and problem-solving in the affairs of government and business, as well as education. Similarly, certain conditions in man's cultural life gave genesis to public oral reading. The medium of drama very early brought special adaptations of the spoken word. More recently, radio and television have imposed even greater adaptive demands upon the forms and uses of speech.

Like life in general, life in the classroom has become increasingly complex. The vastly increased scope of knowledge, together with the sociological ferment and ideological conflicts penetrating every sector of society, has added greatly to the complexity of classroom instruction. It is obvious that today's teaching must be highly adaptable and singularly efficient if it is to meet the educational needs of youth in this complex and changing world. Fortunately the diversity and adaptability of speech make it a particularly valuable tool or method for meeting many of these needs. The question, therefore, is not whether we shall use speech in teaching literature, mathematics, or social studies, but rather what kind of speech shall we use at any given time or with a particular unit of work. The proper use of speech in the classroom, then, starts with intelligent selection of the speech form. Thus the social studies teacher, for example, in considering certain aspects of "right to work legislation," must weigh the advantages of using group discussion, oral reports, lecture, or dramatization. Depending upon a number of contingencies, any one of the foregoing could be a wise choice. What criteria then should be considered in selecting a speech form for use in classroom teaching?

Obviously the teacher's first consideration in the selection of an instructional procedure should be its relevance to and usefulness for achieving one or more of the lesson, unit, or course objectives. *The problem, therefore, is one of prescription.* What activity will get the job done best without creating undesirable side effects? Certainly the teacher's personal preference for a particular form or forms is hardly a defensible basis for selection, unless the choice can be justified on other grounds as well. The following guidelines are offered as useful criteria for selecting a speech form for use in the general classroom: (1) potentials for dealing effectively with the communication problems and needs of youth, (2) amount of available time, (3) specific nature of topic or problem under immediate consideration, and (4) reciprocal relation of the particular subject matter and speech form. In examining each of these bases in further detail, we wish to point out that no special significance should be placed on the order of listing. Circumstances will most likely determine which criterion should receive major consideration in choosing a speech form.

Selecting on basis of student needs and abilities

Here, as in other aspects of learning, it is essential to start at the learner's point of development—his emotional and intellectual maturity—his level of speech readiness. As suggested in Chapter Four, getting to know one's students is paramount to any valid appraisal of such readiness. Thus the teacher makes it his business to determine as well as possible the nature and extent of speech instruction and experience his pupils may have had prior to entering his class. He notes those students who seem to manifest qualities of leadership and those with substandard communication skill. Similarly he notes the extent to which students are reticent or linguistically inept. He takes note of the cohesiveness of his class membership. He is interested in the general level of social sophistication in his group. He is alert to the specific speech habits of his pupils—the orderliness and depth of their thought processes and their manner of speaking in informal contexts. As previously noted, he checks the students' permanent records, particularly those students who present special problems, such as extreme reticence, uncooperativeness, glibness, excessive dominance, and other behavior which tends to interfere with normal personal development and school progress. It should be noted that use of permanent records, in this case, is to gain fuller understanding of pupils as a basis for more prescriptive approaches to their instruction. *Teachers should resist the temptation to use any information thus obtained as an excuse for failure to reach "difficult" pupils.*

Other things being equal, with less experienced pupils, or at the beginning of the school term, the classroom teacher may do well to emphasize informal or group speaking. We suggest a form of speaking which permits distributing responsibility among members of a team and lending moral support to the less confident student who might shy away from solo speaking. Similarly, group activities may be selected if the teacher senses a need for developing cooperative attitudes and group spirit in his class. In another vein, if the class members appear to be somewhat contentious, are inclined to be argumentative but are quite superficial in their reasoning, the teacher might decide to direct these inclinations into profitable channels with some truly well-guided debate experience.

A class of comparatively mature students will generally find a pleasant challenge in individual reports based on intensive research. Or in a literature class such students may gain much satisfaction from an exploratory discussion of Thoreau's philosophy or Emerson's concept of the "Oversoul."

Evidences of general weaknesses in oral projection and articulation might prompt some teachers to select assignments involving reading aloud or choral speaking. An otherwise capable class with poor habits of organizing their thoughts might profit from work on the well-constructed short talk, report, or demonstration.

What we have attempted to stress in the preceding paragraphs is that the teacher needs to know his pupils. He realizes the importance of success in speaking: its relation to speech improvement and to effective learning. He therefore chooses speech activities that are likely to provide successful speaking experiences. At the same time, he is cognizant of student speech weaknesses and needs. So he carefully considers those types of speech activities which can assist pupils in overcoming such weaknesses. *A primary basis for selecting speech activities for classroom use is student speech readiness, capability, and need.*

Selecting in terms of time limits

The amount of time to be made available for speech activity in the classroom is, of course, a question of the relative value of the activity as a medium of learning. Two class sessions devoted to discussion may be worth four periods spent in another method of learning. On the other hand, discussion inefficiently carried out could be a total waste of time. Admittedly, speech activities are time consumers. In polite society one person speaks at a time. If carried out in the classroom, this practice obviously will require a good deal more time than a class-wide written assignment on the same subject. The question we must ask is: What are the objectives being sought at this particular point? Discussion, though more time consuming than some activities, may be precisely what is needed to stimulate the type of thinking and quality of learning desired at this point. Often we need to take time to save time. For instance, many teachers report that well-guided discussion can be a highly useful motivator and preliminary preparation for independent study or writing. This is particularly true for the student who has trouble getting started independently or "doesn't have anything to say" in his writing assignments. Let us repeat: speech activities take time; there is no denying it. It is up to the teacher to determine whether a speaking activity is called for in a given situation and, if so, which one will do the job best. Then, of course, he must see to it that the activity comes off successfully through adequate pupil preparation and appropriate teacher guidance. When this happens, the experience is not likely to take more than its fair share of time in the course schedule. In any event, given a specific amount of class time, the conscientious teacher will strive to select those speech activities which can be expected to achieve the greatest pupil benefit in the time allotment. And having selected a given speech activity, he will take the necessary steps to insure its efficient use, thereby justifying its consumption of class time.

Selecting on the basis of learning situation

As suggested earlier, the needs of a particular situation in man's evolving human relationships have been major incentives for the development of particular speech forms. Just so should the teacher recognize the specific nature of each instructional problem and consider the types of speech activity which are most likely to meet the communication requirements of that situation. An example or two may help illustrate our point.

Members of the class in contemporary problems decide that a good method of gaining a clear understanding of the problem of fair employment in their community is to have a panel discussion on the question: "To what extent are principles of fair employment observed in our city?" Members of the panel include students who represent the points of view of various interest groups, such as city government, business, education, the black community, the oriental population, as well as the lay white community. Or take the example of the history teacher who, in leading his students through a study of the pre-Civil War period, includes student presentations of excerpts from key speeches of that era. With appropriate explanatory introductions students can show how the eloquence of Calhoun, Clay, Webster, Douglas, and Lincoln helped shape public opinion and influence the tide of subsequent events.

A home economics teacher arranges with a group of pupils in her family relations class to enact through role playing a family discussion of a critical financial problem. In a unit on the study of poetry, after appropriate preliminary preparation, an English teacher provides an exciting listening session with recordings by Dylan Thomas, followed by informal discussion. A science teacher, or one of his pupils, chooses the demonstration speech to illustrate the principle of vapor condensation. A student committee in a mathematics class is appointed to make a topographical survey of some newly acquired school property and present an oral report of their findings to the class, using appropriate visual aids and relevant applications of mathematics.

From these few examples, one may glimpse some of the many possible ways in which speech may be used as a method for meeting specific learning situations. For the creative teacher, the possibilities are limited only by time and availability of information. The point we wish to emphasize, however, is that *wise selection of a speech activity must include a careful assessment of the needs of the particular learning situation.*

Selecting on the basis of reciprocal relations of speech and course subject matter[1]

A somewhat less explored basis for prescribing speech forms for classroom use is found in the nature of the subject matter and in the character of its relationship with speech forms. In other words, *prescription* here is derived by discovering the reciprocal and complementary relationships between speech forms and subject matter. To discover these relationships it is necessary, first, to explore the potential contributions of the subject matter to the speech growth of pupils and then to ascertain which speech form by its nature most completely complements and implements learning the content. By taking advantage of such relationship we may not only hope to attain the best utilization of subject-matter learning for the speech growth of pupils, but we may also be confident that we are using that form of speaking which best assists in realizing the objectives of the subject areas through effective integration of learning. In addition, prescribing speech forms on the basis of reciprocal relationship will

---

[1] Oliver W. Nelson, "The Prescriptive Selection and Use of Speech in the Classroom," *The Speech Teacher,* IV (September, 1955), 167–72.

tend to assure all pupils' receiving training and experience in the essential speech forms, since the diverse natures of various subjects will require the use of a variety of speech activities. Such provision can go far toward coordinating the speech work of the regular classroom with the over-all high school speech program.

To illustrate the principle of reciprocity as a basis for prescribing speech forms for classroom use, let us note briefly some of its possible applications to social studies, mathematics, and English.

The social studies have been described as the study of the problems of human relations and of the methods for dealing with such problems. Bining tells us:

> The materials of the social studies provide the basis for making the world of today intelligible to pupils, for training them in certain skills and habits, and for inculcating attitudes and ideas that will enable boys and girls to take their places as efficient and effective members of a democratic society.[2]

The social studies may be expected to help the pupil form wholesome self-regarding attitudes, grow in social understanding and tolerance, appreciate the obstacles to social integration, and to develop social responsibility. These contributions should show up favorably in the pupil's emotional adjustment to speech situations, in his willingness to approach controversial questions fairly, and in his desire and ability to discover and report truth.[3]

Worthy objectives indeed! However, such contributions to the social and communicative development of youth do not occur automatically from a study of history, geography, economics, or government. They occur optimally only when they are given an opportunity to do so in social experience. This opportunity is primarily, if not altogether, a speech act, and in particular that form of speaking called *discussion*. Of the various speech forms, discussion, along with conversation, is most basically social in character. It is, in a very real sense, a social group in action. It is indeed a vital means of integrating social knowledge and skills into the personality and behavior of the learner.

---

[2] Arthur C. Bining and David H. Bining, *Teaching the Social Studies in Secondary Schools,* 3rd ed. (New York: McGraw-Hill Book Company, 1952), pp. 3–4.

[3] See also Edgar B. Wesley and Stanley P. Wronski, *Teaching Social Studies in High Schools,* 5th ed. (Boston: D. C. Heath & Company, 1964), pp. 77–80.

Social studies in themselves can provide pupils only with knowledge *about* human relations; it remains for speech, particularly discussion, to furnish pupils with knowledgs *of* and skills *in* human relations. When applied as problem-solving it may for the maturing student become a technique for living. It is democracy in action.

McClendon[4] strongly supports this view when he says : "The teacher of social studies should concentrate on students' development of the kinds of speaking skills needed by effective, but reasonably typical, citizens in situations where oral communication regarding public affairs is appropriate." In this connection, he cites discussion, parliamentary procedure, and sociodrama as particularly appropriate speech forms. On the principle of reciprocity, then, such prescription would promote the direct application of the learning to the pupils' social behavior and would, at the same time, afford pupils an opportunity to secure meaningful guided experience in an important form of speaking.

Speech and mathematics also have intriguing reciprocal relationships from which the pupil may gain significant rewards in both speech and general learning. However, as in the case of social studies, the transfer of learning from mathematics to speech or any other aspect of social learning is not spontaneous. To secure transfer of training in mathematics, this subject must be taught with transfer or application in mind.

Since the thought process in mathematics is not essentially different from straight, analytical thinking required in other fields, transfer should be quite possible for students who have been taught to do more than memorize algebraic and geometric facts and formulae. The pupil who has been trained to think mathematically should manifest this trait in his behavior when confronted by non-mathematical problems calling for solution. This view finds support in a report of a joint committee on mathematics which states in effect that the study of mathematics may (1) contribute to the ability to think clearly as shown in gathering and organizing and representing data, drawing conclusions, and establishing and judging claims of proof; and (2) help develop desirable attitudes, including social awareness and open-mindedness.[5] We believe such contributions are

---

[4] Jonathon C. McClendon, *Social Studies in Secondary Education* (New York: The Macmillan Company, 1965), Chapter 3 "Objectives of Social Studies."

[5] *The Place of Mathematics in Secondary Education*, Fifteenth Yearbook of the National Council of Teachers of Mathematics, pp. 22–34.

most likely to reach fruition when implemented through oral processes.

To facilitate such contributions, including the transfer of mathematical thinking to nonmathematical contexts, one speech form in particular possesses features which render it especially appropriate. That form is the short extempore speech—with its major purpose the analysis and application of methods of inference. The use of extempore speaking can be illustrated in such examples as (1) the oral presentation of a mathematical problem showing the method of reaching a solution —i.e., of drawing an inference; and (2) presentation of the solution of a mathematical problem, together with an analogy of a social problem and its suggested solution. Extensions of these examples will be found in Chapter 14.

Speech experiences and instruction in mathematics can be integrated in such a manner as to expedite the study of mathematics and yield speech growth in pupils. Since the focal point here is the thought process, the principal effects of the integrated instruction will be observed in the rational behavior of pupils. The short talk aimed at the analysis and application of inference is highly recommended for special prescription in mathematics classes, for it can be shown that this form most nearly complements the nature of mathematics and facilitates its instruction.

It is not difficult to find reciprocal relations between speech and English. English can make indispensable contributions to the speech development of youth, and speech experiences, well chosen, can implement the teaching of English. A cursory examination of the subject of English, together with the nature of certain speech forms, will reveal how these contributions are possible.

One major portion of the study of English is traditionally concerned with the linguistic aspects of communication: in particular, grammar, vocabulary, and syntax. Since language is a fundamental element of the speech process, it lies within the scope of English instruction to make a primary contribution to this aspect of the speech development of youth. *However, this contribution can be made optimally only by providing for it through oral experience.* Speech forms and activities which best seem to foster speech growth and a corresponding development in writing skills are the oral sentence and the oral paragraph. In the former, attention should be given primarily to structure, appropriate usage, and vocabulary building. In oral paragraph practice, phrasing of topic sentences, together with their orderly and unified development should be stressed.

As Quintilian pointed out centuries ago, careful attention to writing can be highly instrumental in developing language facility in speaking. Conversely, pupils may improve their skills in writing with preliminary exercises in speaking. The small unit of activity which one finds in the oral sentence and oral paragraph provides a highly effective, manageable device for implementing the speech and English language development of youth.

Another equally important aspect of the content of English is the study of literature. Here the teacher is concerned with such objectives as developing pupils' comprehension of the written word, increasing interest in and enjoyment of good literature, and motivating pupils to do independent reading. Although many types of speech activity may be helpful in attaining these objectives, two speech forms have demonstrated their preeminence as implements for teaching literature. These forms are oral interpretation and dramatization.

The outstanding utility of oral interpretation is doubtless due to the fact that "The materials of literature courses are the materials of all courses in oral interpretation; and the oral expression of those materials is a natural expression, especially for poetry and drama."[6] Reading aloud can make the dead symbols of the printed page come alive—stir the imagination, quicken the emotions, take hold of the listener in ways that merely talking about, reading silently, or formally dissecting a selection rarely can achieve.

In much the same way, dramatization can implement the teaching of literature. By extending the experience of oral reading to group reading or actual enactment of scenes from dramatic literature, pupils may derive a personalized understanding of the author's purpose, may secure deeper appreciations of the aesthetic values of the work, and learn more fully the forces which motivate human behavior as illustrated in the interaction of the personalities characterized in the selection. Oral reading and dramatization are "naturals" for teaching literature. These particular speech forms, together with practice in oral sentence and oral paragraph work, constitute major prescriptions for speech in English classes from the point of view of reciprocal relations.

---

[6] Clara A. Hargis and Donald B. Hargis, "High School Literature and Oral Interpretation," *The Speech Teacher*, II (September, 1953), 205–208.

While the preceding example and the illustrations pertaining to social studies and mathematics are admittedly lacking in detail, it is hoped that they serve to clarify the principle of "reciprocity" as one basis for prescribing the use of speech in the classroom. We strongly emphasize that following this principle in practice need not or should not limit the teacher's use of speech in the classroom to the forms designated in the illustrations. It has been our intention mainly to stress the importance of judicious selection of speech activities for implementing classroom learning. The four principles presented here offer sound bases upon which to make such selection or prescription.

MINIMAL REQUIREMENTS FOR WISE USE OF SPEECH IN THE GENERAL CLASSROOM

Prescriptive selection of speech forms as media for classroom instruction and learning is the first important step in securing their wise use. Implicit in making wise choices is a knowledge of the nature and instructional potential of the several speech forms. Information about them is presented in the following chapters. Wise choice obviously also requires a knowledge of one's students, their level of speech sophistication and adaptability, as well as academic status.

Equally as important as wise selection of speech forms is the assurance that the selected activity will be carried out effectively. To accomplish this objective the teacher must command a working knowledge of the essential preparatory steps for using each of the basic speech forms in the classroom. Such steps include methods of assigning topics, limiting subjects, and carrying out appropriate research. In addition, steps must include guidelines for organizing and presenting material, and in cases of group activities, attention must be given to the responsibilities of the leader and participants, as well as to methods of forming groups and selecting leaders.

Finally, wise use of speech activities in the classroom involves appropriate attention to listening, the responsibilities of the "audience," and, of course, evaluation of the oral presentation. All of these factors pertaining to effective preparation, participation, and evaluation will receive detailed attention in Part Three.

SUMMARY

In this chapter we have considered some of the basic principles for selecting and guiding speech activities in the secondary school classroom. We have seen that selection is fundamentally a matter of prescription based on the criteria of: (1) student needs, (2) availability of time, (3) nature of topic under consideration, and (4) reciprocal relations of speech and subject matter. We have pointed out that the intelligent use of speech in the classroom requires a functional knowledge of the steps of adequate preparation and an ability to guide and evaluate the activity during and following presentation.

SELECTED READINGS

Fessenden, Seth A., and others. *Speech and the Creative Teacher.* Dubuque, Iowa : William C. Brown Company, Publishers, 1968. Part IV "Creative Activities and Experiences."

McClendon, Jonathon C. *Social Studies in Secondary Education.* New York : The Macmillan Company, 1965. Chap. 3 "Objectives of Social Studies."

Phelps, Waldo. "Integration of Speech with English and Social Studies." *Bulletin of National Association of Secondary School Principals,* XXXVI (May, 1952), 79–88.

7 *evaluating the speaking-listening act*

As any experienced teacher will testify, few of his functions are more essential to pupil growth than appraising the results of instruction and educational experience. In their role as monitors, evaluation and criticism are the handmaidens of goal-setting and motivation. As such, they help determine the direction of instruction and the quality of learning.

Experienced teachers will also just as quickly attest to the difficulties of appraising products of instruction, and therefore of necessity the methods of instruction. Evaluation of learning is difficult because it involves making a choice—a mental calibration, as it were. Some types of behavior, particularly those of speech, are not easily quantified. As a result, the evaluations are for the most part subjective; literally, *judgments*. The difficulty of evaluating speech is heightened by the absence of absolute standards, the evasiveness of the spoken word, and the complexity of the speech event, not to mention the psychological factors resident in the evaluator which may affect his attention and attitude.

Difficult or not, evaluations must be made and criticisms must be offered at appropriate times. Having thus spoken, let us quickly add that it is a wise teacher indeed who knows *when not to evaluate, when not to criticize.* For instance, evaluating when the situation calls for a permissive, free discussion, may be a sure method of stifling creative thinking. Obviously in this chapter we are concerned with *timely,* as well as *effective* evaluation.

In keeping with the theme and purposes of this textbook, we shall consider evaluation and criticism as serving two related functions; first and foremost, judging the worth of a unit, procedure, or activity in achieving the objectives of instruction, irrespective of subject matter; second, appraising the speaking-listening achievement of pupils or groups of pupils, whether viewed as a by-product or as an integral object of instruction in any school subject. While the functions of evaluation and criticism are closely related, it is helpful to consider them separately but as two stages of one continuous process. We shall identify evaluation as *the process of appraising the quality, the level of excellence or effectiveness of a procedure or behavior.* Evaluation provides the data for criticism : *The act of conveying the results of evaluation to those who may stand to profit from the information.*

JUDGING THE WORTH OF AN INSTRUCTIONAL UNIT OR TEACHING PROCEDURE

Obviously, even when applied subjectively, judging the worth of a teaching-learning procedure is dependent upon: (1) having a set of objectives, understood by pupils and, when appropriate, evolved by them; (2) relating the teaching-learning procedures to the agreed-upon objectives; (3) having the means for gathering evaluative data: e.g., observing, listening, testing; (4) taking time to contemplate and having the ability to judge the data in light of the objectives.

Admittedly the relative worth of a unit of learning, a procedure, including, for instance, a dramatization, teacher-led discussion or interpretative readings, cannot be precisely determined even with use of an experimental design. Most teachers, however, are likely to conclude that a unit or a procedure has been worthwhile when (1) it appears through tests and observation most pupils have comprehended the basic concepts inherent in the experience; (2) most pupils give evidence of interest and purposeful participation; (3) most pupils show indication of growth in perceptiveness, sense of responsibility, and knowledge; and (4) most pupils evidence growth in communicative skills.

Two basic modes of evaluating the worth of a unit or teaching-learning procedure merit our attention: first, the written or oral test covering the substance of the learning experience; and, second, written and/or oral evaluative analysis of the experience. The test is particularly appropriate for measuring concepts, command of factual information, and the ability to draw inferences from this information. Validity of such instruments is increased when they are applied both before and after instruction and the responses compared. Measurement specialists remind us that tests are considered acceptable when they provide a worthwhile learning experience, when their contents reflect the items, concepts, attitudes deemed most important in the material covered; when their design suits the nature of material being tested; when the questions enable the tester to distinguish the relative merits of answers given by different pupils; and when they are so constructed that when scored, the tester will have obtained meaningful information regarding the depth and breadth of learning stimulated by the unit or procedure covered in the test.[1]

Many teachers prefer to employ an open-end written or oral analysis of a learning experience, either as a supplement to or a substitute for the conventional test. The oral form of this type of experience is discussed later in the Chapter on *Discussion*. For the moment, the list of questions below suggests one approach to an open-ended class evaluation of a unit of learning. Generally it is advisable to have pupils write their reactions to the questions and then, using the questions as an agenda, to lead the class in a general evaluative discussion of the unit, project, or activity. As in the case of the conventional subject matter test, it is essential to relate the evaluative questions to the purpose and objectives of the unit. The reader will observe that the following questions are essentially extensions of those presented in Chapter Eight under "using discussion for planning a unit."

GUIDE QUESTIONS FOR EVALUATING A UNIT

1. What can we honestly say we have achieved in this unit? What new knowledge have we gained? Has it changed any of our concepts of or our attitudes toward issues included in the unit? How?

---

[1] See, for example, Alfred Schwartz and Stuart C. Tiedeman, *Evaluating Student Progress in the Secondary School* (New York: Longmans, Green and Co., 1957), Chap. 5 "A Measurement Rationale."

2. What source materials did we find most helpful? Least helpful? Why?
3. What specific experiences connected with this unit (reports, discussions, readings, trips, etc.) contributed most to our learning? To our enjoyment of the unit? Least? Why?
4. What can we say regarding the general worth of this unit to the course as a whole? To us as individuals—i.e., how did it measure up to the original objectives of the unit?
5. What recommendations can we offer for making such a unit more interesting? More worthwhile?

While the foregoing questions are intended for evaluating an entire unit of instruction, they may easily be modified to meet the needs of an individual lesson or basic procedure, such as a symposium, a dramatization, or an oral reading program.

In a very real sense, the worth of a learning experience, whether that experience be a single assignment or an extended unit of study, should be judged to a large extent upon the basis of the desired change it engenders in individual pupils. For this reason alone we may justify evaluation and criticism of individual speech behavior. Equally important, however, is the evaluation of speech behavior as an end in itself. That is to say, if speech behavior as a legitimate object of instruction is to be improved, it will require guidance and evaluation.

EVALUATING SPEECH BEHAVIOR

Foci of speech evaluation

Regardless of whether speaking is employed as a medium of learning and instruction or as practicum for the improvement of speaking ability, with minor exceptions, evaluation should be centered first on the content of the message : "Good speech is concerned with the substance of ideas." Thus, following a pupil's oral report, we may quite appropriately ask: Were the speaker's topic and information geared to the class assignment? Was his information apparently accurate? Did it contribute something to our present knowledge?

Having satisfied ourselves regarding the substance of the speaker's message, we may rightly turn to his method of presentation. Here we may recall that how something is said is quite intimately related to what one says: one's manner of emphasis, for instance, helps to convey the intended meaning of a message. We shall have occasion to enlarge upon this point in Chapter 10 and in Appendix A. Suffice it to say here that no teacher, regardless of the speciality of his teaching field, can in conscience or in the interest of sound pedagogy afford to ignore the responsibility for evaluating the speech behavior of his pupils.

Guidelines for speech evaluation

As in evaluating a teaching-learning unit or procedure, so in speech evaluation, it is essential first to establish the desired objectives for the speaking assignment. Normally these should not exceed four or five major points: e.g., two points covering content and the remainder on some aspects of delivery. It is often advisable to arrive at the list of objectives through teacher-class collaboration. The objectives of course should have been chosen when the assignment is initially made and reviewed immediately before the speaking experience begins.

The evaluator should strive to maintain objectivity in observing, listening, and judging, making an effort to appraise speaking effectiveness on its own merits. Similarly, the evaluator should maintain his focus of attention in observing and listening. It is easy to allow one's self to be drawn away from the immediate objectives to other factors in presentation, important in themselves perhaps, but not included in the agreed-upon objectives.

The judgments should be recorded promptly, accurately, and concisely, both for immediate and future reference. Recording may take the form of a series of comments, an anecdotal paragraph, notations on a check-sheet, or a check-sheet with comments. Checking scales are convenient time-savers; they assist in maintaining focus upon the designated objectives and help provide pupils with a useful guide when they are serving as peer evaluators. However, check-sheets cannot be expected to improve the quality of one's rating ability. A scale is only as good as the evaluator using it. Several sample rating sheets will be found in later chapters dealing with the major speech forms.

Although the teacher should accept the major responsibility for evaluating speech behavior of his pupils, he need not always be the sole evaluator. With appropriate guidance, a committee of students or the entire class may be made jointly responsible for evaluation. This is especially helpful and appropriate in classes stressing speech improvement as a major objective.

If it is to perform its rightful function in the improvement of speech learning, evaluation, obviously, must be communicated to the pupil whose speech is being judged. This brings us to the important though delicate task of criticism.

Guidelines for criticizing speech behavior

Effective criticism, of course, is dependent upon sound and insightful evaluation. However, much of its effectivness depends upon how it is presented. Indeed, criticism is an experience in interpersonal communication of the first order; it is a strategic form of student guidance not to be entered into lightly. From these remarks it will readily be noted that when we speak of criticism we have much more in mind than mere fault-finding, a connotation all too frequently associated with this activity. What then are some of the qualities of *good criticism?*

Criteria for Effective Criticism: First and foremost, good criticism is *constructive;* it is positive rather than negative. The critic seeks to help the learner to recognize his strengths and weaknesses, and to discover the means for further improving his speaking ability. Good criticism leaves the student with self-respect and a challenge to move forward toward the next objective. Second, good criticism is *relevant.* It is based upon the agreed-upon objectives and the nature of the assignment. Third, good criticism is *individualized:* it is specific and applies particularly to the needs of a given pupil and is communicated in a fashion that is calculated to "reach" this particular pupil. Fourth, good criticism is *timely.* It is given at a point in time that enables it to produce maximum impact on the learner. Usually this means immediately following the speech event, or at the end of the class period. Fifth, good criticism is *impartial.* It is fair : it judges the presentation on its merits, but does not fail to relate achievement to pupil potential. Thus, two pupils may "turn in" essentially equal performances, yet merit different criticism because of differences in their potential, past performances, and relative excellence of their present achievements. Criticism, however, must be honest; it must be based on an honest appraisal of the strengths and weaknesses of the speaker. But in being honest, criticism must also be tactfully given. It is plain that the teacher-critic, to be effective, must know his pupils, weigh his words, and anticipate the consequence of his counsel. Finally, good criticism, of course, must be *clear*. It must be presented in terms that are comprehensible to the learner. He must be able to visualize, to understand the import of the criticism. It must be specific. There is no place in criticism for "sweeping generalizations." Such comments as, "That was fine, John," mean nothing. John wants to know what was fine. Was it *all* fine? He has a right to know wherein he excelled and in what ways perhaps more improvement is needed.

Should the reader be intrigued by mnemonic devices, he may be pleased to discover that the traits we have pust enumerated add up to a good CRITIC.

Suggested methods of criticism. Criticism may be given either orally or in writing or by both methods. Oral comments, of course, are preferred when an immediate response is desired or when the evaluator wishes for various reasons to personalize the comment or make the criticism public. Many teachers prefer to use written comments which can be handed to the student at the end of the class hour. Most experienced teachers employ both methods: oral for immediate response and the written critique for greater detail and for providing both pupil and himself with a record of the evaluation.

Criticism may be offered by the teacher, by class members, and the speaker himself. Although, as suggested earlier, it is the teacher who is ultimately accountable for criticism, when used properly, peer criticism can motivate responsible class listening and can provide a valuable learning experience for all concerned. Robinson and Kerikas suggest that student criticism may be used with profit when:

1. the members of the group demonstrate that they know enough about criteria and standards of speech to criticize intelligently;
3. the students know how to present criticism acurately and tactfully.[2]
   established and the class views criticism as a welcome part of it;
3. the students know how to present criticism accurately and tactfully.[2]

---

[2] Quoted from Karl F. Robinson and E. J. Kerikas, *Teaching Speech: Methods and Materials* (New York: David McKay Co., Inc., 1963), Chap. XI "Diagnosis, Evaluation, Testing and Criticism."

Criticism may be given either publicly or privately, depending upon the circumstances. Some public comment following each talk or reading is usually desirable. However, a criticism should be made public when one wishes to stress a point which might be of benefit to the entire class or to help build the speaker's self-esteem. Obviously, certain criticisms are better shared privately.

Remembering that criticism at its best is a form of counseling, the teacher will wish to employ, when appropriate, some form of non-directive guidance. In such a method the teacher, through skillful questioning, causes the speaker to discover for himself not only his strengths and weaknesses, but also possible steps for improving his speaking. This technique, when thoughtfully and skillfully handled, has much to commend it, not the least of which is its capacity for teaching pupils a method of objective and healthful self-monitoring, which will add to their sense of self-reliance in future speech experiences.

Although it may not always be necessary or appropriate to assign grades for speech performances, generally some recognition or credit should be given. Certainly when speech improvement is the major object of instruction, as in certain English classes, or when effective communication is considered an integral part of class learning, grades should be given for substantive speech-listening activities. At the very least, a grade furnishes the student with a statement of relative worth: he is told how his effort relates to what he has done before or to what others have done or to an expert's view of effectiveness. At best, a grade serves as a stimulus to modification or reinforcement of speech behavior.

SUMMARY

Evaluation and criticism are basic teaching tools. When applied to speech, they may very well determine whether such experiences dwindle to mere passing events or rise to truly profitable learning activities. Effective evaluation and criticism require a combination of three fundamental ingredients: (1) a knowledge of and interest in one's pupils; (2) a knowledge of evaluation procedures; and (3) skill in communicating the results of evaluation to the learner, along with skill in creating an environment which enables the learner to discover the bases for healthful self-evaluation. Evaluating and criticizing are among the teacher's most important, if difficult, functions. Because of the highly complex and personal nature of speech, speech criticism presents an especial challenge to the teacher-critic. To return to an earlier statement: It is a wise teacher who knows when not to evaluate —when not to criticize. However, when they are called for, it is the teacher's responsibility to see to it that evaluation and criticism are provided, not perfunctorily, but effectively and responsibly.

SELECTED READINGS

Holzman, Paul. "Speech Criticism and Evaluation as Communication." *Speech Teacher,* IX (January 1960), 1–7.

Reid, Loren. *Teaching Speech,* 3rd ed. Columbia, Mo.: Artcraft Press, 1960. Chapter 12, "The Art of Criticism."

Robinson, Karl F., and E. J. Kerikas. *Teaching Speech: Methods and Materials.* New York: David McKay Co. Inc., 1963. Chapter 11 "Diagnosis, Evaluation, Testing and Criticism."

Schwartz, Alfred, and Stuart Tiedeman. *Evaluating Student Progress in the Secondary School.* New York : Longmans, Green and Co., 1957.

Wrightson, J. W., Joseph Justman, and Irving Robbins. *Evaluation in Modern Education.* New York : American Book Company, 1956.

METHOD

PART III *key speech forms*

8 *discussion*

In recent years no speech form has gained wider acceptance as a classroom teaching-learning method than *discussion*. In one form or other it is almost certain to appear daily in one or more classrooms of any given high school. Textbooks on teaching methods give proportionately more space to the treatment of discussion than to other speech forms. This general acceptance of discussion as a basic classroom procedure can readily be accounted for. In the first place, certain experimental studies have established its value as a superior method of learning particularly when applied to a problem-solving situation.[1] Then, too, discussion is recognized as a basic method of democracy and an invaluable tool of the business world. It seems only logical that high schools should provide instruction and experience in this important speech form as essential preparation for meeting "civic responsibilities" and developing "economic efficiency," as well as an effective method of learning.

As with speech in general, discussion has no magical power to enable it to perform educational wonders. However, properly understood and competently used in the classroom, it can make unique and valuable contributions to teaching and learning. Improperly conceived and carelessly applied, discussion can result in chaos, frustration, and a waste of class time. Responsible teachers do their best to prevent such catastrophes. In this chapter we cannot hope to deal comprehensively with the subject of discussion. We are interested primarily in its potentials for teaching-learning method. Accordingly, we shall concern

---

[1] R. Victor Harnack and Thorrel B. Fest, *Group Discussion—Theory and Technique* (New York: Appleton-Century-Crofts, 1964), p. 22.

ourselves with basic concepts regarding the nature of discussion, offer some guidelines for its effective use in the classroom, and suggest a number of specialized sources for readers who desire a more detailed and comprehensive treatment of this speech form.

DEFINITIONS

In spite of the widespread use of discussion, or perhaps because of it, there is considerable semantic confusion associated with the term itself. For example, a good deal of talk billed as *discussion* is actually *debate*. The person who says, "I had a heated discussion with my neighbor last night," probably is referring to an *argument*. The picture is further confused by equating *discussion* with *oral communication* in general. Thus, we may hear a social studies teacher announce, "Tomorrow I shall *discuss* the issues involved in the first Constitutional Convention." In this case, the term is used synonymously with *lecture*. Most of us are quite familiar with the all-too-frequent practice of referring to the *question-answer type* of *oral recitation* as classroom *discussion*. Another semantic confusion arises from errors in identifying subforms of discussion. For example, the announced *panel* discussion proves not to be a panel at all but rather a *symposium,* with set, prepared speeches on segments of a common theme or topic. Indeed, there are almost as many concepts of *discussion* extant as there are definitions of *speech,* or even of *writing*. For instance, at some point in a textbook, the author is almost certain to include one or more versions of "We shall now discuss. . . ." "In this chapter our discussion concerns. . . ." Fortunately confusions of nomenclature, though frequent, are not as likely to produce the undesirable results in the classroom comparable to those arising from misguided and incompetent *use* of discussion. Nevertheless, it is highly essential that we come to some agreement regarding the meaning of the term *discussion* as it applies to a particular speech form.

Discussion as a speech form has been defined by McBurney and Hance as *"the cooperative deliberation of problems by persons thinking and conversing together in face-to-face or co-acting groups under the direction of a leader for the purposes of understanding and/or action."*[2] Other authorities, while offering variants of this

---

[2] James H. McBurney and Kenneth G. Hance, *Discussion in Human Affairs* (New York: Harper & Row, Publishers, 1950), p. 10.

definition, generally agree that the purposes of discussion are to pool ideas, to cooperatively weigh opinions and facts in an effort to come to an understanding of a problem, to reach an agreement about a problem, or to decide on a course of action with respect to a problem.

Viewed superficially, it is not surprising that discussion is frequently confused with informal serious conversation or debate. All three may have some elements in common. As indicated in our definition, we should expect at least certain kinds of discussion to resemble conversation—enlightened conversation. And at times discussion may assume some of the qualities of good debating. Discussion, however, possesses a number of characteristics which make it unique as a speech form. As a rule, unlike most serious conversation, discussion is pre-planned, follows an agreed-upon agenda, and proceeds in an orderly fashion toward some specified goal. Though structured to some extent, discussion differs from debate in both procedure and motivation. In debate the procedure is highly formalized with affirmative and negative speakers striving to maintain or controvert a proposition by argument. In debate the spirit is competitive, the method argumentative, the object: persuasion. In discussion, on the other hand, while following certain agreed-upon rules of procedure, participants are all members of the same team working together toward the better understanding or "solution" of a problem. In discussion, the spirit is cooperative, and the method analytical, the object: understanding and, in some cases, problem-solving. Although cooperative spirit should prevail, it should not be assumed that there is no place for difference of opinion or dissent in discussion. Indeed, errors of thinking must be checked, facts carefully examined, and opinions appraised if the discussion is to have any validity or its findings any meaning or utility.

Since we are interested in the improvement of discussion procedure, it is essential that we identify those qualities which normally should be present in *good* discussion.

QUALITIES OF GOOD DISCUSSION

1. *Good discussion is concerned with worthwhile subjects.* It deals with subjects which are of intrinsic and instrumental value to parties concerned. In the secondary classroom, discussion subjects are worthwhile if they are important to youth, if, when studied, they contribute to the education and welfare of students, and if they, in other respects, relate appropriately to the course content in which it is used. Moreover, the subject is worthwhile for discus-

sion if it can be approached more effectively through collaboration than by independent study.

2. *Good discussion manifests careful preparation.* It gives evidence of a thorough study of the question and an appropriate command of the discussion process. It proceeds cooperatively and gives evidence of clear, analytical, objective thinking. Members function as a team in an orderly, purposeful manner. It observes and respects time limits of the occasion.

3. *Good discussion meets acceptable standards of speaking.* The comparative informality of discussion must not lead participants into habits of careless enunciation, projection, and use of body, or inaccurate, colorless language. Speakers must be easily heard, readily understood, and be as interesting as possible. Presence of an audience in discussion magnifies the importance of these qualifications.

4. *Good discussion makes progress toward achieving its objective(s).* It provides at least some of the answers to the question under consideration; it moves the thinking of the group forward in constructive ways. It advances the work of the course or program with which it is identified. It contributes to communicative development of participants.

Generally speaking, then, *discussion* can be viewed as one of the major forms of collective speaking, cooperative investigation, and teamwork. And while it may serve other useful purposes, therapeutic as well as social, its major objectives are to enlighten, to explore, to instruct, and to solve problems. However, to understand the nature of discussion, one must be acquainted with at least some of its subforms and variants. For example, it is possible to describe discussion in terms of *its physical and contextual features;* it may be characterized in terms of *fundamental purposes;* and when applied particularly to classroom use, it may be classified with respect to *type of leadership involved.*

Physical and contextual determinants divide this basic speech form into two major categories: *public* and *private* discussion. In the former, the event takes place in the presence of and primarily for the benefit of an audience, which may or may not participate actively at some point in the proceedings.[3] On the other hand, private discussion,

---

[3] Here the term *presence* is meant to include members of *unseen audiences* (radio and television), as well as those physically present, since both determine or strongly influence the conduct of the discussion.

also known as face-to-face, group, or committee discussion, is group deliberation on a problem with participants interacting with one another somewhat informally with no audience present, except perhaps in the role of observers.

The two most widely used forms of public discussion applicable to classroom use are the *panel* and *symposium.* Besides being audience-oriented, both panel and symposium have a leader or moderator, usually include four to six participants, and may follow similar agendas. However, they differ procedurally. In the symposium, the more highly structured of the two, participants present planned talks, which may cover various phases or aspects of a single subject-problem, such as the topics of *timber, water, wildlife,* and *soil* as subdivisions of the general subject *conservation.* Or they may present various points of view regarding solutions to a problem, such as one might find in a discussion of "fluoridization of central water supply." In this context, discussants might offer points of view of the Dental Association, City Health Department, City Water Department, and citizen organizations known to have made a study of the fluoridization problem. In panel discussion, however, participants, following an agreed-upon thought sequence, examine a problem or issue in much the same fashion as that employed by interacting members of private problem-solving discussion. That is to say, members, under the guidance of a leader, interact more or less informally, but do so in the presence of and for the edification, guidance, or stimulation of an audience. A *forum* period may follow panel and symposium discussions, in which case the audience participates by asking questions, adding further information, or challenging statements of discussants. Other variants of *public discussion* include *colloquy, dialogue,* and *student congress.* Information regarding these adaptations may be found in Selected Readings at the close of this chapter.[4]

Discussion may also be described in terms of its *psychological qualities or purposes.* Contextual factors, of course, tend to influence the purposes of discussion. For example, we may expect that public discussion will normally serve the purpose of instructing, informing, or crystallizing thought for possible action. Private discussion, on the other hand, is likely to be concerned with the purposes of investigating,

---

[4] See particularly: H. L. Ewbank and J. Jeffrey Auer, *Discussion and Debate* (New York: Appleton-Century-Crofts, Inc., 1951), Part IV; and James McBurney and Kenneth Hance, *Discussion in Human Affairs* (New York: Harper & Row, Publishers, 1950), Part IV.

exploring, and policy formulating. What is most significant in this connection is that *different purposes call for different thought sequences and discussion agendas.* The sample forms included later in this chapter illustrate some of the most common agendas.

Other legitimate purposes of discussion of interest to teachers are those of *process-learning, catharsis,* and *sociotherapy.*[5] While discussions should be concerned with worthwhile subjects, more than likely a good deal of the information uncovered and communicated in the process will be forgotten in a relatively short while. More important educationally is that students shall learn a method of attacking problems, of working together cooperatively: such learnings are basic to the business of living. This is, in effect, teaching youth a way of thinking, of learning—a way of life.

At times, discussion can be an effective *catharsis.* Sessions which allow pupils to bring into the open anxieties, gripes, opinions, and beliefs regarding issues or conditions, may help to relieve tensions or create a favorable climate for subsequent more thorough-going and deliberate investigation of the problem associated with the hurt.

Discussion can be *therapeutic.* It can serve the purpose of studying and illuminating group dynamics, individual motivations, and self-regarding attitudes. Through role-playing participants can learn to observe personality traits objectively, develop some understanding of why people behave as they do, and gain further appreciation of what is involved in transforming a collection of individuals into a unified, productive group.

Finally, because of its particular significance to teaching, we have included a third basis for classifying discussion: namely, its *type of leadership.* Three variations concern us here—leaderless, student-led, and teacher-led discussion. As a rule, discussion functions best when guided by a qualified leader. So-called leaderless discussion is most successful with mature students well schooled in the ways and responsibilities of discussion. It is noteworthy, however, that experiments with "leaderless" discussion indicate that leaders tend to emerge as a natural consequence of interpersonal communication and group dynamics. We recommend that leaders be appointed or elected when the group is formed, especially where relatively inexperienced all-student groups are involved.

---

[5] For an excellent treatment of the latter two purposes of discussion, see especially Margaret E. Bennett, *Guidance in Groups: A Resource Book for Teachers, Counselors, and Administrators* (New York: McGraw-Hill Book Company, 1955).

Discussion, of course, may be teacher-led. In fact this particular adaptation is doubtless the most widely used *variant* of classroom discussion. In shifting to teacher leadership, it is not necessary to alter the basic characteristics of discussion. What is changed, however, is the teacher's role in the classroom procedure. Whereas in student-led discussion, the teacher stands by as an active listener, consultant, and critic, in teacher-led discussion, he assumes the major responsibility of moderating and guiding the discussion. Although certainly the teacher may act as a leader of student panels, symposia, or small face-to-face groups, generally speaking, we think this role should be performed by students. The exception might be a demonstration for instructional purposes. It is our view that active teacher-leadership is most appropriate for guiding *class-wide* discussion. In this role, the teacher follows procedures similar to those normally found in the fact-finding, exploratory, instructive, problem-solving variants of group discussion. We shall have more to say on this point later in this chapter.

VALUES AND LIMITATIONS OF DISCUSSION

We have alluded to several of the educational values of training and experience in discussion. Mention has been made of its contributions to creative thinking, to motivation, and to developing group spirit, as well as its value for dealing with emotional adjustment problems of youth. Reference was also made to its role in securing optimal transfer and application of learning beyond the confines of classrooms. Special emphasis was given to the importance of discussion in teaching the social studies. Further appreciation of the potential values of discussion can be gained from a review of the qualities of *good* discussion included in this chapter.

Teachers will discover that such values will not accrue uniformly in all classes or with all types of discussion. Students vary in their ability to grasp and apply the principles of discussion. Moreover, discussion as method is not a panacea for all classroom needs. It has its limitations, as well as strengths. It is essential that these limitations be recognized, particularly those that arise from unwise selection and faulty use of the form. First of all, discussion takes time. Admittedly, the use of discussion in teaching will consume more time than the lecture, written lessons, or question-answer type of recitation. Some information can be communicated far more quickly and efficiently through lecture, silent reading, or some other form of independent study. However, when the topics or questions coming before the class are discussable or when discussion appears to be the most feasible and educationally profitable method of dealing with such problems, the teacher should employ some form of discussion as classroom method in spite of the fact that it may take more time than an alternate procedure. Obviously it is incumbent upon the teacher to make sure that this time is used wisely and economically.

Discussion, especially the class-wide variety, *may reduce individual pupil responsibility.* The reticent or unprepared pupil seldom volunteers. The problem is compounded by the few students who are always prepared, like to talk, generally have something worthwhile to say—keep things going. Active participation by the few may serve to cover the agenda in scheduled time, but fail to foster optimal *class-wide* discussion.

Prestige differences among participants can reduce effectiveness of discussion. Studies of power status in social groups have added a good deal to our knowledge of factors which influence intragroup and inter-personal behavior. As noted in a previous chapter, self-regarding factors are equally important in determining the psychological texture of a group.[6] Of particular significance, in this connection, is the role of the teacher. Position automatically grants him higher prestige status than that of pupils. Question: How can the teacher so conduct himself as to encourage free and responsible student interchange of ideas? Where is that fine line that separates permissiveness from autocratic domination? In short, how can he retain control of the classroom while seeming to entrust most of it to his students? These are fundamental questions for which there is no simple answer. Wholesome self-esteem is a start in the right direction.

These then are some of the acknowledged limitations of discussion. It is significant that in all cases the limitations stem from misuse or misapplication of discussion, not from the form itself. Thus if we are to reduce the factors which limit the effectiveness of discussion and increase the possibilities of its contributions to learning, we must command a functional knowledge of its use in the classroom.

---

[6] Dorwin Cartwright, ed., *Studies in Social Power* (Ann Arbor: University of Michigan Press, 1959).

GUIDELINES FOR USING DISCUSSION

Skillful use of discussion involves a knowledge of methods of selecting topics, choosing the appropriate discussion form, selecting participants, instructing pupils in preparation and presentation of discussion, and evaluating student performance in discussion.

Finding topics for discussion

Ordinarily little difficulty will be experienced in locating problems for discussion particularly in such areas as social studies and English. However, it must be remembered that not all problems lend themselves ideally to the discussion method. The discussability of a problem may be determined by examining it in the light of the following questions:

1. *Is the problem important?* The problem should, above all, be important to pupils. Its importance will be found in the extent to which the problem impinges upon pupils' daily lives and upon matters affecting their security, their well-being and happiness, and the welfare of those who are dear to them. Subjects relating to health hazards, student government, employment practices, family relations, national defense, and crime are likely to yield questions that appeal to youth. Pupils will also be likely to consider important a question whose fuller understanding is essential to the solution of a larger, even more important problem incident to classwork or community life. However, one certainly cannot assume that a given topic will be universally regarded as important. Because of the variability of mores and sophistication in community populations, topics which may seem important in one school may be regarded as trite or trivial in another.

2. *Is the question clear—does it suggest a definite purpose for discussion?* Does the question appear to require mainly the marshaling of information? In other words, is it a *fact inquiry* question? For example: "What is the organizational structure of the United Nations?" Or, does the question seek to *evaluate?* Do we wish to test the worth of something? For instance, "How well does Steinbeck's *Grapes of Wrath* meet the tests of good literature?" is a question which calls for an evaluation. Finally, does the question call for a formulation of *policy?* Does it imply a search for a course of action or a remedy for a problem? For instance, in the question: "How can we best deal with the traffic problem in this city?" discussants will strive to discover

a best policy upon which they can agree as the basis for recommended action.

3. *Does the question call for some form of deliberative thinking? Or is it a question concerning which our knowledge is inadequate or our thinking is confused?* With reference to the former, the problem should be one which encourages or requires reflective thinking. Such problems are those for which the solution is not a matter of immediate decision, but rather one which presents the possibility of multiple choices. An example is the "policy" question : "What can be done to strengthen student government in our school?"

In the case of the latter, the question may be one about which the present understanding and beliefs of the group are either confused or at variance and for which areas of common understanding and agreement are socially desirable. Such questions as "What does the balance sheet on the Peace Corps Program reveal?" and "What is being done to deal with problems of civil rights in our community?" are good examples.

As a rule, questions which encourage taking sides or which call for mere personal opinion should be avoided. For instance, such questions as "Should capital punishment be abolished?" actually call for debate, not true discussion; and such queries as "Who has the more pleasing personality, Dick or John?" are actually not discussable, since judgment of personality is largely a private affair.

4. *Is the question one which calls for group study: can it be approached best through collaborative effort?* Does the question deal with a problem which is of concern to a considerable segment of the immediate population? Is it one which calls for collective judgment or whose solution is more likely to be applied if arrived at through group deliberation? Also is it the kind of problem which is either so complex or so comprehensive that it can be more thoroughly and economically studied by a team rather than one person? Explaining how to drive a car is not a job for a committee. On the other hand, such questions as "How can we best eliminate unethical advertising methods?" might be most effectively approached by a group pooling their information and bringing the benefits of collective, diversified, and creative thinking to the solution of the problem.

5. *Is the question one for which there is an abundance of reliable and useful data?* As indicated earlier, discussion may occasionally be employed as an airing-out process, in which case participants will draw primarily from their present knowledge and reflect their current

feelings. Most discussion, however, should be something more than the bandying of private opinions and the airing of prejudices. A major criterion of good discussion is that it have substance, that evidence introduced be reliable and representative and that the thinking be orderly and logical. Before a question is finally admitted for discussion, a thorough canvass of source materials should be made.

6. *Is the question one which lends itself to reasonably adequate coverage within the designated time limits?* In general, the question should be sufficiently limited in scope to permit its discussion in one class period, allowing some time for audience participation. When necessary or it is deemed profitable to do so, broader subjects can be divided and presented in a series of discussions involving a succession of class periods.

Choosing the type of discussion

To achieve optimum educational results with discussion in a given learning situation, it is important to choose the most appropriate of its several forms. As indicated earlier, group or face-to-face, and two forms of public discussion, the panel and symposium, have been proposed here as the most useful and readily adaptable for classroom purposes. However, in addition to these, some teachers will wish to employ other forms of discussion, such as lecture-forum, hearings, and parliamentary discussion. Information regarding the nature and uses of these forms may be found in the references listed at the end of this chapter.

When teacher and pupils are faced with a problem which calls for straight information or when the teacher believes the audience comprehension of the discussion will be greater through a series of unified speeches, the symposium may be preferred. On the other hand, when the teacher desires a more informal atmosphere, wishes to give greater opportunity for interpersonal action and reaction, he may wish to employ the panel. If, however, it seems wise to carry out simultaneously several projects in group thinking and planning, one may choose the face-to-face or group discussion. In the civics class, the instructor may wish to organize his group on the basis of a legislative body following parliamentary procedure.

Selecting participants for discussion

So far as possible, participation should follow interest and desire of a particular group of pupils to discuss a specific topic. However, there will be times when three or four topics are to be discussed within a given instructional unit or period of time. In this instance, natural choices may not produce an equitable division of the class. Under these circumstances, it will be well to have pupils list their first, second and third choice of topics. On the basis of these choices, the teacher may assign various members of the class to the several discussion groups. In so doing he should be careful to avoid producing initial homogeneity with regard to both general abilities and attitudes toward the subject. Since the teacher looks upon discussion as a social learning situation, he will strive, when possible, to provide opportunities for maximum learning to occur. Getting to know one's students obviously is of paramount importance in forming groups. The use of sociometric devices may prove helpful in gaining useful information about class members.

Choosing the chairman

Much can be said for allowing the members of the group to choose their own chairman. This arrangement often makes for greater intra-group harmony than might result from a teacher appointment. On the other hand, when the procedure is new to the pupils and when the teacher does not wish to risk the disintegration of the discussion because of poor leadership, he would do well to choose his chairman from the group on the basis of proven leadership ability. We should expect, of course, that opportunities for group leadership will be made available to as many members of the class as possible during the year. As pupils gain familiarity with the discussion process, rotating leaders within a given discussion sequence may prove highly interesting and rewarding.

After class members have been given an opportunity to select problems for discussion, have agreed upon the type of discussion to be employed, have formed groups and selected their leaders, they should receive guidance in preparation for discussion.

Guiding pupils in preparation for discussion

The teacher should make it perfectly clear that the functions of participating in and leading discussion carry with them certain responsibilities, foremost of which is the duty to "search for and have high regard for the facts." The teacher, therefore, must lead pupils to find and use those sources which will yield the most pertinent and accurate information on their topics. Naturally, the teacher should have a ready command of these sources. Then, too, he should be able to give direction and purpose to individual research by furnishing or evolving with participants a study guide. This guide will approximate the basic steps to be covered later in the discussion itself. The following outlines are suggestive:

GUIDE FOR PREPARING TO DISCUSS
QUESTIONS OF POLICY[7]

1. Statement of the question.
2. Description of problem.
    a. Symptoms. (What events show the nature of the problem? What harmful effects do these events have?)
    b. Size of problem. (How large and serious is the problem?)
3. Analysis of problems. (What are the major causes of these symptoms?)
4. Suggestion of possible solutions. (On each: 1. What desirable results would we have a right to expect in handling the problem by this plan? 2. What drawbacks or inadequacies would we have to expect?)
5. What suggestions can you make for putting the solution into action?

In practice, the teacher may wish to extend the number and detail of questions in the above outline, depending upon his estimation of the creativeness and resourcefulness of his pupils.

---

[7] Adapted from materials developed by Laura Crowell, University of Washington, Seattle.

GUIDE FOR PREPARING TO DISCUSS EVALUATIVE
QUESTIONS

1. What is the question?
2. What terms in the question need clarifying or defining?
3. What is the nature of the problem?
   a. Why do we wish to test the worth or value of this thing, project, etc?
   b. What criteria can be used in judging its value?
4. What information concerning this thing, project, etc., will assist us in judging its value or worth?
5. What general conclusions and what possible recommendations can be made from these findings?

When the discussion follows the pattern of dividing a general topic into phases and when the purpose is largely *to inform,* the following study guide may be used:

STUDY GUIDE FOR PARTICIPATING IN EXPOSITORY
SYMPOSIUM

1. General topic :
   a. My subtopic :
   b. Other subtopics of the discussion :
2. Time allotted for my presentation :
3. What general plan of approach, if any, has been adopted by the group? (e.g., agreed-upon items to be covered in each of the talks, outline structure, etc.)
4. What sources will be most helpful in furnishing information for my discussion?
5. What information will most adequately meet the requirements of : accuracy, interest, pertinence, and conciseness?
6. How can I best arrange this information in keeping with the group plan so as to accomplish our general purpose?

Broadly speaking, not less than three days should be allowed pupils for research and preparation for discussion. Actual amount of time required will depend upon the complexity of the problem, availability of data, scholastic abilities of pupils, and degree to which participants understand the discussion process.

Advising pupils in the ways of discussion

When discussion is first introduced as a class method at the beginning of the school year, the classroom teacher will need to instruct or reinstruct his pupils in the functions and responsibilities of participation and leadership. The following information may be helpful in providing this instruction.

Leading the discussion. Regardless of the approach taken in the discussion, in addition to being well-informed on the subject under consideration and on the process to be employed, the leader should manifest to the best of his ability: (1) a sense of responsibility for the functioning of the group, (2) respect for the integrity of the individual participant and the validity of ideas, (3) objectivity and fairness, (4) enthusiasm for the subject and the occasion, and (5) patience and restraint—the ability to get things done without doing all of them himself.

In coactive or public discussion the leader's functions will nearly always include: (1) opening the discussion with a statement of the problem, (2) introducing the panel or symposium speakers, (3) announcing the method to be followed in the discussion, including provision for audience participation at the close of the formal presentation, (4) guiding the discussion to its conclusion, and (5) conducting the question period following the discussion.

When the discussion pattern calls for set talks, the leader's specific functions are generally reduced to introducing the problem, stating the issues or reasons for discussing it, introducing the speakers, and managing the question period. However, when the discussion pattern does not call for planned speeches, as in face-to-face and panel discussion, it remains for the leader to take a more active part in guiding the participation along the lines of the discussion outline. In this instance, his functions become more detailed and significant. In addition to stating the problem clearly, the leader must *keep the discussion moving forward* by: (1) discerning and checking irrelevant excursions, (2) securing adequate treatment of relevant issues, (3) getting all important matters considered, (4) recognizing agreements and exploring differences, and (5) providing a sense of direction through transitional questions, stock-taking summaries and final group-achievement summaries. The leader must also keep the thinking of the *group valid.* This he can do by (1) probing generalizations for examples,

(2) testing assertions for supporting material, (3) scanning sources of opinion for competency and bias, (4) assessing single instances for their typicality, and (5) restating emotionalized statements more objectively.

Moreover, in order to get things done, the leader *must secure the most efficient functioning of all the members.* This he does by (1) setting an example of sincerity, consideration, clarity, good will, and purposefulness for the group; (2) encouraging the reticent or silent member; (3) preventing ready talkers from monopolizing the time, (4) appreciating the contributions of members, and (5) providing a hospitable reception for all viewpoints. Finally, the discussion leader *must be able to bring the deliberations to a satisfying close on time.* Generally this is accomplished with a restatement of principal agreements reached and, perhaps, of areas to be explored further.[8]

Participating in the discussion. Participating in discussion, likewise, carries with it definite responsibilites. To begin with, discussing a problem requires of the participant as thorough a knowledge of the topic as time for preparation will permit and as complete an understanding of the discussion process as he can command. If he has faithfully followed his study guide, he should possess adequate knowledge of the subject. It remains for him to become acquainted with his duties and responsibilities for actual participation in the presentation of the discussion.

When discussion calls for planned talks, the participant following his outline, will present as directly, clearly, and interestingly as possible his individual contribution to the total effort and lend his support at all times in the remaining moments of the discussion to a fair hearing of the problem. In face-to-face and panel discussions, the participant will have opportunity to bring wholesome social attitudes and skills into greater play than that permitted in a symposium situation. His abilities to consider the welfare of both his immediate group and larger class audience, to assume with restraint his fair share of responsibility in the deliberation and to listen receptively and creatively to the viewpoints of others, all contribute to a participant's effectiveness in discussion.

When the discussion is concerned with problems of policy or is

---

[8] Based on materials developed by Laura Crowell, Department of Speech, University of Washington. See Crowell, *Discussion: Method of Democracy* (Chicago: Scott, Foresman & Company, 1963), p. 287.

one in which differences of opinion are expressed, Wagner and Arnold point out that:

> It is especially important that participants possess an honest desire to make objective judgments, show a genuine respect for honest differences of opinion, indicate a desire and ability to locate and remove elements of misunderstanding whenever these lie at the root of disagreement; possess a desire and ability to locate and reduce the areas of actual disagreement to specific, clearly understood points, and indicate an earnest desire to achieve the maximum degree of agreement consistent with integrity of belief.[9]

Above all, the participant should continually remind himself that discussion is not a process of persuasion but *the cooperative deliberation of a group sincerely seeking the answer to or solution of a problem.* The success of the discussion method depends on concession and consensus, not on contradiction and coercion. The successful participant, quite possibly, will yield more often than he will seek to win a point.

Guiding the audience for discussion. When coactive or public discussion is employed as classroom method, all class members who are not affiliated with the group making the presentation comprise an audience. For successful discussion, this audience must also assume certain responsibilities, among which is the willingness to listen constructively. When the purpose of discussion is to explain or to inform, the purpose of the listener should be to listen *for information*—for key characteristics and for specific traits, qualities, or definitive attributes. When the purpose of discussion is to deliberate upon a question of policy, value, or disputed fact, it becomes the duty of the audience to adopt a constructively analytical attitude.

When discussion does not involve planned speeches, the audience has the special task of synthesizing into a meaningful whole the informal and often disjointed contributions of the various speakers. Obviously, in this situation concentrated listening is paramount. Then, too, when discussion includes the processes of reflective thinking, the audience must listen not only to learn, but to evaluate and to draw inferences regarding a problem. Members of the audience, therefore, must "test" evidence and "weigh" the soundness of the logic employed

---

[9] Russell H. Wagner and Carroll C. Arnold, *Handbook of Group Discussion* (Boston: Houghton Mifflin Company, 1950), p. 124.

by the speakers individually and collectively. Some tests which the listener may apply in his evaluation of *evidence* include:

1. Trustworthiness of its source as determined by its reliability and validity.
2. Relevance of the facts to the problem under consideration.

Likewise, the listener may apply certain additional tests for evaluating the soundness of the speaker's *reasoning*. For instance, he may ask:

1. Are there enough true, typical instances to justify this particular conclusion?
2. Is this example typical of the general statement with which it is related?
3. Are the cited causal relationships invariable?
4. Are these instances comparable—are they alike in all essential respects?

Evaluating discussion and discussers. Like other classroom procedures, discussion as method must be continuously evaluated in terms of its contributions to the objectives of the course and its worth in promoting pupil speech growth. Such worth is best determined through a study of individual pupil behavior manifested in several discussion situations. The teacher may find the following check sheets useful in carrying out such evaluations.

EVALUATING LEADERSHIP[10]

Leader's name   Date

(On the basis of 5 points for *superior*, 4 for *excellent*, 3 for *good*, 2 for *average* and 1 for *poor*, assign numerical evaluations to each of the

---

[10] Adapted from Crowell, *op. cit.*, pp. 219 and 288.

criteria listed below. Justify your evaluation with a comment in the space at the right.)

Skill	Value	Comment
In opening discussion		
In securing effective functioning of all members		
In keeping discussion moving forward		
In keeping thinking valid		
In bringing discussion to a satisfying close		
In communicating orally		
In handling question period		

Over-all score_____Rating_____

General comments: _____

_____

_____

EVALUATING MEMBER PARTICIPATION

_____   _____

Member's name   Date

(On the basis of 5 points for *superior*, 4 for *excellent*, 3 for *good*, 2 for *average* and 1 for *poor*, assign numerical evaluations to each of the criteria listed below. Justify your evaluation with a comment in the space at the right.)

Criteria	Value	Comment
Sensitivity to other members		
Objectivity of contributions		
Worth of information presented		
Acceptance of share of group responsibility		
Worth of thinking on basis of group (or own) information		
Skill in oral communication		

Over-all score_____ Rating_____

General comments:
_____
_____
_____
_____

Identifying teacher roles during discussion

We have said a good deal about the teacher's responsibilities in preparing students for discussion. At this point a further word or two concerning the teacher's role during discussion would seem to be in order.

Teacher's role during student-led discussion. If advance student preparation has been thorough, the teacher may find it quite unnecessary to do more than listen, observe, and enjoy the discussion, taking such notes as may be useful for an evaluation of both discussants and members of the audience. If, on the other hand, the discussion begins to falter, wander from the agenda, lose focus, or if communication wanes, the teacher may quite properly intervene. However, he should be careful not to assume the group's or leader's responsibilities or appear to take over and in so doing give students the feeling of having failed. When the members of the discussion group seem to be trying, are reasonably well prepared, but are having trouble with group process, the teacher may tactfully interrupt by saying : "Let's stop for a moment and take stock, shall we? You have some very good material; but I think you sense that you might do more with it." (Standing by the leader), the teacher might add, "We are learning. And one thing we are learning is that discussion isn't easy. John, just where are we now on the agenda? What are we doing at this point? What do you think we need to do better to make our discussion most worthwhile?"

In the foregoing, note that the teacher avoids telling the group what to do. Rather, through questions he helps the group discover the procedural difficulty and what could be done to meet it. He preserves the integrity of the group and protects the prestige of the leader. Of course there will be occasions, hopefully not many, when it is perfectly clear that the group isn't ready—the signs of unpreparedness are evident from the beginning of the unfortunate event. In this case the merciful thing to do would doubtless be to stop the massacre and say, "I think you know what's wrong, don't you? You simply aren't prepared, are you? Now there must be a good reason for this." Then if the occasion will permit it, the teacher should sit down with the group in the rear of the room and go over the trouble spots. Or he may schedule a conference with the leader. Complete cancellation of the discussion should be avoided if possible. However, students should never be given the impression that second, third, fourth trials are always possible if their first presentation fails to materialize or falls flat. To sum up, the teacher's special role during student-led discussion is that of consultant, resource person, and sensitive analyst.

The teacher's role in leading discussion. As suggested earlier, the teacher's role in leading discussion is theoretically similar to that assumed by students in this position. It is applied most generally in class-wide discussions when it is desirable to engage members in an investigative, exploratory, evaluational, or problem-solving approach to some aspect of learning, such as the study of a poem, a play, an art object, a person, a vital issue, an editorial, or a local problem.

Leading a successful *class-wide discussion* demands a great deal of *skill, sensitivity,* and *patience.* It requires skill in planning, skill in wording provocative and penetrating questions, and skill in listening. It calls for sensitivity to pupil strengths and limitations, sensitivity to the delicate balance of permissiveness and control, sensitivity to the proper depth and breadth of probing a given point so that meanings are made clear without redundancy. It calls for patience. The teacher must not hurry the thought process merely for the sake of conforming to a time schedule. Of course, interest must be kept alive, but the teacher must use every possible means to draw out the information from his pupils. He should resist the temptation to answer his own questions, talk too much, or prejudge answers. He must allow pupils *time to think, to judge, to respond.*

Although certainly not inclusive, the following guidelines prepared by a committee of graduate speech students at the University of Washington may be useful in helping the classroom teacher improve the quality of his class discussions.

GUIDELINES FOR LEADING CLASS-WIDE DISCUSSION

1. Select the appropriate purpose for the discussion : to investigate, evaluate, to solve a problem, etc.
2. Always clarify with your pupils the procedures to be followed in the discussion.
3. Emphasize the need for critical listening. Illustrate by example if necessary.
4. Stress open-mindedness, willingness to volunteer, sound reasoning.
5. Phrase your questions clearly, concisely.[11]
6. Make each question serve a specific purpose in the discussion : to help the group extend or clarify its line of thinking, bring in additional relevant points, or move to a new line of thinking.
7. Guide pupils to fruitful lines of thought and effectively reasoned choices by appropriate questions rather than by dictatorial pronouncements.

---

[11] Consult Stanley L. Payne, *The Art of Asking Questions* (Princeton, New Jersey: Princeton University Press, 1951) or M. J. McCue Aschner, "Asking Questions to Trigger Thinking," *National Education Association Journal,* L (September, 1961), 44–46.

8. Be quick to echo a pupil's effective phrasing, or to provide a handle for a troublesome, fuzzy idea, or to summarize when necessary.

9. Treat disagreement *as differences of* IDEAS, not PEOPLE, whenever possible.

10. If some pupil's idea is seemingly worthwhile but rejected by the others, try the method of SPEAKER'S PRIVILEGE.[12] Give the floor to this pupil to explain his viewpoint without contradiction or comment of any kind from the others; then let them speak up but only with questions of clarification (WHEN YOU SAID . . . , DID YOU MEAN THIS? or WHAT DID YOU MEAN WHEN YOU SAID . . . ? or DID YOU SAY . . . ?) or questions of difference (HOW IS THIS IDEA DIFFERENT FROM . . . ? or IS THIS IDEA LIKE . . . ?). During this period of SPEAKER'S PRIVILEGE, the teacher must allow no refutation or argument. Only when the point of view is understood similarly by all does the teacher declare the period of SPEAKER'S PRIVILEGE ended and the discussion begun again.

11. In all cases the class *must* know when the teacher *is using* the teacher-led classroom discussion method so that they will understand their privileges and responsibilities.

12. In all uses of classroom discussion the pupils must know how long the classroom discussion activity is going to last so that they can regulate their efforts most usefully within the time limitation.

Thus far in this chapter, attention has been given primarily to the theory and processes of discussion as method in teaching. Let us now consider some suggestions for applying this method of teaching.

GENERAL CLASSROOM APPLICATIONS OF DISCUSSION

As indicated in Chapter Six, *discussion* has special significance for teaching the social studies. However, because of its wide adaptability, it is quite capable of serving a number of instructional purposes and may be applied in almost any classroom in a variety of learning situations. For instance, it may serve as basic method or the chief ingredient of the so-called *problem method of instruction*. It may provide the

---

[12] From Irving J. Lee, "Procedure for Coercing Agreement," *Harvard Business Review*, XXXII (January-February, 1954), 39–45.

implementing procedure for *planning a unit of work*. It may become the fundamental procedure for achieving the purposes of each of the several steps of *unit development*. And not the least important, discussion may serve as a technique for carrying forward *daily or special lessons*.

Discussion as basic method

Problem-solving discussion is the core of the problem method. Following Dewey's five steps of reflective thinking, it may furnish the primary means for dealing with an entire unit-problem or any portion of it.

Social studies, for example, present the learner with two types of problems: those for which society has already found an answer, though imperfect, and those for which it has not. Both of these types of problems offer a wide range of investigative possibilities. The first presents opportunities for verifying present solutions, as well as occasions for pursuing additional, more acceptable solutions. The second offers opportunities to explore the relatively unknown, an experience which calls for the highest type of creative and constructive thinking. Frequently the problem-unit will grow out of the subject matter of the course. More likely to be stimulating, however, are those which are suggested by a community difficulty, a question facing youth, or a national dilemma. The problem can be either teacher- or pupil-initiated. The latter, when well guided, would seem to insure a higher degree of pupil motivation. The following problems are illustrative of pupil-initiated questions which found expression in various areas of study in one high school.

Economics: "How can labor-management relations be improved?" (Arose from effects of a major strike in that particular geographical area.)

Geography: "How can we improve our relations with South American countries?" (Given impetus through pupils' reading newspaper reports of anti-American demonstrations in several South American cities.)

History: "How can we best employ manpower for the security of our country?" (Arose out of the problems of draft and universal training facing high school seniors.)

Civics: "How can we strengthen democracy in our city?" (Initiated by a report of a recent election which revealed that only 25 per cent of the eligible voters had cast ballots.)

All of the above questions, it will be noted, arose from felt difficulties. The alert teacher will strive to create in his pupils sensitivity to such problems.

Developing each of the subsequent steps of problem-solving, however, may vary from one teaching situation to another. For instance, one teacher, after general class-wide discussion on method, divided his class into "Buzz" groups. Each of these groups, with its leader, gathered around a table in the classroom for approximately thirty minutes of each class period for a week, devoting roughly one meeting to each of the several steps in the problem-solving discussion. At the conclusion of the buzz session series, the chairmen of the various groups formed a symposium and reported their individual group findings and recommendations to the class as a whole.

Another teacher chose to approach a problem by dividing his class into panels, each group being responsible for one of the major steps in the discussion sequence. For example, *Group One* defined the problem and discussed its symptoms and their implications. *Group Two* explored the problem as to its causes and established criteria for solutions. *Group Three* presented solutions. *Group Four* evaluated the solutions in light of the criteria. Finally, the entire class, under the direction of an able student leader, chose what they believed to be the best solution of the problem and considered measures for its implementation. The teacher then led his pupils in an evaluation of the unit experience. In this instance, the pupils, for the most part, agreed that while discussion took time and made them work to get information, "it was fun," "learned a great deal about the problem," and "learned how to see the other fellow's point of view."

Discussion in planning a unit

Effective motivation lies at the heart of all successful teaching and effective learning. Too frequently teacher-contrived and -imposed units of work fall short in inspiring motivation. On the contrary, units developed through pupil planning or teacher-pupil planning generally have high motivational potential. The concept of "our problem" is normally more challenging than that of the "teacher's problem."

The work of planning a unit can be carried out most efficiently by a committee of pupils and the teacher rather than by the class as a whole. The committee, however, should be selected by class members. Meeting with their instructor during study period, before or after school, this committee will become acquainted with and seek solution to their problem: *How to organize and approach a unit of study.* Since high school pupils possess little knowledge of unit construction, members of the committee are likely to flounder and accomplish little, unless the leader (teacher or strong pupil) is equipped with a working outline for guiding the group's deliberation and research. Given a general pattern to follow, members of the group will have sufficient latitude to think creatively and constructively. And while the teacher will need to guide and supplement the group's thinking regarding objectives, materials, and resources, members of the planning group, being pupils themselves, are likely to choose wisely those procedures that will appeal to the class as a whole.

The following guide questions are suggested for assisting the student committee in planning the unit:

1. What is the subject of our study?
2. Why is the study of this subject necessary or desirable?
3. What specific benefits should each of us gain from its study?
4. What sources, references and informational aids are available for our work?
5. What, specifically, do we wish to find out or learn?
6. How will we start our study of this subject?
7. What activities can we engage in to secure the desired information?
8. What kinds of activities will enable us to share this information with one another and use it to achieve our major purpose?
9. How much time shall we give ourselves to complete this unit?
10. How can we determine how much we have learned and how well we have learned it?

Unit planning is obviously not an easy task for youngsters and should be entrusted only to pupils who are unusually mature, creative, and resourceful. However, as a means of providing such pupils with a challenging learning situation—one which presents the individual with real discussion opportunities—unit planning experience has few peers.

Discussion as a fundamental procedure for accomplishing the steps of a unit

First, a phase of discussion can be used in *initiating a unit.* This might assume the form of a class-wide deliberation on locating and defining a problem and determining basic approaches to the problem. Second, discussion can be used as one of the several activities incident to the *development steps of a unit.* For instance, buzz groups may be employed to study individual questions or subproblems and the symposium may be used to present resulting information to the class as a whole. Third, discussion can be employed *in the culminating phase* of unit procedure. For example, one class studying the subject of conservation on a national scope concluded its unit with a problem-solving panel discussion viewing the question in its application to a local situation. Finally, discussion, teacher-led on a class-wide basis, may be a useful means of evaluating results of the unit study. When this application is employed, it is advisable for the teacher in the early stages of unit study to assign to individual committees the task of observing achievement of unit objectives as work progresses. Thus when called upon at the conclusion of the unit, each committee will be prepared to present its report regarding individual and collective accomplishments with respect to the particular objectives set for the unit.

Discussion as a technique for teaching daily lessons

As a *systematic method of review* discussion has much to offer. It can provide wide coverage of a subject, stimulate general participation, and provide continuity and wholeness to a unit of work, thus aiding pupils in organizing materials for better understanding. Furthermore, it is considered by many teachers as a valuable means of diagnosing pupil weaknesses.

Discussion can function as an integral procedure in *making an assignment.* For instance, in teacher-pupil planning, the discussion process may serve to lay plans for an excursion or a project, to probe the extent and nature of library research needed to investigate a problem. All such activities may lead to cooperative assignments essential to a study of the larger, more inclusive problem or class project.

Discussion, moreover, provides an excellent setting for *asking questions*—thought-provoking questions incident to good problem-solving. In discussion, leaders, participants, and audience members ask questions when they wish (1) to have meanings clarified, (2) to probe implications of an idea or statement, or (3) to secure areas of agreement. Such questioning, for the most part, is educationally superior to the formal teacher-question, pupil-answer recitation whose chief value lies in its testing potential.

Discussion has been advanced as an outstanding avenue for *individualizing instruction*. Group organization attained by dividing the class into small instructional units, makes possible greater attention to individual pupil needs and abilities. One of the major aims of good discussion method is to assure a high level of individual participation by assigning to pupils duties commensurate with their abilities.

Discussion also affords pupils *opportunity to follow individual aptitudes and interests*. For example, one group of youngsters, studying a unit in United States history entitled "The American Industrial Giant," presented a symposium with the following division of responsibility: (1) a pupil interested in shop work showed how specialization of jobs has made mass production possible; (2) one student planning to enter business presented the advantages of large and small business units; (3) a pupil interested in government and politics discussed government regulation and business; (4) another pupil interested in international relations explained how American business has affected our relations with other countries; (5) a socially minded pupil showed how the industrial age was responsible for growth of cities and how this growth created new social problems.

Finally, discussion is a valuable *means of testing knowledge*. Discussion provides the teacher with opportunity to observe, in part, the extent to which knowledge incident to the unit is understood by pupils and integrated in their behavior. Evidences of growth in personality and matured behavior are, in the final analysis, among the most reliable indices that learning is taking place.

SUMMARY

In this chapter, discussion has been presented as a basic speech form with high potential as a classroom method of instruction and medium of learning. It was defined in general as "the cooperative deliberation of problems by persons thinking and conversing together in face-to-face or coacting groups under the direction of a leader." Variant forms were considered in terms of the influences of *situation, purpose,* and *leadership.* Its values, together with its limitations, for use in the class-room were reviewed. Stressed in particular was the point that valuable as discussion is as a method of instruction and learning, it is neither a panacea for meeting all classroom instructional problems nor a self-activating process. Discussion must be wisely chosen and competently guided if it is to achieve desired results. To this end, considerable attention was given to identifying the skills essential to effective use of discussion in the classroom. Included were: (1) Finding suitable topics, (2) Choosing the appropriate type of discussion, (3) Selecting partici-pants, (4) Choosing the chairman, (5) Guiding pupil preparation, (6) Leading the discussion, (7) Participating in discussion, (8) Guiding the audience in discussion, (9) Evaluating discussion, and (10) Identifying teacher roles during discussion. The chapter concluded with brief descriptions of some general classroom applications of discussion.

SELECTED READINGS

Boyd, Gertrude A. "Role Playing." *Social Education,* XXI (October, 1957), 267–9.

Chrisman, Richard. "Use of the Panel Discussion in Teaching of Social Science." *High School Journal,* XXIV (March, 1941), 106–110.

Crowell, Laura I. *Discussion: Method of Democracy.* Chicago : Scott, Foresman & Company, 1963.

Hoffman, Randall W., and Robert Plutchik. *Small Group Discussion in Orientation and Teaching.* New York : G. P. Putnam's Sons. 1959.

Keltner, John W. *Group Discussion Processes.* New York : Longmans, Green and Co., 1957.

McClendon, Jonathon C. *Social Studies in Secondary Education.* New York : The Macmillan Company, 1965. See especially Chapter 16 "Conducting Oral Activities."

Overcoming Obstacles in Discussion of Current Affairs. Junior Town Meeting League, 356 Washington St., Middletown, Conn., 1957.

9 *dramatization*

Dramatic instinct runs deep in the life of man. Whether we take as an example the ritualistic dance of primitive peoples, the festival revels of Elizabethan England, the religious rites that persist to this day, or the formal drama of ancient, medieval, and modern times—all give evidence of man at play, man involved with the cosmos, or man in conflict with himself, his fellowman, or with nature. And as all of us know, the basic urge to pretend appears early in childhood: playing house, playing school, and cowboys and Indians are but a few of the make-believe experiences of children that illustrate the dramatic urge.

Sophocles and Aristophanes knew it; Marlowe and Shakespeare felt it; Shaw, O'Neil, Sherwood, and all worthy playwrights, as well as Thespis, Burbage, Ellen Terry, the Barrymores, and the host of other great actors of all times—all knew the power of drama and acting for touching life through man's imagination. All have known the potential of the play for moving participants and audience to thought, to deep feeling. Through direct involvement, a player identifies with the character; he enters into the conflict of the play, and serves the purpose of its author. If there is an audience, it emphatically shares in this experience. This propensity for touching the thoughts and feelings of participants by catching their attention and enlisting their participation makes dramatization a valuable method of teaching and learning in the classroom. If, as the educational psychologists inform us, "we learn best by doing," then *drama,* which from its original derivation means "to do," should command high priority as a learning procedure in all classrooms, regardless of subject matter.

In keeping with the philosophy and aims of this textbook, this chapter will present what we consider to be the essentials of dramatics as a basic method of learning. And while our objective is not stage-worthy dramatic productions, we shall hope that imaginatively applied, our suggestions may be instrumental in making classroom learning both enjoyable and meaningful. Dramatization has great potential for developing appreciation and understanding of human nature and deeper insight into the nature and resolution of human problems.

DEFINITIONS

The terms *dramatics* and *dramatization,* of course, are derived from the word *drama,* meaning "the art or profession of writing, acting, or producing plays."[1] The word *dramatics* is frequently used with reference to plays produced and performed by amateurs; the term *dramatization* includes the processes of adapting, arranging, reporting, and presenting a concept, event, problem, or story in the form of a play. In the discussion which follows, therefore, we shall be using the terms *classroom dramatics* and *dramatization* more or less interchangeably. In the sense that classroom dramatics, rightly conceived, is a highly creative activity and for this reason educationally significant, it is also appropriate to equate our terms in a general way with *creative* and *educational dramatics.*

It is generally agreed that to be *dramatic* an episode or situation must possess two major ingredients: two or more interacting agents—usually human beings—and some form of conflict. This conflict may be a struggle for or against someone or something. It may be man's struggle with himself, as in *Macbeth,* or it may involve groups of people in conflict with each other for political, social, economic, or religious reasons. Structurally, a dramatization resembles narrative prose and narrative poetry: it possesses a main current, the story, composed of a series of related events leading to a climax and resolution of the basic conflict. In dramatization, however, the story normally unfolds through the action and dialogue of the characters of the play rather than through a narrator. Like oral interpretative reading, dramatization is also a creative (or an interpretative and re-creative) process. However, dramatization involves acting, which possesses

---

[1] *Webster's New World Dictionary* (New York: World Publishing Co., 1964).

certain unique qualities that distinguish it from reading aloud, including the kind of *speaker-audience relationship,* the *amount* and *kind of action* employed, and the *physical arrangement for presentation.* In addition, the speech and action of dramatization may be supplemented with costume, scenery, special lighting, and makeup.[2] In *dramatization,* the player attempts to represent a character. He improvises or memorizes his lines; he moves and speaks—acts—as he thinks the character would under the circumstances. In short, dramatization seeks to create credible illusion of reality. The degree of identification with character and situation for both actor and observer is likely to be the measure of the depth and scope of their intellectual and emotional experience with the story or episode.

The process of dramatization is not limited to the *enactment* of the episode or story. For example, group discussion may be used in planning dramatic experiences, interpretative reading is often a preliminary step to acting a part; creative writing is frequently employed in composing original dramatic materials.

It is both significant and fortunate that the study of and participation in dramatics can be approached in a number of different ways and on several levels of sophistication, all with equally satisfying results. We shall be concerned here with three types of dramatics: *informal* (commonly referred to as *creative dramatics*), *semiformal,* and *formal dramatics.* It is our view that all three forms are creative but each offers its own unique opportunities for creativity. For our purposes, we believe it more appropriate to classify *dramatics* in terms of degrees of formality-informality than on a continuum of creativity.

Informal dramatics refers to an activity in which participants creatively and spontaneously act out an experience. Although participants may have planned the general structure of the play, action and dialogue are extemporized rather than written and memorized. Instead of directing the activity, the teacher motivates and guides the pupils. Normally informal dramatization is not presented for an extramural audience. Emphasis is on the total development of the participants and the activity itself, not on achieving a finished performance. It can be enacted with or without scenery.[3]

---

[2] Of necessity, if not by preference, these elements may be kept minimal, suggestive rather than realistic.

[3] Winifred Ward, *Playmaking with Children,* 2nd ed. (New York: Appleton-Century-Crofts, 1957), pp. 9–10.

An important variant of this form of drama is role-playing in problem-solving situations, particularly when applied as socio- or psychodrama.

Semiformal dramatics includes all types of creative adapting or developing of plays from ideas, situations, or stories leading to the writing of the dialogue and suggested action, together with enactment of the play. It resembles informal drama in its initial stages but is more structured in its subsequent development. Examples include developing an original sketch for a special event, such as Memorial Day, or in behalf of a cause, such as civil rights; or depicting an incident in the life of a famous person.

Formal dramatics refers to all activities pertaining to the selection, preparation, and presentation of either published or unpublished plays.

As we have said, all forms are creative and potentially educational. Certainly the opportunities for creativity are virtually limitless in the minimally structured *informal drama;* similar potentials are present in *semiformal dramatizations,* which include the experience of writing; and *formal drama* invites creativity through its challenge to analytical thinking, original presentation, and vivid character delineation.

VALUES AND LIMITATIONS
OF DRAMATIZATION

As previously suggested, a major value of dramatization lies in its inherent capacity for motivating and involving pupils—both essential for effective learning. In addition, dramatization rightly guided can contribute to the development of the pupil's imagination, his ability to concentrate, and his use of language. As a means of reaching the reticent child and guiding the apathetic or rebellious boy or girl toward constructive learning, dramatics probably has no peer.[4] And for many teachers it is one of the most effective means of developing cooperative attitudes in the classroom. Doubtless its greatest value, however, is its capacity for enlivening the spirit of learning in the classroom. It has been said "Dramatization is to touch life with life."[5]

[4] See, for instance, M. Jerry Weiss, *Guidance Through Drama* (New York: William Morrow and Co., Inc., 1954).

[5] Eleanore Hubbard, *The Teaching of History Through Dramatic Presentation* (New York: Benjamin H. Sanborn and Co., 1935), p. 41.

Like all speech activities, dramatics also has its limitations as a classroom procedure. First of all, of course, dramatization is time consuming. Even though the intention is not to produce polished performances, dramatizations must be carried out reasonably well if they are to warrant the time taken. Then, too, guiding dramatic activities calls for considerable imagination and skill from the teacher. Few, other than drama, English, and speech teachers are likely to have received training in this activity. Less frequent perhaps is the limitation which may result from misinterpreting the purpose of classroom dramatics. It should not be forgotten that dramatization is here conceived as a classroom experience, not a preparation for public exhibition. Should the experience be extended beyond the classroom, such extension should be an incidental outcome not the major purpose of the activity.

In all events, choosing dramatization as a class procedure calls for weighing its advantages against its limitations in light of the demands of a given learning situation. Whenever the nature of the material to be covered, pupil interest, and time available make dramatization a logical and desirable choice, then this activity in one of its variant forms should be seriously considered as a teaching-learning procedure. The following sections are calculated to help teachers guide pupils in the use of this exciting speech activity.

GUIDELINES FOR USING DRAMATIZATION

Selecting the type of dramatization

Although it is difficult to lay down hard and fast rules for selecting the type of dramatization, it can safely be said that: (1) The choice should be guided by the nature of the subject or learning experience under consideration. For example, illustrating a safety principle in a health class might best be accomplished through use of informal dramatization, such as a short improvisation. The nature and importance of fair employment practices being discussed in a history class might be effectively portrayed in a role-playing discussion. A class in English literature or social studies might wish to try their hand at writing and acting out an original play or sketch and thus make use of semi-formal dramatics. Or they may prefer to use professional material

—formal drama—as a means of studying drama and the art of play-writing. (2) The choice may be influenced by the amount of time available. Obviously an improvisation will require less total time than a rehearsed play, even though their respective presentation times may be comparable. (3) The choice may be influenced by the interests and capabilities of the students. Writing, staging, and acting out a play call for a wider array of talents than merely improvising a sketch. (4) Closely related to the latter, the choice may be determined in part by the teacher's special capabilities. Many teachers possess unusual creative abilities and are able to stimulate creative responses in their pupils. For instance, some teachers have found their skill with puppets has paid high dividends in class motivation. Other teachers, because of their basic interest and skill in teaching problem-solving discussion, find that role-playing in sociodrama is an excellent device for teaching comprehension of certain problems. (5) The choice may be determined by the availability of formal drama in school and community. Television, films, and community theater may all become means for students to enjoy the benefits of good drama and good literature, and to gain deeper insights into some of the problems that beset mankind. Most high schools have access to numerous excellent films of standard works, including Dickens, Shakespeare, and Shaw. Excellent professional recordings of plays are also available for classroom use. And while experts in learning theory remind us that participants usually derive more benefit than observers from dramatization, we must not minimize the educational values of seeing and hearing good drama. In some instances, the chief value of a play is its power to stimulate a penetrating discussion of the problem with which the play is concerned.[6]

Let us say, then, that the choice of dramatization will depend largely upon the immediate learning objectives, availability of time and appropriate materials, student interest and abilities, and the breadth and depth of the teacher's dramatic sophistication. Having made a choice of the type of dramatization, the teacher is then faced with the responsibility of guiding his pupils in a rewarding use of that particular play form. Although the three types of dramatization included in this chapter have many features in common, they differ sufficiently to warrant separate consideration.

---

[6] Consult Lydia G. Deseo and Hulda M. Phelps, *Looking at Life Through Drama* (New York: Abingdon Press, 1931).

Guiding informal dramatic activities

Many pupils and teachers find that, of the three types of dramatization, *informal drama* applies most readily to general classroom use. As suggested above, it is less time consuming and for limited purposes it is an excellent method of applying principles of dramatics to the improvement of teaching and learning. It can be limited to pantomime or employed with both action and dialogue.

Choosing materials for informal drama—criteria for selection: For successful playing (1) the material must have dramatic appeal, i.e., possess some element of conflict; (2) the characters should be comprehensible to the pupils who are to play them; (3) the situation should require movement and pantomime; (4) the material should impel dialogue when speaking is wanted; the dialogue should seem to flow naturally from the situation and action; (5) the subject should appeal to adolescents.

Adolescents, as noted earlier, are interested in adult problems, in ethical and philosophical questions, as well as in situations that call for action or sparkle with good humor. In fact, their interests are many and varied, ranging from those of preadolescence to those of adult life. Interests tend to reflect levels of mental and social maturity. Many adults have childish interests. Children who have had the benefit of enriched environments are likely to have adult-level interests.

Sources. Fortunately sources for providing materials which meet most of the foregoing criteria are abundant. News items, pictures, an incident in the life of a famous person, ballads, folk tales, short stories, and episodes from longer narratives have been found to yield excellent material for informal dramatizations.

Planning the dramatization. Planning sessions incident to the actual presentation of an informal play are frequently the most educationally valuable phases of the dramatization experience. Basically problem-solving in nature, these sessions have great potential for developing creative and analytical thinking, as well as cooperative spirit among participants. They may be guided by the teacher or, in some cases, entrusted to a talented student who has the respect and cooperation of his peers.

Although not all authorities agree on either the sequence or methods of planning, the following steps in the order presented here have wide currency. Comments and questions accompanying each step are merely suggestive; teachers with training and experience in drama will doubtless prefer to follow their own tested procedures.

Step One: *Motivate.* In spite of the fact that youngsters enjoy make-believe and engage in some kind of play-acting every day, dramatizing a story or a ballad in class in the presence of one's peers may meet with some resistance unless it is skillfully approached. When the teacher senses reticence among his pupils or in other ways feels that the class is not psychologically ready to try dramatizing a story, he should start with comparatively simple problem-improvisations.

Adolescents are familiar with charades. Variants of this game can provide boys and girls with exciting and worthwhile exercises in effective communication. The teacher might begin by pantomiming a simple problem situation, such as buying an item in a department store, waiting on a fussy customer at a gas station, or opening a can of beans. The teacher would then invite members of the class to experiment with similar problems. The following are illustrative:

1. A student performing a hazardous experiment in chemistry.
2. A boy reporting to his father that he has had an accident with the family car.
3. A golf teacher giving a lesson to two beginners—one who is quick to learn, the other, an awkward dub.
4. A boy or girl being interviewed for a job.
5. Acting out a news item.
6. Dramatizing a picture : Showing the picture, ask what has preceded this scene? What is happening in the scene? What will ensue?

Beginning with Suggestion Number 4, pupils should be urged to include some dialogue which to them seems appropriate to the situation and characters. As experimentation progresses, more careful attention should be given to details in pantomime and movement: imaginary objects handled should seem to have weight, size, dimension, texture; movements should express thought and feeling—motivation. Having students work in pairs or small groups frequently encourages the more reticent pupil to "let go." Pupils who have had pleasant experience with creative dramatics in elementary school can help immensely in building classroom atmosphere conducive to informal dramatization. The indirect approach just described is frequently used to prepare less experienced or socially reticent pupils to approach willingly and freely the somewhat more demanding task of *informally dramatizing* a story, ballad, or biographical episode. The experienced or socially sophisticated pupils perhaps will not require this preliminary introduction. In any event, let us now turn to a more directly motivated approach to the *dramatization of a short story.*

Frequently student interest in dramatizing a story develops spontaneously from a silent reading and class discussion of a narrative. Or the desire may evolve from comments by the teacher. He might say: "I am really impressed by what you seem to have gained from this story. You have raised some very interesting questions concerning the motivation of the leading characters. Would it help us to visualize these people more vividly if we acted out a scene or two from the story?" There is a good chance the pupils will respond affirmatively.

Some teachers who enjoy reading aloud or telling a story, find that both methods are excellent introductions to a dramatized version of the story. These methods are particularly successful when the story poses a problem or an unsolved climax, as in Stockton's "The Lady or the Tiger." When the desire to dramatize has been established, participants are ready for the next constructive step.

Step Two: *Plan the structure of the sketch.* Through group discussion plan the number and location of scenes and what is to take place in each episode. Do not record the decisions; encourage concentration, good listening; cultivate an atmosphere of freedom and purposeful informality so as to invite constructive contributions.

Step Three: *Designate the essential characters.* Determine through discussion the leading characters, their motivations and their essential qualities. Discover how they feel toward one another, how their natures affect their movements, speech, listening habits; and determine what supporting characters, if any, are needed to help tell the story. What dominant moods must the characters strive to create? How will each character help achieve the purpose of the dramatization?

Step Four: *Assign students to roles.* Parts can be assigned by the teacher-leader with assistance from the group. Whenever possible, choices should be made on the combined bases of what the experience may contribute to the players and what the players may be expected to bring to the roles. Though the "performance" will not be public, it should be a total classroom experience, hopefully, a constructive learning experience for all concerned.

Step Five: *Initiate the playing.* (First Scene) Have players take their places, and, on signal, begin to "tell the story" through pantomime. If the students appear to be ready for it, they should include improvised dialogue with the action. Remind players that their task is to convey the sense of the story and to share with the class audience their interpretation of the roles being played.

Step Six: *Indirectly assist in the process.* As in group discussion, the teacher may find it unnecessary and unwise to participate in any way during the "play" except to listen and observe appreciatively. Some teachers react with words of encouragement, praise, challenge. Occasionally when things are going badly, it may be necessary to call a halt and, again as in discussion, lead the group in a self-analysis. Do not try for polished performance; sincerity of purpose, honest involvement, some evidence of creativeness: these are the essential qualities for which to strive.

Step Seven: *Evaluate.* After each scene or, preferably, following the entire presentation, the group, with the cooperation of the class, should evaluate the project. In the evaluative discussion, led by the teacher or a talented group chairman, students will wish to give thought to two kinds of questions: first, those pertaining to *subject matter,* and second, those relating to *process.* With respect to the former, it would be appropriate to inquire, in what ways, if any, has the dramatization added to an understanding of the problem, event, or persons dramatized? What new insights have been gained? Have attitudes toward the problem or people involved in the dramatization been modified in any way as a result of this experience? Why or why not? What questions, if any, remain unanswered, what points are still unclear? What can be done to gain further understanding of the problem with which the dramatization was concerned?

With regard to *process,* the following questions are pertinent: Was the story or incident made clear? If not, why not? What could have been done to improve the clarity? Did the dialogue and action seem consistent with character and purpose of the play? How might they have been improved? Were the characterizations believable and consistent? Did the players appear to have clear impressions of their roles, and did they remain in character consistently? How well did everyone work together in the project, including members of the "audience"? Was there good team spirit? In terms of procedure, what was learned that might be useful in another such project?

In *informal drama* usually no props except tables and chairs are used. Players are urged to imagine, to observe, to capture and share the message of the story or incident and salient qualities of the characters. Because of its informality, this type of dramatization has much to offer pupils in the ways of emotional release, creative thinking, effective interpersonal communication, and wholesome enjoyment of playing and learning together.[7]

Earlier in this chapter, *role-playing* or *sociodrama* was mentioned as an important variant of *informal dramatics*. Because of its growing acceptance as a procedure for problem-solving, its potential for fostering interpersonal communication, and its capacity for investing the classroom with life, this variant deserves attention beyond that already given *informal dramatics* in general.

Whereas in most dramatization our chief concern is with content and the personal satisfactions which may derive from playmaking, in sociodrama our major interest is in process : a group experience in dealing with problems of human relations. As a classroom activity, it has been described as a group method that enables young people to explore, in spontaneous enactments followed by guided discussion, how they intend to solve a problem, to consider alternatives available to them, and to weigh the possible personal and social consequences of the various proposals.[8]

GUIDELINES FOR ROLE-PLAYING

Materials of role-playing

The substance for role-playing is to be found in life itself. Textbooks, stories, poems, plays, news items, actual events provide a wealth of material which may be approached through role-playing, particularly when the story or event concerns a vital problem of human relations. Regardless of source, the problem should be one that impinges upon the participants, has relevance to their age and their interests, and is consonant with the general purposes of the course in which it is used.

---

[7] Viola Spolin, *Improvisation for the Theater* (Evanston, Ill.: Northwestern University Press, 1963). Though written for drama specialists, this book offers a refreshing approach to the subject and a host of ideas for "problem" improvisations, many of which can be adapted to classroom use.

[8] Fannie R. Shaftel and George Shaftel, *Role-Playing for Social Values* (Englewood Cliffs, N.J.: Prentice-Hall Inc., 1967), p. 9.

All good dramatic situations involve conflict and are motivated by the need for a solution of a problem. In sociodrama the problem generally concerns a question of *value*. Hopefully, the experience in role-playing offers participants opportunity to develop a core of values—the substance of personal integrity.

Although most role-playing problems are introduced to a group in the form of an unfinished story, the following brief "situations" perhaps will suggest the kind of material from which sociodrama or role-playing may emerge:

1. You have to return a borrowed object that you broke. How do you do this?

2. One of the boys in the class has taken your pocketbook and hidden it. You think you know who it is, but when you ask him about it he says that he didn't take it. How can you get it back?

3. Your parents tell you that they don't approve of some of your friends of the same sex. They think these friends are a bad influence on you and insist that you stop seeing them. You like these friends, enjoy being with them, and want to continue to see them. What can you do to influence your parents? Enact the scene where you and your parents discuss the problem.

4. A young boy, about fourteen, is in the courtroom for stealing some groceries from a large store to get food for himself and his family. The main characters are the judge, the boy, the boy's mother, a lawyer defending the boy, and a lawyer prosecuting the case. The scene can be acted out by high school students with minimal instructions and no prearranged dialogue. The discussion can concentrate on the attitudes other students have regarding this situation or on the feelings of each actor as he approaches this event.[9]

The following outline, adapted from Shaftel and Shaftel[10] indicates in a general way the purposes and basic procedures identified with *role-playing* dramatizations.

---

[9] Quoted from Mark Chesler and Robert Fox, *Role-Playing Methods in the Classroom* (Chicago: Science Research Associates, 1966).

[10] Shaftel, *op. cit.* © 1967 by Prentice-Hall, Inc. Adapted by permission of the publisher.

Step One : Orienting the group—warm-up.

    Purpose :

    a. To develop mental and physical flexibility.

    b. To introduce ways of dealing with a problem.

    c. To help individuals identify with persons experiencing a problem.

    Procedures :

    a. Select a problem that is important to pupils and with which they can readily identify.

    b. Express the problem vividly : e.g., relate a problem story, or cite a problem incident.

    c. Hold brief discussion on "nature of the problem," issues involved, motivations in the conflict.

    d. Lead into the problem for which the warm-up is intended : e.g., say that you are now going to read a story that is similar in certain respects to the one just discussed. This time you will not finish the story—finishing it will be up to the pupils. Suggest that when you have finished reading the story some members of the class may wish to show how they think the person or persons in the story may solve the problem.

    e. After reading the unfinished story, help the group move toward role-playing by asking pupils what is happening in the situation and what they think will happen. The discussion which follows will not only bring out interesting possibilities for "solutions," but will offer clues as to which pupils have identified strongly with the characters in the story.

Step Two : Selecting the players.

    Criteria :

    a. Select on the basis of helping pupils gain a needed experience or an opportunity "to better understand the other fellow's point of view."

    b. Select on the basis of potential for enactment of motivations in the story.

    Procedures :

    a. With questions, discover what kind of persons the characters are. Invite pupils to play roles with which they have identified.

    b. Appoint pupils who appear to have strong convictions concerning the issues involved. Be cautious about assigning roles to youngsters who have been "volunteered' for those roles by others, unless there are compelling reasons for doing so.

Step Three : Planning the action.
    Purpose :
    To orient the players sufficiently to begin the role-playing.
    Procedures :
    a. Have players decide on a general line of action, but do not prepare any dialogue.
    b. Remind each player of his role.
    c. If essential to the enactment, decide time and place of action.
    d. Determine what characters are doing when "the curtain rises."

Step Four : Briefing the "audience."
    Purpose :
    a. To involve the entire class in a learning situation.
    b. To teach good listening and observing.
    Procedures :
    a. Always have pupils listen *for* something.
    b. Assign one group in the audience to "follow" one character; another group a different character, etc., *or*
    c. Have entire audience respond to the role-playing as a whole : was it believable?
    d. Remind class to be thinking of other solutions to the problem, which might then become the bases for second and third enactments.

Step-Five : Acting-out the problem.
    Purpose :
    a. To explore reality, not to reveal acting ability.
    b. To develop social sensitivity.
    c. To provide experience in decision making.
    Procedures :
    a. Suggest, when advisable, one character's line of action so as to enable others to react to something reasonably definite.
    b. Encourage players to play their roles as believably as possible, to play the roles as they see them.
    c. Remember, "the way an actor portrays a role has no reflection upon him as a person."
    d. Avoid slanting the outcome of the process with value judgments of your own.

Step Six : Discussing and evaluating the enactment.
    Purpose :
    a. To weigh the strengths and weaknesses of the "solution."
    b. To draw out and refine the learnings of the enactment.
    c. To probe alternative solutions.

Procedures :
a.   Pose such questions as : "What happened here?" "How does
     the (mother, father, principal) feel?" "Is there another way
     of resolving this situation?"
b.   Ask audience groups to report their observations.

Step Seven : Replaying.
  Purpose :
  a.   To provide opportunity for viewing alternative solutions.
  b.   To promote the experimental approach to problems.
  Procedures :
  a.   Have same players reenact their "performance" in light of
       the discussion following their first playing; or
  b.   Have other players demonstrate their "solution" to the
       problem.

To sum up, informal dramatics, while the least structured of three,
requires thoughtful, creative planning and quidance, ranging from
selection of appropriate materials through the seven steps of
preparation and enactment, followed by evaluation.

Guiding semi-formal dramatics

It is but a short step from informal to semiformal drama with its
additional structuring, including writing and using a script. When
this added dimension is deemed important as a learning experience,
semiformal drama should be considered for classroom use.

Few schools normally include in their curricula systematic instruction in playwriting. However it is virtually certain that every year in
many high schools, skits, short plays, and even pageants are written,
sometimes by teachers, often by pupils. The teacher who can provide
incentive and guidance in writing such materials is helping to bring a
valuable learning experience to pupils, while deriving much personal
satisfaction from the project.

Composing dramatic material, as with all creative writing, requires
considerable discipline. In lieu of a course in playwriting, the teacher
can learn the essentials from reading a number of good one-act plays,
studying model sketches, and consulting some special sources on the
art of playwriting, such as Kenneth MacGowan's *A Primer of Playwriting* and *Constructing a Play* by Marion Galloway. Meanwhile

some general guidelines for composing original plays and sketches are suggested here for the classroom teacher who may wish to try his hand at elementary playwriting or guiding students in such activities.

Writing sketches and short plays. First of all, one should have some knowledge of play structure. In a general way, this includes an understanding of such fundamentals as: introduction, development, climax, resolution of the conflict, and the conclusion of the story.

The *introduction* provides the audience with all the basic information concerning time and place of action, what has gone before, the theme of the play, and the leading characters. The *development* carries the plot forward through a series of episodes or incidents, which must express conflict, i.e., reveal the leading character in a struggle of some kind. The development leads to a high point of interest or place in which the struggle or conflict reaches its highest peak of excitement and the nature of the outcome begins to become evident. Following the *climax,* the conflict undergoes an unraveling action: equilibrium is restored and questions about the leading characters are satisfactorily answered.

One of the most manageable and rewarding experiences in elementary playwriting can be found in adapting a short story to dramatic form. The following procedures developed from ideas suggested by J. R. Dyce[11] illustrate basic steps for converting a short story to a one-act play.

Step 1. Read and reread the story silently for the plot, climax, setting, characters, and mood.

Step 2. Write an outline of the story.

Step 3. Decide on what parts of the story can and should be selected for a scene or scenes.

Step 4. Determine content of each scene—what takes place and what characters are needed to tell the story.

Step 5. Assign students to various characters; discuss each character —nature, motivations, etc.

Step 6. Perform scene(s) in pantomime; add dialogue as the situation demands. Repeat until dialogue and action begin to take definite shape.

---

[11] J. R. Dyce, *Speech and Drama in the Secondary School,* Book I (Melbourne: Thomas Nelson and Sons, Ltd., 1963), pp. 105-110.

Step 7. When actors feel they have established the action and dialogue sufficiently well, they may appoint a committee to record the lines and stage movement. One person should be responsible for editing the materials—for clarity and consistency.

Step 8. Prepare copies of script for all participants.

Step 9. Rehearse the play as constructed.

Step 10. Evaluate the project with entire class participating. Give attention to the play itself, the production, and the players. Set goals for future "experiments in playmaking." (For evaluative questions see the conclusion of the section on Informal Dramatics.)

Working from a good short story such as O. Henry's *The Last Leaf* or *The Ransom of Red Chief,* teacher and pupils have the benefit of situation, good plot, and the rudiments of dialogue already available. With imagination and some skill in composition, they can select, arrange, enlarge upon, and redesign the original author's material so that it can be presented as a play. An interesting variant is an arrangement for radio or closed-circuit TV with appropriate sound effects and scene bridges. The production can be tape-recorded, auditioned, and evaluated.

A somewhat more demanding playwriting task is that of starting with an idea or situation and developing a full-fledged sketch or play with appropriate action and dialogue. Examples of suitable subjects might include the dramatization of an incident in the life of a famous scientist, explorer, or artist, such as Paul DeKruif, Lewis and Clark, or Michelangelo; an exciting historical event, such as a Salem witchcraft trial or the discovery of gold in California.

In dramatizing nonfiction material such as the foregoing, care must be taken to preserve authenticity, at least insofar as basic facts can be determined. Actual dialogue, when not known, should be made consistent with the characters, the situation, and the times. In the preparation of such plays, therefore, the first step, after a choice of subject has been made, is researching the incident for the facts of the case : the nature of the problem, source of conflict or struggle; basic action, climactic event, principal persons involved, bases for suspense; time, place, special conditions of any kind.

From the assembled information, a synopsis of the proposed play should be sketched from which a scenario may be developed. If the project is being carried out by a student committee, the group procedure suggested for transcribing a short story may be followed. If, however, the work is being done by the teacher himself or by one student, that person then continues with the project by writing the dialogue and working out the stage movement for the play. The dialogue and action should quickly establish the situation or problem, lead the audience along with an interesting revelation of how the characters set about dealing with the problem, move with some suspense toward a climax and resolution of the conflict. The action and lines should be well motivated and consistent with the story and people involved. The dialogue should sound like people conversing. The action should help tell the story; at times, it becomes the primary means of telling the story.

When the author has carefully checked his manuscript for clarity, interest, consistency, and readability, he may wish to have it reviewed and evaluated by members of the class.

Guiding formal dramatics

Thus far we have been concerned primarily with *informal* and *semi-formal* dramatics in the classroom. Both are particularly appropriate learning activities when creative planning, composing, and acting are deemed especially desirable or essential. There are occasions, however, in which *formal* drama is preferable. For example, when a class is studying the structure of dramatic literature, or is concerned with a particular author's approach to a given problem, or when the class wishes simply to enjoy the excitement of working with a well-written professional play, then the choice should be one of the many excellent ready-made plays suitable for classroom study and acting.

The field of *formal drama* is as broad and complex as it is old. In this chapter we can hope only to touch on those fundamentals of the subject deemed most essential to directing *formal dramatics* in the classroom. As we have suggested earlier, it is not our intention that the classroom teacher become a professional play director or his students professional players. However, if time is to be taken for dramatics we ought to be certain that it is used wisely, profitably.

Choosing a play. Most of the one-act plays in standard courses of study of typical high school English curricula provide excellent material for class play production. Such plays as O'Neil's *Ile,* Jacob's

The Monkey's Paw, The Valiant by Middlemas and Hall, *A Marriage Proposal* by Chekhov, and Rachel Field's *Three Pills in a Bottle* are good examples. Scenes or single acts from longer plays by Ibsen, Goldsmith, O'Neil, Sherwood, and MacLeish are also excellent possibilities. Many history teachers find scenes from such plays as *Abe Lincoln in Illinois, Joan of Arc, The Devil and Daniel Webster,* and other plays that deal with historical episodes or moments in the lives of great scientists, writers, and statesmen add much to classroom interest. In all events, the selection of a play or segment of a play should be guided by the needs and nature of the present classroom learning situation or subject matter, a knowledge of the talent and basic interests of class members, the literary value and challenge of the play, and the length of the play and the number of characters. For classroom use, the play generally should be chosen for the benefit of the participants. A play that stimulates thoughtful discussion of a basic human problem or illustrates playwriting at its best is especially appropriate for classroom production. Other things being equal, one should select plays with relatively short speeches, a single scene, and with no more than six or seven characters.

Assigning parts. In classroom play production the physical and vocal attributes of players are not as crucial as they are in casting for public performance. Nevertheless some attention should be given to the relative physical appropriateness of the individual to various roles. And while potential ability to do justice to a part should be given consideration in assigning students to various roles in classroom plays, opportunity should be afforded students for optimal self-development.

Scheduling rehearsals. Taking class time for play rehearsal must be considered carefully in terms of its relative value to pupil growth and its contribution to the objectives of the larger unit of learning in a particular course. Preparing a one-act play, if only for classroom presentation, generally requires several hours of rehearsing. It is doubtful that a teacher, other than an English, drama, or speech instructor, can justify taking much class time for rehearsing a play. Therefore, in most cases, extra time in the school day must be found for at least some of the rehearsals. We suggest, when possible, using free periods, excusing members of the cast from regular class period work to rehearse in another room with a student-director, or meeting after school hours. Adjoining work rooms, when available, offer excellent facilities for play rehearsals. The rehearsal schedule should not be extended beyond two or three weeks. Concentration of effort so as to maintain interest must be balanced with other essentials in the course of study. Needless to say, effort must be made to prevent waste of time and energy. To compensate for time devoted to rehearsals, pupils may need to give more attention to, and receive supplementary help in, regular classwork.

To expedite the work of rehearsal and final presentation, the teacher may wish to appoint a stage manager and prompter. The former assumes responsibility for setting the stage and seeing to it that all necessary properties are accounted for and on hand. The latter holds the book at all rehearsals and during the performance. If costumes and makeup are to be used, someone should be assigned to cover these items. Once the preliminary arrangements for producing the play have been completed, the teacher- or student-director is ready to begin actual work on play preparation.

Rehearsing the play. For convenience, we have arranged the production schedule in seven steps covering the equivalent of twelve sessions. The general content of each step is outlined below.

Step 1. *Analyzing the play* (two sessions).
The play may be read aloud by the teacher or the assigned characters. Following the reading, the teacher should conduct a discussion along the following lines : What is the purpose of the play? What is the plot? Initial situation? Rising action? Climax? Falling action? Conclusion? What is the general mood or feeling of the play? What are the essential qualities of each of the characters? What special production problems, if any, does the play present? i.e. staging, character portrayal, unusual language, pace, transitions (if more than one scene)?

Step 2. *Blocking the basic action of the play* (one session).[12]
Before serious work on character development and memorization of lines is begun, the action of the play should be blocked. The play is a series of incidents, pictures, if you will; blocking is the process of laying out the entrances, exits, crossings, and various positions of the actors in coordination with

---

[12] In some cases, this may have been done as a class-wide activity prior to deciding to act out the play. In this event, rehearsals will begin with a rereading of the play, discussion of characters, followed by blocking of the action. If time permits, the teacher-director may invite the players to assist in the blocking process. Their participation often helps them to gain fuller appreciation of the problems of acting and directing, as well as offering them opportunity for creative activity.

the dialogue. Movement and position are based upon the plot itself, motivation of characters, and the pictorial effects which give balance and emphasis to the visual aspects of the play. In blocking the play, it is helpful to sketch an *acting area* diagram on the chalkboard, or preferably, on the actual playing area. The figure below illustrates a simple version of such a diagram (C=Center; L Left; R=Right; D=Down; U=Up).

AUDIENCE

DL	DC	DR
L	C	R
UL	UC	UR

With reference to these general areas and his own script on which he has previously entered any modifications of the author's stage directions, the teacher- or student-director has his actors read and walk through the play, noting the reason for the crosses, other stage movement, and relative positions of characters. Each player will make notations in his book from these directions. He will find that with these gross movements worked out in advance, line memorization will be easier and more meaningful. The actor's business, individual pantomime and handling of stage properties will develop with the speaking of the lines and in response to other characters in the drama.

Step 3. *Building character and action* (three-four sessions).
By the fifth rehearsal all players should have memorized their lines so that they may work for concentration, character portrayal, and coordination of movement, business, and lines. Hand props should be used effectively.

Step 4. *Establishing tempo* (two sessions).
Work for appropriate pace; stress picking up cues. Improve character portrayals.

Step 5. *"Dress rehearsal"* (one session).
Costume and makeup, if they are to be used.

Step 6. *Class presentation* (one session).

Step 7. *Evaluation* (one session).
This is generally done informally. Check-sheets such as those included later in this chapter, may be used as a basis for the discussion of the performance.

Helping students with acting. Acting, like oral interpretative reading, is both a creative and re-creative process. The actor must thoroughly understand the play, its purpose, its moods, and the role his particular character plays in the story. If he is to be at all convincing, the actor must understand his character's motivations, his attitude toward other characters in the play. He must develop a manner of speaking, moving, standing, sitting, listening that is consistent with the player's conception of the part.

The same principles which apply to vocal response in oral interpretative reading are applicable to acting, except that in the latter the speaker strives to represent the character and therefore adapts his voice more completely to the nature of the character being portrayed than he does for oral reading. Additional projection may also be necessary in acting since the players generally speak to one another, or seem to; rarely do they speak directly to the audience. In acting, the speaker works with other speakers: he must learn to establish his own characteristic way of speaking, but at the same time his speeches must be properly related to and timed with the lines of other characters, so the total effect is one of believable conversation. Picking up lines on cue is especially important. In interpretative reading, the reader *suggests;* in acting, the speaker represents the character. The actor "asks" his audience to accept him as Launcelot Gobbo, Brutus, Macbeth. Proper emphasis of central ideas, good phrasing, and use of the pause; clarity of articulation and accurate pronunciation are all musts in acting. A tape recorder in rehearsals can be an invaluable means of perfecting one's enunciation. Above all, it must be remembered that the vocal response in acting, as in other speech forms, should spring from thought and feeling: it must not become a mechanical recitation.

As one would suppose, *action* is especially important in the art of acting. The actor's stance, walk, gestures—all tell the audience something about the character being portrayed. Young actors must learn to observe the actions of types of persons they are representing; they must, in all events, imagine how the character would behave; then try to project this concept to the audience. Players must learn to coordinate action and speaking effectively. Speeches and business must complement each other in conveying exact meanings to an audience.

Formal acting, like other art forms, is governed by an extensive system of rules and conventions on which we need not expatiate here. Suffice it to say that acting is a team effort. In amateur dramatics, particularly classroom activities, there is no room for "stars." Play production calls for cooperation. Everyone is important, but no one is indispensable. During classroom rehearsal, the teacher draws the remaining class members into constructive listening and evaluating. Every effort is made to invest pupils with a sense of responsibility and of sharing in the project, even though in the final analysis, pupils know that the basic responsibility for their instruction rests with the teacher.

GUIDING THE AUDIENCE IN DRAMATIC ACTIVITIES

At various points throughout the chapter, reference has been made to the role of the audience—members of the class not directly participating in a play. We have noted that in some instances, particularly in *informal drama,* all members of the class may be drawn into planning, observing, and evaluating. When a play is presented for its informative or educational values, class members comprising the audience should be helped to understand their role in the learning situation. Good acting, good theater, is a perfect blend of sight and sound representing the director's and actor's interpretations of the playwright's meaning. It is therefore the audience's responsibility to "tune in" on both visual and audial "channels": to listen with both eyes and ears. Obviously it is paramount that in speaking his lines the actor sees to it that his voice and body convey the meaning intended, and that nothing is done either vocally or visually to detract from the intended message.

In no speech activity is the factor of empathy more important than in dramatics. A good actor empathizes effectively with the character he portrays. To the extent that all actors in a play achieve this goal will audience empathy likely be favorable. It is evident that here as in all oral communication, both sender and receiver have responsibilities, and as elsewhere, the major responsibility for this communication rests with the sender, since he must somehow make receiving—listening—both worthwhile and pleasurable.

EVALUATING FORMAL DRAMATIC ACTIVITIES

As in all speech activities, the classroom teacher will wish to evaluate formal dramatization. First it is necessary to determine whether the class has learned anything from it; and, second, to discover what growth, if any, has been achieved by the individual participants. The following forms suggest bases for evaluating *formal dramatics*. They may be used by the teacher or members of the class in whatever manner seems most appropriate for a given situation.

EVALUATION FORM: FORMAL DRAMATICS

Project as a Whole

Title of play: ——————— Student director: ————————————————

Participants:

1. Realization of purpose, mood, and spirit of the play:

2. Unity of effort; team spirit:

3. Audience response (degree to which presentation seemed to be appreciated and enjoyed):

4. General assessment of the worth of the play (Was it a wise investment of time and effort?):

5. Notations for future projects:

Acting

Student:_____   Character:_____

1. Conception of character (clarity, accuracy, consistency, creativeness):

2. Vocal response (diction, projection):

3. Bodily response (poise, appropriateness, coordination with speaking):

4. Timing (cues, pacing):

5. Team spirit (contribution to the project during rehearsals and in final performance):

6. Summary
   Notable achievements:

Needed improvements:

(The teacher should also take note of evidence of individual pupil growth : e.g., character traits, motivation, new insights, etc.

As we have seen, selecting and guiding dramatic activities is not a simple task. To repeat: few experiences demand more of participants for their fulfillment; few, however, offer more to the enjoyment and effectiveness of learning than dramatizations. Some typical applications of dramatic activities in the teaching of representative school subjects may serve to illustrate their general usefulness as a teaching-learning procedure.

GENERAL CLASSROOM APPLICATIONS
OF DRAMATICS

Like oral interpretative reading, dramatization is especially applicable to the teaching of English and foreign language. Incorporating an analysis of the play, dramatization is considered one of the most effective ways of teaching understanding and appreciation of dramatic literature. Indeed, drama, like poetry, is meant to be heard; but drama is also meant to be seen, to be acted out. Having students play scenes from *Julius Caesar, Macbeth,* and *Hamlet* is standard procedure for many English teachers who wish to enliven the students' introduction to Shakespeare. English teachers have also found many of the available professional recordings and films of well-known plays excellent means for stimulating pupil interest in drama and for providing subject matter for provocative class discussion. To supplement classroom dramatics, English teachers will wish to encourage their pupils to attend local theatrical productions by resident or touring companies. Many teachers find that a student theater party is a most enjoyable way of sparking pupils' enthusiasm for good theater and drama and providing them with artistic standards for judging this art form.

In addition, the study of good plays is an excellent means of teaching creative writing. The opportunities for composing classroom dramatic sketches, assembly programs, and special occasion features are abundant in today's secondary schools with their emphasis upon creative learning. There is no surer method of stimulating a pupil to extraordinary effort than to make it possible for his writing to come to life in a classroom play or on the auditorium stage, whether the medium be live or staged by puppets.

Dramatics has also demonstrated its worth in teaching social studies. Role-playing in a problem-solving discussion has previously been mentioned as one example of its use in teaching history. Dramatized interviews with famous people, mock trials, and recreated legislative or United Nations Assemblies are prime examples of successful experience with dramatization in history and government classes. Dramatization has long been an accepted procedure in teaching social studies in the elementary school. We are convinced that it has as much educational validity at the secondary school level. Quoting Franklin Bobbitt, Eleanore Hubbard asserts:

> The concrete historical experiences are not to be consciously memorized. They are to be *lived*. A mental residuum then grows up which is normal and healthy. If experiences are abundant and vivid, memories will be normally abundant.[13]

Dramatization, though not the real thing, creates a substantial impression of the real thing: the impressions are vivid, forceful, meaningful—the learning is likely to be more durable. It is obvious, of course, that a more advanced type of dramatization must be employed at the secondary level than that appropriate for elementary grades. This requirement presents no serious obstacle since there is abundant dramatic material available for high school use. We have reference not only to the raw materials from which original dramatizations can be developed, but to ready-made plays, professional films and recordings as well. An excellent example of the latter is Columbia's *"You Are There"* Series.

Dramatization makes equally valuable contributions in other school subjects. A "fashion show," a dramatization of a family discussing a domestic problem, a skit extolling the merits of wise consumer buying

---

[13] Eleanore Hubbard, *op. cit.,* p. 24.

can add interest and vitality to learning in home economics classes. Dramatization of interesting events in the lives of famous scientists and mathematicians, a skit illustrating the operation of a scientific or mathematical formula, or a pageant illustrating the advance of modern science can extend the learnings of the classroom to an assembly program in most effective ways. Dramatizations of the lives of noted composers and painters can add color to music appreciation classes and art history units.

The opportunities for dramatization in the classroom are virtually limitless. There is an abundance of usable ready-made material for classroom play production. But more importantly, the resourceful and creative teacher will find opportunities for discovering the potentials for exciting original dramatic activities in the raw material of the subject matter of his teaching field.

SUMMARY

In this chapter we have considered three types of dramatic activities: *informal, semiformal,* and *formal dramatics,* each offering its own unique opportunities for creativity. *Informal dramatics* was described as an activity in which participants spontaneously act out an experience or incident. Its potential for stimulating creative expression, communicativeness, and wholesome group attitudes was stressed. *Semiformal dramatics* was likened to informal dramatics in basic objectives and initial procedures, but with more formal structuring including the writing of original dialogue which is then acted out as in the formal play. *Formal dramatics,* like oral interpretation, was described as a re-creative process, including the preparation and presentation of published plays.

All forms of dramatics were considered valuable avenues of communication in the classroom, by virtue of their potential for motivating and securing pupil involvement, for stimulating thought, and for modifying attitudes and habits of behavior. Basic principles were outlined for selecting, guiding, and evaluating each of the three dramatic forms with particular regard for their usefulness in helping to achieve objectives of the unit of learning in which they are employed. The closing section sketched some possible applications of *dramatization* in classroom instruction. Specific illustrations of dramatization applied to the teaching of key subject areas are offered in Section Four of this textbook. More comprehensive and detailed discussion of the teaching of drama in secondary schools will be found among the references listed at the close of this chapter.

SELECTED READINGS

General references

Dale, Edgar. *Audio-Visual Methods in Teaching*, rev. ed. New York : Holt, Rinehart & Winston, Inc., 1954. Chapter 3 "Dramatic Participation."

"Dramatics in the Secondary School." *Bulletin of the National Association of Secondary School Principals*, December, 1949. (Entire issue devoted to dramatics in the high school; prepared under editorship of American Theatre Association and Speech Association of America.)

Dyce, J. R. *Speech and Drama in the Secondary School*. Melbourne : Thomas Nelson and Sons, Ltd., 1963.

Hedde, Wilhelmina, William N. Brigance, and Victor M. Powell. *The New American Speech*. Philadelphia : J. B. Lippincott Co., 1963. (Excellent section on Drama in the Secondary School.)

Hubbard, Eleanore. *The Teaching of History Through Dramatic Presentation*. New York : Benjamin H. Sanborn and Co., 1935.

Robinson, Karl R., and Charlotte Lee. *Speech in Action,* 2nd ed. New York : Scott, Foresman & Company, 1965. (Seven very informative chapters devoted to play production in high schools.)

Weiss, M. Jerry. *Guidance Through Drama*. New York : William Morrow & Co., Inc., 1954.

Informal dramatics

Burger, Isabel B. *Creative Play Acting,* 2nd ed. New York : The Ronald Press Company, 1966.

Howard, Vernon. *Pantomimes, Charades and Skits*. New York : Sterling Publishing Co., Inc., 1967.

Lease, Ruth, and Geraldine Brain Siks. *Creative Dramatics in Home, School, and Community.* New York : Harper & Row, Publishers, 1952.

Spolin, Viola. *Improvisation for the Theatre.* Evanston, Illinois : Northwestern University Press, 1963.

Ward, Winifred. *Playmaking with Children,* 2nd ed. New York : Appleton-Century-Crofts, 1957.

Semiformal dramatics

MacGowan, Kenneth. *A Primer of Playwriting.* New York: Random House, Inc., 1951.

Formal dramatics

Lees, C. Lowell. *Teaching Students How to Direct Plays.* College Hill Station, Cincinnati : National Thespian Society, 1946. (A series of seven articles on basic principles of play production, reprinted from *Dramatics.*)

————. *A Primer of Acting.* Englewood Cliffs, N.J. : Prentice-Hall, Inc., 1940.

Ommanney, Katherine A. *The Stage and the School.* New York : McGraw-Hill Book Company, 1960.

10 *the short talk*

None of the speech forms included in this work has a longer, more prestigious record of usefulness in the affairs of man than has public speaking. With its roots in classical rhetoric, public speaking continues to occupy a central place in college and university speech programs; and without question it is one of two speech forms most frequently emphasized in high school speech curricula, whether viewed as rhetoric, oral English, or speech communication. This is understandable; historically, instruction in speechmaking has had a practical, utilitarian orientation. Public speaking has been and continues to be a powerful tool for influencing human conduct. Its uses in politics, religion, and business are well known. Training in public speaking thus somehow has been linked with preparation for life. Granting public speaking a primary place in speech education, moreover, can be explained pedagogically. The canons of rhetoric are well established; the chronology of preparing and delivering speeches is well defined; the steps are both comprehensible and teachable.

Equally important in explaining the central place of public speaking in speech education is the assumption that training in public speaking is an effective means for teaching basic speech skills. Such an assumption is based on the view that the fundamentals of public speaking are at once the fundamentals of speech in general and that what is learned in public-speaking courses can be applied to a large extent in other types of speaking. Although many speech educators question whether public speaking is the most effective means of teaching speech fundamentals, all would agree that it is an important speech form, widely used, and widely taught.

Just as public speaking has occupied a central place in formal speech education in both secondary schools and higher institutions of learning, so has it played and continues to play an important role in the general classroom, whether as lecture, report, explanation, or demonstration. When wisely adapted and skillfully guided, this major speech form, along with discussion, dramatics, and oral reading, can serve as an effective instrument of teaching and learning for most subjects in high school curricula. The principles and procedures suggested in this chapter are aimed at such instrumentation.

DEFINITIONS

In keeping with the purposes and boundaries of this work, we have limited our consideration of public speaking to the *short talk*. This we define as *a presentation by a single speaker, addressing a group of listeners, using relatively continuous discourse for a specifically identified and limited purpose*. We have in mind talks ranging in length from two to ten minutes. We shall also confine our consideration of the short talk to three of its primary purposes, namely: *informing, exploring,* and *advocating*.

Informative speaking, including reports and demonstrations, may take the form of an *explanation,* as in "telling how to solve a problem in geometry," or "explaining how to make a barometer." It may take the form of *description,* as in presenting a verbal portrait of an interesting character in a novel or a place visited vicariously in the pages of such works as *The National Geographic;* or in delineating the salient features of a structure, such as an induction coil, the human ear, or a blade of grass. Informative speaking may also assume the form of *narration,* as in relating an anecdote, tracing an historical episode, or recounting a chemistry experiment.

Exploratory speaking is concerned with the method of inquiry and analysis, though not necessarily leading to the solution of a problem. It takes the audience through an experience of discovery by presenting information designed to clarify the understanding of a problem or to open up new ways of looking at a problem. Such topics as "Poverty," "Alcoholism," and "Freedom of Speech" lend themselves to *exploratory* speaking.

Advocative speaking calls for taking a stand on a specific issue and presenting the case for a particular belief of course of action with respect to the issue. Such subjects as "Lowering the Voting Age to Eighteen," "Eliminating Racism," "The Social Problem Novel" offer opportunities for advocative speaking. Frequently subjects which are initially approached in an exploratory fashion may subsequently be treated advocatively. In other words, a student may wish to present two related talks on the same issue: in the first he analyzes the problem; in the second he offers a solution to the problem. Or students may elect to have one speaker present an analysis speech, followed by other students presenting solution speeches.

QUALITIES OF GOOD TALKS

Quite possibly no speech form has been more frequently abused and misused in the classroom than the short talk or oral report. All too frequently it proves to be an utter waste of time, if not a deterrent to learning. Whether presented by pupils or teachers, short talks should meet tests of good speaking if they are to achieve effective comunication and foster desired learning. Rarely, perhaps, can we expect classroom talks to meet all the following standards. Some such criteria, however, should be kept in mind when using the short talk as a teaching-learning experience.

1. *Good talks are concerned with appropriate and worthwhile subjects.* Subjects should be compatible with the interests and knowledge level of the class and the purpose and content of the general problem being studied. They should contribute something to the students' understanding and appreciation of the topic under study. Of course, the subject should be of special interest to the speaker and not beyond the limits of his ability. It should be a subject for which there is abundant usable, accurate, and interesting data available. And, lastly, it should be a subject which can be dealt with meaningfully and interestingly in the allotted time.
2. *Good talks are carefully and thoroughly prepared.* They are appropriately focused and properly delimited. They contain accurate, interesting information. They are systematically organized and conform to the agreed-upon time limits. They give evidence of appropriate rehearsal for presentation. In short, good talks are based upon thoughtful, thorough, responsible preparation.

3. *Good talks are characterized by effective delivery.* The presentation is direct, purposeful, essentially conversational in manner. The voice is adjusted to the size of the audience and is responsive to thought and feeling. Articulation and pronunciation meet standards of intelligibility and good usage. The physical response is characterized by alertness, purposiveness, and good taste. Ideas are expressed with clarity and vitality and with some measure of originality. They are developed with effective illustrations, examples, analogy, or other appropriate devices. Sentences are well constructed and usage is in keeping with acceptable grammatical standards. In a good talk, the speaker manifests respect for self and his audience. A good talk claims and holds the attention of the listeners—most listeners. It reflects the best qualities of a speaker's unique personality.

SPECIAL VALUES AND LIMITATIONS OF TALKS

As with other speech forms considered in this work, the short talk can be expected to share many of the values already attributed to oral communication as a medium of learning and instruction. However, because of its uniqueness among speech forms the short talk possesses certain important values. Guided experience with the short talk, for example, has marked potential for promoting growth in the habits of independent study, for fostering individual responsibility, and engendering self-confidence. It can assist pupils in developing the ability to think clearly and orderly and can help them form good habits of research, reading, observing, and listening.

As a medium of instruction in the classroom, the talk can add variety to class procedure; it can be a means of enriching basic text information and it can provide opportunities for securing systematic involvement of pupils in class activities. It is a particularly valuable method of conveying factual information not readily available to all members of a class, for giving instructions, for explaining little known processes, and for bringing new interpretation to commonly known facts or concepts.

Obviously these values do not accrue uniformly in all classes or to all pupils. Moreover, as with other speech forms, the short talk has its limitations as a medium of learning. As will be evident, most of the limitations associated with the short talk arise from faulty or indiscreet use of the form not from its inherent nature. For the most part, the weaknesses appear when one or more of the basic qualities associated with *good* talks are found wanting.

Classroom talks are likely to prove disappointing: (1) when they deal with material which might more effectively or easily be obtained by the class through reading or observing; (2) when they are inadequately or carelessly prepared; (3) when they exceed time limits or violate the normal attention span of the audience; (4) when the audience is not appropriately prepared to receive them; and (5) when, in evaluation, more attention is given to form than to the substance of the message. Awareness of these limitations, together with a knowledge of the qualities of the *good* talk, provide us with the means for teaching and using this speech form in the classroom.

GUIDELINES FOR USING SHORT TALKS

Selecting topics

Although sources of topics for short talks, reports, and oral demonstrations are virtually limitless, obviously not all subjects are suitable for classroom use. Topics should be relevant to the unit of work under study. Some examples will illustrate:

"Patch Logging"—in a unit on conservation in a contemporary problems class; "A Day in the Life of the Mayor"— a unit on city government in civics class; "A Mathematical Formula at Work"—student in a geometry class explains how principles of mathematics are applied in building a bridge; "The Anatomy of Humor"—in a unit on the informal essay in an English class; "The Ancient Art of Cloth Dyeing" —in a home economics unit on fabrics; a simulated Lincoln-Douglas debate—paired speakers in a U.S. history class.

As suggested under *Qualities of Good Talks,* the topic should be geared to the interest and comprehension of the students involved— both speaker and listeners. Interest usually springs from factors of timeliness, relevance to immediate personal and group problems, and proper balance between the known and the unknown in the subject being discussed. While certain universality of interest may be found among adolescents, as suggested earlier, specific individual tastes and preferences vary with the school and community, age group, and level of pupil sophistication.

As with subjects for discussion, topics for short talks, as a general rule, should deal with subjects of some importance. But we hasten to add that importance is a relative concept: the significance of a topic depends upon the variables of time, place, and instrumental worth. It seems unnecessary to mention that frequently the teacher may find it necessary to guide pupils toward discovering what is important in a given situation.

Limiting the scope of a talk

Regardless of the length of a speech, some attention must always be given to the scope and focus of its subject matter. With time stringently limited, focusing and narrowing the subject coverage in the short talk become crucial if the speaker is to treat his subject with a respectable degree of thoroughness. The following delineation indicates possible steps for narrowing the scope of topics:

PROGRESSIVE DELIMITATION

Level	Very general	Inclined toward general	Inclined toward specific	Specific
Topics	Student government	Student government in this high school	Our student Council	Should our system of electing student representatives be changed?
	Conservation	Soil conservation	Conserving wheat lands	Crop rotation in wheat farming.
	Choosing a profession	Social professions	Teaching	Why I wish to become a primary teacher.

In stressing the importance of subject delimitation, we do not wish to imply that the speaker should always avoid general themes. At times a survey of a broad subject may be more appropriate than a close examination of one of its parts. Nor should it be assumed that in the delimited talk the speaker never generalizes. Indeed, if at no other point, the speaker is likely to "draw some generalizations" in the conclusion of his talk.

Becoming informed

Many talks in the classroom may be presented without prescriptive preparation. A good example is the short impromptu "one-pointer" given in response to a teacher's question. Hopefully the pupil responding has a background of knowledge of the subject under study, including having read the day's assignment. It would help also if he has had some previous experience with question analysis and thought organization. Talks of a more comprehensive nature, such as special reports aimed at enriching a lesson, or a demonstration designed to clarify a concept, all require special preparation: prescriptive research for locating pertinent and interesting information. As suggested in the chapter on *discussion,* the teacher must be prepared to help pupils locate appropriate data. In some cases this may mean offering a special lesson or two in the use of the library and helping pupils to discover additional sources of information, such as museums, chambers of commerce, government bureaus and offices, public relations offices, and the like. It may also include helping some pupils to take meaningful notes on their observations, interviews, and reading. The methods and patterns normally taught in English classes should be followed when possible.

Pupils need to be reminded that a well-informed speaker invariably assembles a good deal more information than he can or should include in his talk. His image as an authority will depend upon the depth of his preparation, the true nature of which may not be completely revealed until the customary question period following the talk. Choice of material for actual inclusion in the talk will be governed by a number of factors, including: (1) audience receptability, (2) length of allotted time, (3) nature and complexity of the material; (4) relation of material to information already covered or being covered in similar reports, readings, or lectures; (5) purpose of the talk. Selecting data for inclusion will therefore proceed concurrently with organizing the material.

Organizing the talk

Having informed himself, chosen a purpose for the occasion, given thought to the nature of his audience, noted his designated time allotment, the student speaker should select and arrange his information in a design he believes will best accomplish his purpose. Most teachers, of course, are fully aware that many students find outlining and organizing distasteful or difficult, a kind of "busy work." Students, however, need to recognize the connection between careful planning and effective communication, between good thought organization and the economical use of speaking time. They may be reminded that the outline serves the speaker in the same fashion a blueprint serves the carpenter or a map serves the traveler. Good speech organization is known to be an aid to effective communication: it gives focus to the speaker's message; it prevents mental meandering; it supports the speaker's confidence by reducing his fear of forgetting; and it makes possible more effective listening. The following checklist of principles for teaching and appraising speech outlines may be helpful:

PRINCIPLES OF OUTLINING

1. The speech outline should represent the speaker's thought line, together with its major-minor point relationships.
2. The speech outline should constitute a map of the territory to be covered in reaching a particular destination.
3. It should follow major features of a conventional speech outline :
   a. It should have an introduction, body, and conclusion.
   b. The body should rarely contain more than three major points.
   c. Items of equal importance in the outline should be given co-ordinate rank and position in the plan.
   d. Each point should be phrased clearly and succinctly.
   e. Each point should be confined to one specific idea or fact.

The following developed outlines illustrate the application of the foregoing principles:

EXAMPLE A : INFORMATIVE SPEAKING
A One-point Explanation

In a history class the teacher has posed the question: "On the basis of what we have learned about Jefferson earlier this semester and what we have now been reading about the New Deal, how do you think Jefferson would react to much of the New Deal program?" The outline of one pupil's response follows:

Although Jefferson would approve of the goals of New Dealism, I think
he would oppose its basic methods, because:
1. He was a great humanitarian.
2. He believed in the sovereignty of the people.
3. He favored strong local self-government.
Therefore, he would champion social justice, but not at the expense
of making the people subservient to "big government."

EXAMPLE B : INFORMATIVE SPEAKING

A Multi-point Explanation

Subject : Basic Archaeology—a process.
Audience : Classmates—world history (10th grade).
Time limit : 6 minutes.

I. Introduction :
  A. We cannot divorce ourselves from our past.
     1. When man leaves a city, nature covers up his remains.
     2. An archaeologist's purpose is to discover man's remains
        in order to illustrate the course of human civilization.
  B. Today I hope to shed some light on the exacting and time-
     consuming job of an archaeologist.
  C. In doing this I will refer to the processes of the locating,
     excavating, and the preserving of ancient remains of man as
     found in towns and graves.

II. Development :
  A. In locating ancient towns and graves the archaeologist must
     employ the process of "comparative analysis."
     1. Color of earth.
     2. Types of stones.
     3. Formations of earth.
  B. If an archaeologist feels he has found evidence of an ancient
     town or grave, he begins the process of excavating the area.
     1. Organizing the excavation crews.
     2. Digging trial shafts.
     3. Peeling off layers of civilization.
        a. Towns.
        b. Graves.
  C. Once the town or grave has been uncovered the problem
     of preserving the objects becomes extremely important.

    1. Preservation by nature.
       a. Egypt.
       b. Mesopotamia.
    2. Preservation by man.
       a. Plaster of paris.
       b. Muslin and wax.
       c. Tin boxes.

III. Conclusion :
   A. Briefly, I have shown how an archaeologist locates, excavates, and preserves the artifacts of mankind.
   B. Perhaps from this presentation you have gained some interest and insight regarding the fascinating work of the archaeologist.

Bibliography : Lloyd, Seton. *Foundation in the Dust.* London : Oxford University Press, 1947.

Woolley, C. Leonard. *Digging up the Past.* New York : Charles Schribner's Sons, 1931.

The following plans suggest outline patterns for INFORMATIVE, EXPLORATORY, and ADVOCATIVE speaking.

EXAMPLE C: INFORMATIVE SPEAKING

You gain attention and state the purpose.

I. Introduction.
   A. (Prepare an interesting opening statement to catch the attention of your audience.)
      1. (Develop opening statement: e.g., give a reason for choosing the topic;
      2. give a reason for listening;
      3. establish rapport.)
   B. (State the specific purpose in a sentence.)
   C. (Present a presummary of points to be covered.)

You present the information that will accomplish your purpose.

II. Development.
   A. (State in *sentence form* the first point. This will be the first point mentioned in the presummary.)
      1. (List the subpoints needed to develop point A.
      2. Use topics or phrases.)
      3. etc.

B.   (*Using a transition word or phrase,* state in
    sentence form the second major point—
    the second point in presummary.)
    1.   (Follow the same procedure as in
       A–1, 2, 3, above.)
    2.   etc.
    3.   etc.
    (Note: While logically one may have as
           many main points as the topic
           requires or the time permits, for
           best results, covering only two or
           three in the five minute speech is
           recommended. The development
           employed under each of these
           main points will depend upon the
           nature of the subject, purpose, the
           occasion, and time limits. You
           may use *details, examples, illus-*
           trations, comparisons, or visual aids.)

You "round   III.   Conclusion.
off" and   A.   (Restate purpose and review main points.)
close your talk.   B.   (Choose an appropriate clincher sentence
Leave audience   which gives a sense of completeness to
with a clear   the speech.)
impression of
your purpose and   Bibliography: (List sources of information in
major points.   approved bibliographical form. This can
You document   be done on a separate page or in the
your speech.   space following the conclusion.)

EXAMPLE D : EXPLORATORY SPEAKING

I.   Description of the problem.
   A.   Symptoms.
      1.   (What events show the nature of the problem?)
      2.   (What harmful effects do these events have?)
   B.   Size of the problem.
      (How large and how serious is the problem?)
II.   Analysis of the problem.
      A.   (What are the major causes of these symptoms?)
      B.   (What are the maintaining causes?)

III. Present efforts to solve the problem.
    A. (What steps, if any, have been taken with what success?)
    B. (What additional steps have been proposed?)
IV. Conclusions. (What appears to be the status of the problem?)

EXAMPLE E: ADVOCATIVE SPEAKING
Offering a Solution to a Problem

Getting
attention
and de-
termining
the issues.

I. Introduction.
    A. (Gain attention by brief reference to problem; stress points that impinge upon listeners' self-interests.)
    B.* (Review symptoms of the problem, including severity and scope.)
    C.* (Review basic causes which are producing symptoms.)

Defining or
describing
proposed
solution

    D. (Outline the criteria which a satisfactory solution must meet.)
    E. (Identify the proposed solution.)

Meeting the
first
criterion.

II. Development.
    A. (State first major contention in support of plan.)
        (Give details of evidence supporting contention: facts, testimony introduced through examples, statistics, illustrations, quotations, etc.)

Meeting the
second
criterion.
Meeting the
third
criterion.

    B. (State second major contention in support of plan.)
        (Develop as above.)
    C. (State third major contention in support of plan.)
        (Develop as above.)

Activating
the audience

III. Conclusion.
    A. (Summarize.)
    B. (Restress main items in support of plan.)
    C. (If appropriate, suggest immediate steps which may be taken to get proposal into action.)

BIBLIOGRAPHY.

---

* May be reduced to a minimum when this talk follows an analysis speech on the same subject.

Developing and supporting ideas

We have already alluded to the importance of *substance* in speech: the facts, opinions, ideas, the attitudes with which oral communication is concerned. But substance ineptly expressed, for all practical purposes, remains uncommunicated. The speaker who would stir up in his listeners meanings which approximate his own, must command as many of the devices as possible for reaching the minds of his listeners. We have reference to methods of developing, amplifying, clarifying ideas, necessary because they add warmth and human interest to the talk and therefore serve to claim and hold the attention of listeners. Let us review briefly a few of the most useful methods, namely: *illustration, example, analogy; the story, axiom, or proverb; statistics,* and *the quotation.* Another important device, *the visual aid,* is considered in some detail in the appendix.

Illustration. The illustration is essentially an account of an incident or event. It may be either *literal* or *hypothetical*: real or imagined. Its chief value lies in its potential for adding vividness and clarity to thought through the power of suggestion. In a general way, the illustration is a form of implied comparison, a relating of the unknown to the known. The *factual illustration* describes the events and consequences of a particular incident or episode. Its chief requirement is that it be accurate and logically applicable to the point being considered. Although literal illustrations are common and generally well understood, pupils may need help comprehending and applying the "Let us suppose that . . ." or *hypothetical illustration.*

Specific examples. While the *illustration* deals with one major example, literal or hypothetical, *specific examples* provide a number of minute "illustrations" or instances which can be used to clarify a concept or prove a point.

Analogy. The analogy, actually a form of illustration, seeks to show similarities between what is known and what is unknown. As with the general illustration, analogy also may be either *literal* or *figurative*. Using a *literal* analogy, a speaker might endeavor to show that since most of the geological conditions present in Region "A" are similar to those in Region "B" (rich in copper deposits), we might reasonably expect Region "A" to have similar deposits. The *figurative* analogy attempts to draw an inference by comparing two entities of entirely different classes, but whose governing principles may be similar. The reader is doubtless familiar with the following analogy which Lincoln

used in addressing those who criticized his conduct of the Civil War.
In it he compares the position of the government with that of a well
known tight-rope walker:

> Gentlemen, I want you to suppose a case for a moment.
> Suppose that all the property you were worth was in gold,
> and you had put it in the hands of Blondin, the famous
> rope-walker, to carry across the Niagara Falls on a tight
> rope. Would you shake the rope while he was passing over
> it, or keep shouting to him, "Blondin, stoop a little more!
> Go a little faster!" No, I am sure you would not. You would
> hold your breath as well as your tongue, and keep your
> hands off until he was safely over. Now the government is
> in the same situation. It is carrying an immense weight
> across a stormy ocean. Untold treasures are in its hands. It
> is doing the best it can. Don't badger it! Just keep still and
> it will get you safely over.

It will be seen that while the *figurative* analogy may be highly useful
in describing and explaining, the *literal* analogy is likely to be more
dependable as a method of proof.

The story, axiom, and proverb. Every student knows the power of a
story, well told, to enliven attention and to make a point by implication.
Personal experiences are especially effective when used in proper
perspective and with good taste. The short anecdote is also a valuable
device for securing or regaining audience attention and humanizing
an otherwise sterile point. At one juncture in an address entitled
"Toward Understanding through Speech," the speaker, Andrew T.
Weaver, asserted that if the listener did not have in his experience the
stuff out of which the desired meaning could be made, there was no
way in which the speaker could "give" it to him. He said, "I am sure
that should the ghost of Albert Einstein come to me in the hope of stir-
ring up in me the concept of relativity, his mission would be hopeless;
I simply do not have in my experience the ingredients out of which I
could construct Einstein's theory." Weaver then, in a lighter vein,
illustrated his point with the following anecdote:

> A motorist stopped at a farmhouse and inquired the way
> to the Miller place. The farmer said, "Go down the road
> till you come to the Johnson farm—." "but," broke in the
> traveler, "I don't know which the Johnson farm is." "Well,"

said the farmer, "Go down the road till you come to a fence
with some hop vines trailing along the top—." "I never have
seen a hop vine in my life," said the traveler. The exas-
perated farmer looked at him for a moment and then
remarked; "Well, stranger, I guess you just don't know
enough for me to tell you how to get to the Miller place!"[2]

Maxims, parables, and proverbs, when injected at the appropriate
moment can add color and force to one's talk. Lincoln built an entire
speech on the Biblical axiom: "Every city or house divided against
itself shall not stand." Benjamin Franklin's *Poor Richard* has provided
many a speaker with a timely theme. Note also the potential of such
aphorisms as "Freedom is not worth having if it does not connote
freedom to err."—Mahatma Gandhi; "The best of all governments is
that which teaches us to govern ourselves."—Goethe.

Statistics. Statistics have been described as "a shorthand method
of summarizing a large number of examples."[3] While statistics can be
impressive and can be a highly effective means of clarifying a point
or proving a contention, they must be used carefully and responsibly.
McBurney and Wrage admonish the speaker:

> 1. To be accurate in handling statistics: know the
> meaning of the unit being used; base statistics on a fair
> sample; be sure that statistics measure what they say they
> measure.
> 2. To use statistics sparingly and skillfully: avoid
> deluging listeners with too many; to assist recall use round
> figures; translate numbers to percentages or employ
> dramatic illustration.[4]

Statistics can frequently be made more meaningful through use of such
visual aids as graphs and maps.[5]

Quotations. When drawn from a qualified authority in a particular
field, the quotation can be used with notable effect in bringing
credibility to a contention or in adding clarity and authenticity to a
statement or assertion. Pupils should be reminded to be careful in

---

[2] *Vital Speeches of the Day,* XXVIII (February 1, 1961), 244–47.

[3] James McBurney and Ernest J. Wrage, *Guide to Good Speech* (Englewood Cliffs,
N.J.: Prentice-Hall, Inc., 1965), p. 122.

[4] *Ibid.,* pp. 122–24.

[5] See Appendix A–3.

using quotations out of context lest the intention of the author be misrepresented.

All of the foregoing methods of idea development when used judiciously can aid both speaker and listener in achieving effective communication and thus render the short talk a valuable medium of learning. Time taken to help pupils gain facility in such methods is likely to be time well spent. But let us bear in mind that these and other methods of idea development are useful to the degree that they induce active listening. This they do insofar as they offer variety, help to create suspense, relate the unknown to the known, appeal to normal human drives and incentives, stress the specific and concrete, and do not ignore the leaven of humor. *And they are useful insofar as they foster clear, logical thinking and are impelled by socially desirable motives.*

Presenting the talk

Basic principles. One fundamental principle should pervade all speech delivery. We refer, of course, to the principle of communicativeness. Communicative delivery is characterized by an alertness of bearing, directness, purposiveness, adaptability; it is talking *with,* not *at* or *to* one's listeners. In public speaking it may be said to have the essential qualities of good conversational speech: that is, it possesses the same qualities that are present in animated, responsive, direct conversation, but without some of the colloquialisms, lapses in usage, and faulty sentence structure which commonly accompany informal speaking.

Communicativeness is achieved in different ways by different speakers. In all cases, the uniqueness of the person should be preserved to the extent such uniqueness aids communication. We wish to help our pupils to develop as individuals, to be themselves when they are speaking: but *we wish them to be themselves at their communicative best.* Effective communicative delivery is learned. Classroom teachers can help their pupils to achieve good speech delivery by reminding them: (1) to develop and show a sincere interest in what they are saying; (2) to concentrate on ideas, not on words. Following the advice of James Winans, speech teachers urge their pupils "to develop full realization of the content of their words as they utter them and . . . to have a lively sense of communication." A good speaker will let his voice and body work harmoniously and effectively in conveying intended meanings. He will seek to avoid any mannerisms which might distract attention or belie his intentions. He will respect the feelings and sensibilities of his audience and observe the courtesies merited by the occasion.

Delivery may occur in any of four basic modes: *reading from a manuscript, speaking from a memorized manuscript, speaking extemporaneously from a prepared outline, and speaking impromptu*—i.e., improvising. Each may be used in the classroom on certain occasions, although there is likely to be little call for the memorized manuscript. Of the four methods, impromptu and extempore delivery are by far the most flexible and therefore most adaptable to classroom use. Because of their flexibility, they are ~~almost~~ most likely to yield direct, communicative speaking. And while memorized and manuscript speeches enable the speaker to give more attention to composition and the wording of his talk, these methods of delivery are less flexible; and because of this it may be more difficult for a student speaker to maintain active contact with his audience in these modes of presentation. We leave to the teacher's good judgment whether to allow a pupil to write out completely and read aloud his talk or to require him to present his material extemporaneously. Certainly it would be appropriate to permit a student to read his report of a scientific experiment. Likewise, it would seem to be sensible to allow a student to read his speech, if through fear or inexperience be balks at presenting it extemporaneously. If the student is to read his report, however, he should be encouraged to "keep in touch" with his audience as much as possible.

In the classroom, impromptu speaking occurs most frequently in the form of an oral paragraph or a short response to a question posed by the teacher in the oral recitation. Extempore speaking is most appropriate for subjects which require more careful, specific advance preparation. Paradoxically, its chief limitation, arises from its major advantage : flexibility. For some students, talking creatively from an outline may induce careless speech habits, particularly with respect to sentence structure and word choice. Such weaknesses, however, are generally overcome with thorough preparation, including oral rehearsal.

Because of its somewhat specialized nature and because it presents some additional problems in delivery, let us consider for a moment a variant of extempore speaking: *the demonstration*.

The demonstration talk. To demonstrate is to show by emphasizing the major and unique characteristics of an object, process, skill, etc. It is literally showing the nature of something or telling how something is done or how something functions. It differs from most expository talks, which may employ visual or auditory aids, with respect to the degree and manner the spoken word is employed. In the *demonstration,* talk usually serves as commentary, an adjunct, to the action of the demonstration. Action is primary; talk is secondary. In the more conventional oral exposition, speech is primary; the visual or auditory factor, if any, is a supplement to the spoken word. From the standpoint of the audience, demonstrations, for the most part, involve observing, some listening, and quite often, doing. The more typical expository talk involves listening, some observing, and occasionally some doing. The following guidelines for helping pupils to present effective demonstrations have been adapted from Dale :

1. Be sure all apparatus, equipment, materials are accounted for; they should be operable, large enough for all to see during the demonstration; and they should meet all safety requirements.
2. Plan all steps of the procedure carefully in advance.
3. Rehearse the demonstration, preferably with someone. Check for clarity and proper timing.
4. Focus on main ideas : keep the demonstration as simple as possible.
5. Use the chalkboard or flannel board when necessary to highpoint basic steps.
6. Check from time to time to make sure audience is understanding the demonstration. Review; perhaps involve members of the class in an occasional summary.
7. Watch pace of the demonstration. Keep it moving, but don't hurry it at the expense of comprehension.
8. Close demonstration with a brief review of main steps and appropriate word commentary.[6]

Listening to and evaluating the short talk

Assuming that the speaker has done his part in meeting the demands of the occasion, it remains for the listeners to assume their responsibilities if optimal communication is to occur. The degree of genuine listening which takes place in *talk* situations, as in most speaking occasions,

[6] Edgar Dale, *Audio-Visual Methods in Teaching,* rev. ed. (New York: Holt, Rinehart & Winston, Inc., 1954), pp. 144–54.

depends upon the listener's present knowledge of the subject, his basic interest in the topic, his attitude toward the speaker, and his ability to attend, to recall, and to synthesize the parts of the message.

Prior to any report or talk, the class should be asked to consider its part in the event. They may be told that a question period will follow; they may be asked to answer questions on the talk or briefly to summarize the message. Or they may be given opportunity to question the speaker or to comment upon the content of the talk. The teacher may wish to involve members of the audience in a brief constructive evaluation period following the speeches. When this is done, major importance should be accorded the substance of the talk. Skills of presentation, however, should not be overlooked, since they often determine what actually is communicated. The following check-sheet suggests bases for judging the quality of talks and laying the foundation for their further improvement and usefulness as a classroom activity.

EVALUATING THE SHORT TALK

Speaker:_____ Date: _____

Topic and/or purpose of talk: _____

<table>
<tr><td>Content</td><td>Comments</td></tr>
</table>

1. Appropriate (for occasion, audience, speaker).

   High   Low
     5   4   3   2   1

2. Value of information.

     5   4   3   2   1

3. Accuracy of information (support of assertions, credibility of sources).

     5   4   3   2   1

4. Organization (degree to which it aided communication and met requirements of a good outline).

     5   4   3   2   1

Presentation

1. Directness and communicativeness.

    5   4   3   2   1

2. Use of voice in revealing meaning.

    5   4   3   2   1

3. Use of body in conveying meaning.

    5   4   3   2   1

4. Clarity and accuracy of articulation
   and pronunciation.

    5   4   3   2   1

General Assessment and Recommendations:

Qualities of content and/or delivery which made the talk effective:

Items of content and/or delivery which should be improved:

GENERAL CLASSROOM APPLICATION
OF THE SHORT TALK

As has been suggested, the short talk has a broad spectrum of usefulness as a teaching-learning medium in secondary school classrooms. It is particularly valuable in mathematics classes where it may be used (1) to explain how to solve a problem; (2) to indicate how mathematics is applied in various trades, professions, research, etc.; (3) to present a biographical account of a famous mathematician; and (4) to demonstrate applied mathematics.

Similarly, it may be used effectively in science classes (1) to demonstrate a scientific process; (2) to report on a leading scientist;

(3) to describe a recent scientific discovery; or (4) to analyze one of the effects of the advance of science.

The short talk has also proved useful in the social studies for (1) presenting reports on key historical figures and events; (2) presenting simulated debates based on historical incidents; (3) offering short answer responses to teacher or fellow-student questions; or (4) arguing the case for a proposal (e.g., "Create a wilderness area in the North Cascade Mountains.")

In English classes it may appear as either the object of instruction or the means of learning. It offers especially appropriate means for presenting book reviews, analyses of poems, biographical accounts of authors. It is useful for delineating the origin of the English language, American dialects, or for offering an analysis of some problem in human communication. As an object of instruction, the short talk is a convenient and manageable speech form through which to instruct pupils in the fundamentals of speaking.

We have touched on but a few of the possible applications of the short talk in English and other school subjects. The foregoing applications, together with additional examples, receive more detailed treatment in Part IV of this work, where emphasis is given to teaching various school subjects. The short talk is useful whenever the learning situation calls for conveying significant information, for enriching the content of conventional lessons, providing variety to classroom procedures, and giving pupils guided experience in this important speech form.

SUMMARY

In this chapter we have considered three primary uses or purposes of the short talk: *informing, exploring,* and *advocating.* We have reviewed the qualities of *good* talks and observed some of the special values and limitations of this speech form. Guidelines for using short talks in the classroom included selecting and limiting topics, becoming informed, selecting and organizing material, developing and supporting ideas, and delivering the talk. The chapter closed with some suggestions for listening to short talks and for using this speech form in the classroom as a medium of learning.

SELECTED READINGS

Dale, Edgar. *Audio-Visual Methods in Teaching,* rev. ed. New York : Holt, Rinehart & Winston, Inc., 1954.

McBurney, James H., and Ernest J. Wrage. *Guide to Good Speech.* Englewood Cliffs, N.J.: Prentice-Hall, Inc., 1965.

Monroe, Alan H. *Principles and Types of Speech,* 4th ed. New York : Scott, Foresman & Company, 1955.

Rahskopf, Horace G. *Basic Speech Improvement.* New York : Harper and Row, Publishers, 1965.

Reid, Loren. *Teaching Speech,* 3rd ed. Columbia, Mo.: Artcraft Press, 1960. Chaps. 7 and 8.

Robinson, Karl F., and Charlotte Lee. *Speech in Action.* New York: Scott, Foresman & Company, 1965. Chaps. 5-11 "Making a Speech."

Weaver, Andrew T., and Ordean G. Ness. *Fundamentals and Forms of Speech.* New York : The Odyssey Press, Inc., 1957. Chap. 14 "Public Address."

11 *oral interpretation of literature*

Oral interpretative reading, sometimes referred to simply as oral reading, reading aloud, or audience reading, is among the oldest, most cherished, most useful of the speech arts. Though diminished somewhat by the invention of the printing press and its attendant increase in private silent reading, reading aloud, since ancient times, has served variously as a form of heraldry, of instruction, and of entertainment. Reading aloud in the home continues to be a source of great delight for children, a means of instilling a love of books and reading : a major contribution to readiness for formal reading instruction. What parent can in conscience resist: "Mommy, please read me a story." What is more, most teachers know that children from kindergarten through high school enjoy being read to, particularly when the material is "right" and the reading good. And there is ample evidence that many children also enjoy reading to others. What magic is this that makes words spring to life from the pages of a book!

Oral reading can be a source of delightful entertainment, a means of conveying information, and an aid to personal development and life enrichment. All of these ends may be served when oral reading is approached as an instrument of instruction and learning.

DEFINITIONS

Broadly speaking, perhaps all forms and levels of oral reading are at base *interpretative* in the sense that the reader recognizes printed symbols and gives voice to them. The *oral reading* with which we are concerned, however, involves considerably more than mere oral conversion of the printed symbol. The art of *oral interpretative reading*, as we shall refer to it, calls for discovering the author's probable intended meaning and the effective communication of this meaning to one or more listeners. This is to say that we are concerned with the processes of translating printed symbols into speech symbols in such a fashion as to cause others to perceive meanings which correspond as closely as possible to those which the reader has gained for himself.[1] This function is aptly illustrated by an analogy suggested by Weaver and Ness.

> The reader is somewhat in the situation of an interpreter who listens to what a speaker has to say in Japanese and then for the benefit of someone who understands English only, translates the remarks into English. The success with which he does the job is determined by two factors: first, how well he understands what the speaker has said in Japanese; and second, how completely he commands English.[2]

As a basis for the discussion in this chapter we shall define oral interpretative reading as *a process of sharing with others through speech one's understandings of the intellectual and emotional meaning of a particular literary object.* The term *literary object* is used here to denote the *material* being read.

While possessing a certain uniqueness of form, oral reading has much in common with other speech arts. As with other types of speaking, it is primarily concerned with communication, with securing a response from a listener at a given time and place with respect to a particular subject in terms of a particular purpose. Like acting, oral reading is a combination of creative and re-creative processes.

---

[1] Andrew T. Weaver and Ordean Ness, *The Fundamentals and Forms of Speech* (New York: The Odyssey Press, Inc., 1957), p. 367.

[2] *Ibid.*, p. 368.

However, oral interpretative reading is unique in several important respects. First, unlike public speaking, oral reading brings together three important elements in the communicative event: writer, reader, and audience. Unlike the actor, the oral reader does not ask the audience to consider him a character in a play. With benefit of certain theatrical conventions, the actor offers his audience a representational approach to life; whereas the oral reader, depending almost wholly upon voice and subtle bodily response, suggests his understanding of a piece of literature in such a manner that the listener may share in the re-creative experience: the end being, of course, the communication of the intellectual and emotional content of a selection. Although discussion in the present chapter is directed primarily toward oral reading as a solo speaking activity, the form has several group variants, including choral speaking, readers' theater, and chamber theater, all of which we regard as extensions of basic solo reading, and beyond the scope of this textbook.

VALUES AND LIMITATIONS OF ORAL INTERPRETATIVE READING

As an instrument of learning and teaching, oral interpretative reading can perform a number of uniquely useful functions in the secondary classroom. First and foremost is its use in teaching and experiencing literature. It is a commonplace that verse, speeches, and dramatic literature are written to be heard: that creatively they are incomplete until brought to living experience through speech. Similarly, though in less dramatic fashion, oral reading provides a needed dimension to such literary forms as the prose narrative essay, and certain other expository material.

Grimes and Mattingly remind us that "literature makes a distinctive contribution to knowledge, and interpretation is a way of discovering this contribution."[3] Effective oral reading does much to bring the flavor and impact of the author's actual or imagined experiences, the fullness of his wisdom, and the technique of his craftsmanship to both reader and listener. Especially can oral reading,

---

[3] Wilma H. Grimes and Althea Mattingly, *Interpretation: Writer, Reader, Audience* (San Francisco: Wadsworth Publishing Co., 1961), p. 5.

effective oral reading, bring vividness to (and thus added enjoyment of) the pictorial, rhythmic and acoustic properties of language. At its best, oral reading becomes a means of sensitizing participants to forms of beauty, whether such beauty lies in the subject of the literary object, in the manner in which it is treated, or in the interpretative process—all to the end of inspiration and elevation of the human spirit. It is well to realize that the values of oral reading in the study of literature are not confined to English, but may apply with equal significance to the study of foreign languages.

The use of appropriate literary models has long been a standard practice in teaching written composition. By highlighting many of the essentials of good writing, oral reading can be an effective means of enhancing the value of literary models in teaching creative writing.

Beyond its contributions to the study of literature and the teaching of composition, oral reading possesses other instrumental values of interest to classroom teachers. As one of the essential speech forms, along with public speaking and discussion, oral reading, as suggested earlier, is a basic means of communication, and as such, it has many practical applications, some of which will be mentioned later in this chapter. In addition, as an art form, oral interpretative reading may serve as a truly delightful means of public entertainment. Whether arranged merely for classroom use or extended to the school auditorium or a community program, it can be employed as the basis for pleasant and worthwhile listening entertainment.

Finally, through experiences in oral reading, whether "on stage" or in the classroom, we may expect general improvement in pupils' individual speech skills, including growth in discriminative thinking, vocal responsiveness, and bodily control, as well as improvement in ability to listen appreciatively to material read orally. Indeed many speech educators are of the opinion that, since the content is provided in reading, this speech form offers an especially strategic opportunity for the student to concentrate on improving specific speech skills, particularly those involving voice and articulation.

Valuable as oral reading may be as a medium of learning and teaching, like all speech forms, it too has its limitations. As we have said, bringing life to someone else's writing calls for imagination and specific speaking skills. Since oral reading is not an activity in which all pupils may participate with notable success, teachers often reject it in favor of a speech form which holds greater promise for more general class involvement. But it should be remembered that learning also accrues for those who listen. Naturally no speech form, including oral reading, prospers from inept performance. We believe that every teacher should possess some ability to read aloud, should enjoy reading, and should take occasion to read appropriate materials to his pupils or enlist the assistance of competent readers, live or recorded, when it is feasible and profitable to do so. In all events, every effort should be made to guide all pupils toward a sincere and creditable oral reading experience if optimum results from this type of speaking are to obtain.

Another limitation may arise from inappropriately prescribing oral reading for a particular learning situation. Not all written material profits from being read aloud. Most factual reporting, textbook material, statistical data and the like are normally better left to silent reading and possibly to discussion. An exception might be the oral reading of an occasional difficult passage of textual material as a means of "drawing out" the meaning more effectively. The limitations of this speech form, then are those which arise from unwise prescription and inept uses of the form. Let us therefore review some of the qualities of *good* oral reading which must be sought if the form is to serve its purpose in the classroom.

QUALITIES OF GOOD ORAL INTERPRETATIVE READING

1. *Good oral reading deals with worthwhile and appropriate materials.* Materials should be suited to the needs of the situation and the interests of those participating. They should have "high readability" for those concerned. At the same time, with the exception of announcements and the like, in so far as possible, materials of oral reading should meet recognized standards of good literature. One should ask whether the idea expressed has a certain degree of *universality,* has potential interest for most people because it "touches on a common experience." One should also ask whether the idea is expressed with originality, *individuality.* Is there a freshness and uniqueness of presentation? And one should inquire whether the writing has high *associational* value. Does the writer leave something for the listener to do, but give him adequately clear "directions" for doing it through his use of imagery and allusions?

2. *Good oral reading is well motivated.* It is marked by thoroughness of preparation and sincerity of attack.

3. *Good oral reading is technically and artistically effective.* It effectively presents the reader's understanding of the author's intentions as gained from a thoughtful study of the material and its

author. It reveals the successful unity of mind, voice, and body in the act of speaking.

4. *Good oral reading is purposeful* and can generally be expected to achieve its purpose of securing audience interest, understanding, and approval.

GUIDELINES FOR USING ORAL INTERPRETATIVE READING

Effective prescription and use of oral reading in the classroom require that the teacher have a functional knowledge of (1) appropriate materials, (2) methods of instructing pupils in preparation and presentation of these materials, and (3) methods of evaluating oral reading performance.

Selecting materials for oral reading

The materials of oral reading extend from simple but essential school announcements, news items, feature articles, or parts thereof, quotations incident to public speaking, the texts of or excerpts from selected speeches and orations, to the almost unlimited resources of the world's great literature, as expressed particularly in the forms of essay, narrations, poetry, and drama. In English classes, of course, there is a wealth of material which lends itself especially to oral reading. The only limiting factors may be the availability of time, length of selection, and readability. In social studies, appropriate essays, editorials, excerpts from feature articles, poetry and dramatic literature relating to historical subjects, as well as famous speeches on important issues in critical periods of history can be used with profit. In other classes, teachers and pupils may find excerpts from essays and feature articles appropriate for enriching regular class procedures.

In English classes, of course, oral reading becomes a major approach to the study of poetry, essays, dramatic literature, and much narrative prose material. When selecting material for oral reading as a means of course enrichment, teachers should be guided by (1) pupil interest and comprehension levels, (2) relevance to topic or problem under consideration, (3) literary quality and amount of time available. In all cases, the test of *readability* of the material should be given careful consideration. Literature, as a rule, has high readability if it is rich in imagery, has a comparatively familiar structure, and employs language that is generally comprehensible.

Selecting readers

Ideally, teachers should strive to engage all pupils in some form of oral reading activity sometime during the school year. Teachers must face the probability, however, that most pupils will not be able to read aloud well, unless they have received prior training in speech or English classes or in some other context. The creative classroom teacher "takes pupils where they are" and guides them toward an effective and rewarding use of this speech form, just as he must with other speech activities.

Guiding pupils in preparation for oral reading

In assisting pupils to prepare for oral reading, teachers should make it perfectly clear at the outset that the reader does not assume the role of the author, unless, of course, he is in fact the author of the material. When reading the works of other authors, the oral reader, as suggested earlier in this chapter, is an *interpreter,* a representative; hopefully, faithful and effective. With the author as original creator, the reader enters as a re-creator and in some respects a creator in his own right since he brings his own insights, skills, and art to bear upon the selection and occasion, much as does a pianist in addressing himself to a musical composition.

If the reader is to be a faithful interpreter of a literary object, he should endeavor to meet the following responsibilities :

1. To secure a full and accurate understanding of the meaning and purpose of the selection chosen for the occasion.
2. To command the essential skills for communicating this understanding to a given audience.

This is to say, the reader must first discover the meaning of the selection. Then through the medium of speech, he must cause the listeners to approximate those meanings. The following constitute recommended steps for securing an understanding of the meaning and purpose of a selection. Specific application will depend upon the complexity of the material. Obviously not all steps need apply to every selection; a simple announcement will obviously not require the study given to a poem, story or speech.

General guidelines for subjective preparation. Having chosen an appropriate selection and having made whatever adaptations seem advisable, the reader should:

1. Read and reread the selection silently to fix the purpose and general idea. Note who is talking? to whom? at what time? about what? with what point of view and attitude? Then read it aloud several times to discover more specific meanings, to study the structure, and to become familiar with the mood, phrasing, emphasis, and rhythm of the material.

2. Inform himself regarding the author and the circumstances bearing upon the writing of the selection. For example, in preparing to read "Lincoln, Man of the People," it would be useful to know that the poem was Edwin Markham's fulfillment of a commission on the occasion of the dedication of the Lincoln Memorial in Washington D.C.

3. Find out what leading critics have said about the author and the selection.[4]

4. Check meanings and pronunciations of all unfamiliar words.

5. Look up all literary allusions, such as "When the *Norn Mother* looked down," "To hear old *Proteus* blow his wreathed horn," "He doth bestride the world like a *Colossus.*"

6. Reflect thoughtfully upon the selection—its direct and possible symbolic meanings.

7. Paraphrase or write a precis of the selection in order to personalize the author's language.

8. Note the especially important passages : those which seem critical to the expression of meaning and feeling.

9. Observe special problems for reading aloud, such as inordinately long sentences, unusual structure, difficult pronunciations, shifts in mood, thought transitions, etc.

---

[4] See, for example: *Saturday Review, Harpers, Newsweek, Time.*

General guidelines for objective preparation. To achieve effective communication, the reader should :

1. Determine what is to be his point of contact with his audience. Normally when reading essays, speeches, or informative announcements, the reader should adopt a straightforward, direct relationship with his audience, as in extempore speaking. Whereas in reading poetry and dramatic literature, he may, in some cases, employ a more indirect contact with his listeners. In this instance, he may be said to be reading *for* rather than directly *to* his audience.

2. Prepare an appropriate introduction for the selection, when such is needed to establish a context for and a receptive attitude toward the material and the reader.

3. Rehearse the entire presentation thoughtfully, concentrating upon the *ideas,* the *purpose,* the *mood* and *feeling* of the message. To visualize the presentation, rehearse with the specific audience in mind. (Many readers find that a double-spaced typed copy of the script is easier to read).

Since the major burden of preparation for actual reading rests with the *act of reading* itself, let us examine this step in further detail.

Weaver and Ness remind us that discovering as well as revealing meanings in oral reading is primarily a function of the imagination: that is, it is a largely symbolic experience—"living in terms of symbols."[5] And since both writer and reader know that the basis of experience is sensation, they realize that if they are to discover and reveal meanings symbolically, they must employ language in such ways as to stimulate the senses.

Note for example the author's use of sensory images in the following lines from "Work Without Hope" by Samuel Taylor Coleridge:

> All nature seems at work. Slugs leave their lair—
> The bees are stirring—birds are on the wing—
> And Winter, slumbering in the open air,
> Wears on his smiling face a dream of Spring !
> And I the while, the sole unbusy thing,
> Nor honey make, nor pair, nor build, nor sing.

---

[5] Weaver and Ness, *op cit.,* p. 384.

Here the reader and subsequently the listener are reached through visual, thermal, and auditory sensory appeals. And again in the following passage, perceive how through the use of figures of speech the author strengthens his imagery, thus adding to the clarity of his intended meaning:

> The sky immense, bejeweled with the rain of stars,
> Hangs over us.
> The stars like a sudden explosion powder the zenith
> With green and gold;
> Northeast, southwest, the Milky Way's pale streamers
> Flash past in flame;
> The sky is a swirling cataract
> Of Fire, on high.
>
> John Gould Fletcher, *Night of Stars*[6]

Meaning is rarely expressed merely by words as isolated elements, but by words in contexts. More specifically, meaning is expressed by words arranged and revealed in *phrases—thought units*—groups of words that convey a unit of an idea, which when considered in proper relation with other units, express a larger more complete idea.

Essential to the identification and functioning of the phrase, of course, is the pause. The pause can be likened to the mortar in a house of brick or stone: it separates the units, but serves a more useful function of binding the units together in meaningful, functional wholes. Observe, for example, the following passage marked to indicate one person's judgment of appropriate phrasing and pausing. Note how meanings tend to stand out through such phrasing.

> I do not assert / that the jury trial / is an infallible mode of ascertaining truth.//Like everything human,/it has its imperfections./I only say/that it is the best protection for innocence / and the surest mode for punishing guilt / that has yet been discovered. // It has borne the test of a longer experience, / and borne it better / than any other legal institution that ever existed among men.
>
> Jeremiah S. Black, *Trial By Jury*

But phrases are composed of words, some of which are more important than others; that is, some words carry the burden of mean-

---

[6] Used by permission of Mrs. John Gould Fletcher.

ing while others merely accompany, give support or aid, as it were, to the leading words. For instance, in Shakespeare's lines:

> The fault, dear Brutus, is not in our stars,
> But in ourselves, that we are underlings.

Key words doubtless are intended to be *fault, not, stars, ourselves,* and *underlings.* These words normally are stressed with added force, pitch change, or other appropriate modes of emphasis. Whereas words like *the, dear, is, in,* and *our,* are unstressed, subordinated, because they are less essential to the imagery and because by unstressing them, we actually, by contrast, lend greater strength to the key words.

In a similar way, phrases relate to one another. Some carry more weight of imagery than do others. When reading a complete thought, one does not merely pronounce a series of phrases; one must sense the connection or relation between phrases. For example, note how pointless it would be to read all phrases in the following example from Jack London as if they were complete self-sustaining units themselves.

> It was the green heart of the canyon, / where the walls swerved back from the rigid plan / and relieved their harshness of line / by making a little sheltered nook / and filling it to the brim with sweetness / and roundness / and softness. // Here all things rested. /
> Even the narrow stream / ceased its turbulent downrush / long enough to form a quiet pool. // Knee-deep in the water, / with drooping head and half-shut eyes, / drowsed a red-coated, / many-antlered buck.

All the parts, the phrases, combine to form the total image. The reader reveals the interconnections of phrases through sustaining the thought vocally. Observe, for example, in the following line from Emerson in which he omits certain connective words, how important are correct phrasing, use of pause, and appropriate vocal response to correct revelation of thought:

> Books are the best things / well used; // abused, / among the worst.

Phrase and pause are inseparable teammates: In one respect, the pause serves the role of oral punctuation as do the period and other marks in written communication. And while written punctuation is not the only determinant of pause and phrasing, note how it determines grouping, placement of pause, and helps to reveal meaning in the following:

1. Woman without her man would be a savage.
   a. Woman! without her, man would be a savage.
   b. Woman without her man—would be a savage.
2. The professor says the student is stupid. Or: "The professor," says the student, "is stupid."

It is no exaggeration to assert that proper phrasing, discreet use of the pause, and various modes of emphasis constitute the reader's principal means of revealing his understanding of an author's intended meaning. In guiding pupils to develop skill in and enjoyment of oral interpretative reading, priority should be accorded these elements.

General guidelines for presentation. Allowing for the individual variations of occasion, the nature of material, and the personality of the reader, certain principles can be outlined for the presentation itself, the first of which relates to the *fundamentals of communicating meaning.* Assuming that the reader, through careful study, has discovered the probable meaning of the selection, he must now at the moment of presentation recapture with full realization the meaning previously discovered. This requires concentration. He will attempt to meet the demands of the situation with poise. He will not only attempt to recapture the best of his rehearsal; he will strive to improve upon it in response to his audience. He will apply techniques of emphasis and subordination—he will reveal his discovered meanings with appropriate modulations of volume, pitch, and rate. In all cases, he will strive for intelligibility, vividness, and interest. He is mindful that his reason for reading may be *to inform, to move,* or *to entertain.* He remembers that *his presentation is not an exhibition of skill, but an experience in communication.*

Although the reader actually does not deliberately memorize, he has his material very well in mind, so that he is free to relate effectively with his listeners. His *eye contact* assists him in achieving effective *mind contact* with his audience. His total bodily response, beginning with alert posture, supports with appropriate gesture, movement, and facial expression, the verbal symbols of the message. In their textbook

Communicative Reading, Aggertt and Brown summarize the effective oral reader's communicative task in this fashion:

> The oral interpreter can facilitate his expression of meaning by means of good platform technique. He establishes favorable audience attention by means of a well-planned, but spontaneous, introduction, and closes his reading in such a way as not to distract his audience from the content of the material. In addition, he uses a manuscript which he can handle with ease and which will actually add to the effectiveness of his reading. If he memorizes, he will learn the sequence of thought in the words of the author: he will not be satisfied with mechanical memorization. If he does not hold the book in his hands, he uses a reading stand which will not interfere with his communication. He maintains contact with his audience directly with the eyes whenever the reading materials demand conversational communication: he never buries his nose in a manuscript. He does all he can to avoid letting his reading seem mechanically prepared, for he knows that spontaneity and freshness are necessary for the audience's enjoyment of his reading. He never lets technique become an end in itself. He enjoys reading to others, for he has prepared well.[7]

With the foregoing discussion of *general* principles as our base, we may now appropriately turn our attention to some of the *specific* features and corresponding reading requirements of those materials most frequently read orally in secondary classrooms. As representative of prose materials we have selected the announcement, the essay, the speech manuscript, and the narrative.

Special requirements for reading prose

Announcements and other factual prose should be read straightforwardly and objectively with appropriate attention to major purpose and key details essential to the understanding of the message. Phrasing, rate, distinct ess of utterance, and projection are especially important in this type of reading. Except in cases when oral reading is being

---

[7] Otis J. Aggertt and Elbert R. Bowen, *Communicative Reading,* 2nd. ed. (New York: The Macmillan Company, 1963), p. 48.

used for testing and diagnostic purposes, the reader should be sufficiently familiar with the material to enable him to maintain contact with his listeners in much the same manner as in extempore speaking.

In reading the essay, additional attention should be given to the point of view and attitude expressed in the material. Care should be exercised to preserve the stylistic features, mood, and intellectual tone—whether straightforward, satirical, whimsical, fanciful, or starkly realistic. Since both intellectual and emotional qualities are essential features of such literature, the reader must give himself time to reveal his impressions of these qualities.

Reading a speech, either one's own or another's, requires essentially the same approach as that applied to essays. However, since speeches are purposefully prepared to be heard, particular care must be taken to observe the structure and pace, as well as the point of view of the material. In preparing to read a speech, the student should be advised to apply a modest but thoughtful rhetorical analysis to the selection. The following outline is suggested for such an analysis:

A. Identifications.
  1. Title of speech.
  2. Speaker.
  3. Setting : Place and date delivered.
  4. Source of text (e.g., *Famous American Speeches,* 1964).

B. Analysis.
  1. The speaker : personal data; qualifications to speak on the subject.
  2. The audience : size, makeup, attitudes toward speaker, subject, and speaker's point of view.
  3. The speech.
     a. Issues with which speech was concerned.
     b. Purpose of speech.
     c. Principal theme.
     d. Logical appeals and supporting evidence.
     e. Emotional appeals.
     f. Style : (e.g., simple, direct, decorative, clear, ponderous, etc.).
     g. Known effects of the speech.
     h. Other factors which may have influenced outcome of the speech.

C. Summary : (What useful or new information or insights regarding the major problem being considered in class has your study of this speech given you?)

To help "set the stage," the reader will wish to incorporate some of the analysis data in his introduction for the presentation of the speech itself. In his delivery he should not attempt to impersonate Lincoln, Adlai Stevenson, or Churchill—to represent the original speaker. He should think of himself as an interpreter, a faithful translator of the purpose, thought, and feeling of the speaker he is representing. In reading a speech, the student should be advised to maintain direct, communicative relations with his audience. He should try to read as one conversing with his listeners. Thorough preparation will go far in assisting him to secure and maintain this contact.

Finally, a word concerning adapting material: Many essays and speeches are too long for effective oral reading in the classroom and, therefore, require cutting and adapting. In such editing, care must be taken to preserve the tone and intention of the full text. Appropriate transitional remarks will often be needed. Occasionally, of course, all that may be wanted from a particular speech will be a brief excerpt as documentation for a point in a talk or in group discussion. In this case, the material should be treated like any other citation.

In the oral interpretation of narrative prose, the reader in a sense joins with the author in the role of storyteller. The more closely his reading sounds like good storytelling the more it is likely to be enjoyed. Since narrative material contains not only narration, but descriptive passages and probably some dialogue, it presents special challenges to the reader. Also in reading narrative, the movement of the story must be made clear, the climax sensed and properly focused; the critical descriptions must be read with vividness, and the characters suggested with appropriate vocal and bodily response. Again, the reader is not expected to impersonate the characters: he suggests in his voice and body his impression of the characters' dominant traits— their strengths, weaknesses, personal qualities. Unless the reader wishes to achieve a ludicrous or comical effect he should not attempt to "pitch his voice" to depict a man, a woman, or a child. We believe that stressing the qualities of individual character rather than emphasizing the physical differences, is both aesthetically and educationally preferable.

As with essays and speeches, narratives may often require cutting. This is particularly true in the case of the book review in which only passages are selected to be read in conjunction with an oral report or review. In the more general adapting of a story for oral reading, care must be taken to preserve the total effect of the narrative. The plot must stand firmly, the characters must emerge vividly, and the over-all style and feeling must be sustained. When "bridging" over the sections deleted by cutting, the reader should strive to catch as faithfully as possible the author's own style. In all cases of cutting, the reader, in his introduction, should make it clear that for the purposes of the assignment he has abridged the original text.

Special requirements for reading poetry[8]

It is generally conceded that of all literary forms, poetry demands most from the reader; but it is also generally agreed that with the exception of drama, of all the types of literature, poetry profits most from the interpreter's art. What is the uniqueness of poetry that makes its reading a special challenge to the interpreter? Most authorities agree that it can scarcely be said to be wholly one of form, rhythm, and meter; some prose soars poetically and some poetry has the freedom of prose. Critics do agree, however, that the exclusive quality of poetry rests in the uniting of three factors: *selectivity, concentration,* and *form.* The poet employs greater selectivity than other writers in presenting a scene. Whereas a novelist might require several pages to describe an action sequence, the poet may cut through the event with a stanza or two. The poet also concentrates a great deal of emotion and feeling in his language through giving particular attention to word choice, especially to their image-making propensity. Finally, in poetry the author always employs rhythm, including meter, and often, rhyme to achieve the desired effect. These elements add considerably to the oral reader's problem. It is essential, therefore, that we give due consideration to these factors, among others, in assisting pupils to prepare for reading poetry. However, lest we err in the direction of sterile over-

---

[8] The authors gratefully acknowledge the influence of Weaver and Ness in both the content and organization of this section.

analysis, it would be well to accept the counsel of Professor Charlotte Lee:

> Instead of beginning at once to work on the poem, let the poem work on you. Enjoyment is a good starting point for appreciation, even if you cannot immediately formulate in words your reason for liking the poem.[9]

From this preliminary experience with the poem, we may turn to more profitable analysis of the selection. Such analysis must, as implied earlier, include careful attention to the interrelation of content and structure, for in poetry these factors are inseparable and interaffective. As experience, even imagined, a poem, we are told, "is a blending of idea and emotion—of sense and sound."

In considering guidelines for the oral reading of poetry, three poetic forms will claim our attention: *narrative, dramatic monologue,* and *lyric.* With narrative poetry, such as "The Highwayman" or "The Battle of Blenheim," the reader approaches his analysis much as he does with narrative prose. But in poetry he must study the sound pattern to determine how it assists in advancing the story. In "The Highwayman" the rhythm and meter add an air of excitement, galloping to doom, as it were. In "The Battle of Blenheim" the rhythm is more controlled, quiet, an air of innocence mixed with irony.

Many plays are written in verse to heighten their dramatic appeal and to enhance their emotional vitality. Shakespeare's plays, of course, are prime examples. Although in a less formalized manner, poetry may also be dramatic when it involves a character in a dramatic situation as in the monologue "My Last Duchess." Here the reader's special tasks are to become thoroughly acquainted with the character whom the poet has created outside his own personality and who appears to be conversing with other characters in the development of the episode.

Unlike either dramatic or narrative poetry, the lyric does not present a story. Rather it is a symbolic representation of the poet's personal emotional experience. Since the essence of lyric poety is largely subjective, symbolism, imagery, and sound structure become particularly important.

---

[9] Charlotte Lee, *Oral Interpretation* (Boston: Houghton Mifflin Company, 1959), p. 390.

Let us briefly examine some of the additional specific steps which should be taken in preparation for the oral reading of poetry. First of all, the highly concentrated nature of poetry demands that the reader treat the text with extra fidelity. To pass over key words hurriedly or to skip lightly over important phrases might destroy an entire segment of meaning. Meanings should be felt, experienced, and their impact on the reader revealed. Rhythm, meter, and rhyme must be observed with discretion so that they heighten the emotional impact without overriding the sense of the poem. In order to preserve this delicate balance, some teachers have their students transcribe poems into prose form, retaining, of course the original language and sentence structure. Reading the selection a few times from this less stylized form and then returning to the original pattern may prove helpful when other measures fail to keep rhythm and meter in balance. Rhyming, another reading pitfall, often causes the inexperienced reader to grant unmerited emphasis to the rhymed words—the result, an unnatural detraction from the sense of the poem. To combat this tendency the reader might be advised to read as if the selection had no rhyme. This advice would be particularly valid in cases of the continued line, such as

> A thing of beauty is a joy forever :
> Its loveliness increases; it will never
> Pass into nothingness; but still will keep
> A bower quiet for us, and a sleep
> Full of sweet dreams, and health, and quiet breathing.
> John Keats

GUIDING AUDIENCE PARTICIPATION IN ORAL READING ACTIVITIES

Thus far, we have devoted major attention to the responsibilities of the reader: what about the responsibility of the audience?

Studies in group psychology, as well as empiric evidence, inform us that the behavior of persons in groups is likely to differ from their behavior as individuals. This phenomenon can be both an advantage or a disadvantage to the oral reader. Two or three unusually receptive listeners can "infect" the other members of an audience with their

response. Unfortunately even one distractor or "disbeliever" can sometimes play havoc with an otherwise good oral reading situation.
Obviously it is the reader's responsibility to make listening a profitable
and enjoyable experience for his audience. Nevertheless, the listener
can and should bring something to the event if the values of oral
reading are to be fully realized.

Students may soon discover that good listening, including
supportive feedback to a reader, often stimulates the reader to do his
best. Thus for his investment of supportive response the listener is
likely to reap a special dividend. What then constitutes effective
listening to oral reading? First of all, such listening is similar to
listening to other types of speaking: it is an active thought process;
it requires a certain willingness to "tune in"; it demands a considerable
measure of concentration. In short, it calls upon the participant to
make an honest effort "to translate" as faithfully as possible the author's
message as presented by the reader. Pupils should be instructed not
merely *to listen,* but to listen *for* something: *to listen with* a specific
purpose. Purposive listening may include listening for simple enjoyment, as in the case of a humorous story, poem, or essay. In drama it
may involve listening for clues in character analysis; in poetry it may
include listening for sensory appeals, for rhythms, and symbolism. In
the narrative it may call for understanding of the plot and movement;
in the speech, the point of view and the steps of logical thinking.

If the listener is to share the vicarious experience into which a
reader enters, he, too, must become involved. This he does
empathetically. That is, the listener identifies himself with the reader
by entering into the emotions, mental excursions, and, in a limited way,
physical reactions of the reader. Obviously it is essential that the
reader provide his listeners with appropriate empathetic stimuli and
that he observe the audience's responses to make certain that he is
securing the intended empathetic response: a response in harmony
with the intended meaning of the literary object.

A brief introduction which provides the audience with a "back-
drop" for the presentation will frequently assist the otherwise passive
listener to "tune in." Instruction in the nature and structure of poetry
is conducive to appreciative listening to poetry; often it is simply a
case of adjusting one's listening habits to a new or different way of
saying something. This principle is illustrated when we find ourselves
listening to a dialect different from our own. Listening to a fast-paced
British movie is a case in point.

In any event, pupils cannot be forced to listen: they should want to listen; they should be *invited to listen* and given something definite to do in listening. And in the discussion which may follow an oral reading, listeners should have opportunity to react honestly but tactfully to the selection and its presentation. Since poetry may present the greatest listening challenge, we may be well advised to heed again the advice of Charlotte Lee noted earlier in the chapter: "Let the poem work on you before you work on it." In all cases, care should be taken to select material which is likely to have optimal audience appeal. Pupils should be instructed in techniques of presenting the material effectively and receiving it with understanding if not with appreciation. There is no place for intimidation. Enjoyment, understanding, and growth in appreciative listening to spoken literature eventually must come willingly or not at all.

EVALUATING ORAL READING

While the basic principles and procedures for evaluating speech performance in general as outlined in Chapter Seven may be applied to appraising oral reading activities, it is essential that we identify specific criteria for judging such activities. The following check-sheets contain appropriate evaluative criteria and suggest a method of applying them. They may be used in their present forms; however, they are provided here mainly as points of departure from which the teacher may construct patterns more suited to the needs of his particular classes. In all cases, the evaluator should not lose sight of the wholeness of the reading. Looking at its separate parts can frequently lead one away from the essence of the selection and its presentation.

Suggesting forms for evaluating oral interpretative reading

Comprehensive Form

1. *Choice of selection.*

1	2	3	4	5
Unsuited to occasion, speaker, and audience.		Acceptable choice.	Excellent choice. Very appropriate.	

2. Degree to which *intellectual meaning* was communicated:

1   2   3   4   5
Not at all.   Partially.   Consistently well.

3. Degree to which *emotional meaning* was communicated:

1   2   3   4   5
Not at all.   Partially.   Consistently well.

4. In view of the nature of the material, occasion, and audience, the reader's vocal response with respect to:
   Use of pause and phrase.

1   2   3   4   5
Wholly inadequate.   Generally good.   Insightfully used.

Pitch variety.

1   2   3   4   5
Monotonous.   Generally good.   Excellent response
                                                            to thought and
                                                            feeling.

Audibility.

1   2   3   4   5
Inadequate.   Inconsistent.   Excellent response
                                                            to thought and
                                                            feeling

Vocal quality.

1   2   3   4   5
Unresponsive.   Basically good but Highly responsive
                                        unresponsive.   to feeling and
                                                            moods.

Articulation and pronunciation.

1   2   3   4   5
Unintelligible.   Inconsistent.   Consistently good.

Rate.

1   2   3   4   5
Inappropriate.   Generally good.   Very appropriate
                                                            for material.

Bodily response.

1   2   3   4   5
Inappropriate.   Balanced but   Alert, poised,
                                        unresponsive.   supportive.

Eye contact.

1	2	3	4	5
Inadequate or inappropriate.		Appropriate but inconsistent.	Highly effective and suited to material.	

Summary: Score——————————— Grade———————————————

Commendable features:

Suggestions for improvement:

Limited Forms

Narrative Prose

1. Introduction: (Appropriate content, length, effectiveness of presentation.)

2. The material (literary object): (Suitability for reader, audience, and occasion; effectiveness of cutting, if adapted; special relevance to project or unit being studied).

3. Reader's understanding of material: (Evidence of careful analysis, comprehension of author's purpose, theme, attitude, mood).

4. Reading skill: (Ability to use voice and body to convey author's meaning; communicativeness, audience contact).

5. General impression: (Particularly outstanding qualities; items which may need improving).

Poetry

	Rating				
1. The selection (literary object): (Suitability for occasion, audience, reader; and relevance to unit being studied.	1	2	3	4	5
2. Introduction: (Usefulness in creating audience readiness and willingness to listen; effectiveness of presentation).	1	2	3	4	5
3. Reader's comprehension of intellectual content of the material: (As shown by emphasis, subordination; phrasing, use of pause).	1	2	3	4	5
4. Reader's comprehension of emotional content of the material: (As shown by emphasis, vocal quality, bodily response, handling of rhythm, response to connotative factors).	1	2	3	4	5
5. Specific vocal elements: (Projection, pleasantness, variability, intelligibility).	1	2	3	4	5
6. Audience relationship: (Appropriate selection; ability to empathize and secure empathy).	1	2	3	4	5
7. General impression:	1	2	3	4	5

It has been said that in poetry, language achieves its highest form. However, to bring full realization to this language as communication, it must be brought to life through oral reading: insightful, sensitive, effective oral reading. In preceding sections of this chapter, we have indicated some of the essential guidelines for leading pupils toward effective oral reading of poetry and other selected literary forms. The treatment, consistent with the aims of this textbook,[10] has dwelt on

---

[10] In keeping with this volume's nontechnical approach to speech in the classroom, we have purposely omitted discussion of the various metrical forms in poetry. Teachers of English normally are introduced to this subject in poetry courses; others who wish to pursue an interest in the matter may find useful information in the sources listed under "Selected Readings" at the close of this chapter.

the minimal fundamentals of oral reading, fundamentals which, if applied in the classroom, may be expected to make oral interpretative reading a useful means of teaching and learning. The following section provides a number of examples which illustrate its usefulness as a classroom procedure.

GENERAL CLASSROOM APPLICATION OF ORAL INTERPRETATIVE READING

As suggested in Chapter Six, oral reading is especially suited to the needs and nature of English classes with their particular emphasis upon language and the study of literature. It is here that oral reading attains its greatest instrumental value, and it is here that oral reading may quite appropriately be considered an object of instruction in its own right. That is to say, because of its high implementive value in the study of English and because as a speech form it is considered one of the "language arts," English teachers normally accept the responsibility of teaching principles of oral reading as an essential and integral part of their work.

A number of "oral reading" approaches are available to the English teacher. For example, using the oral interpreter's system of analysis, he may lead his pupils toward an oral experience of literature; he may illustrate and teach by example through his own reading; he may use some of the excellent recorded material available to him;[11] he may be fortunate enough to obtain outstanding guest readers; he may be located in an area served by college or university readers' theater groups. As suggested earlier in this chapter, the English teacher will find oral reading a valuable accessory to the book review; he will wish to use it in motivating interest in writing skill through observing the techniques of good writers. Whatever may be said of its uses in English classes may also be applied to a large extent in teaching foreign language classes.

Oral reading also has several practical applications in the social studies. In an earlier chapter, mention was made of the use of speeches and orations to illuminate the study of history, economics, and govern-

---

[11] A list of selected recording publishers will be found in the Appendix. Consult their catalogues in local outlets.

ment. Oral reading of excerpts from the speeches of Clay, Lincoln, Churchill, Hitler; of Franklin D. Roosevelt, Adlai Stevenson, Norman Thomas, or John L. Lewis, to name but a few, can enhance pupils' understanding of the role of speech in shaping and interpreting the policies of a nation, as well as help them to gain a fuller appreciation of the historical, economic, and political issues with which the speeches were concerned. Classes in government, organized along parliamentary lines, will provide occasion for effective reading of minutes, reports, correspondence, and announcements.

Oral reading may offer teachers and pupils in other classes, such as mathematics, science, fine arts, the means of communicating much useful information and giving specific instructions. Oral reading of news items, excerpts from editorials, feature articles, and specialized pamphlets, has potential value for classroom instruction.

Finally, oral reading, as a product of classroom instruction and experience, can be extended to school assemblies, radio and television, and community programs. When programmed for a readers' theater, oral reading has much to offer as a means of bringing good literature as "living experience" to an audience. Inventive and resourceful teachers will find additional uses for oral reading in their classes. Here we have attempted merely to indicate something of the nature and direction of such applications. In Part Four of this volume, we shall observe a number of detailed applications of oral reading in teaching selected secondary school subjects, some of which are developed operationally.

SUMMARY

We have defined oral interpretative reading as *the process of sharing with others, through speech, one's understanding of the intellectual and emotional meaning of a particular literary object.* Primary among the several values attributed to oral reading as an instrument of learning and teaching in secondary school classrooms is its use as a means of studying literature. Other values accrue from its use in furnishing models in teaching writing, its contribution to improving speech skills, as well as its usefulness as a mode for communicating information. Its limitations arise chiefly from improper application and inept performance. *Good* oral reading was defined as that which (1) deals with worthwhile and appropriate materials, (2) is well motivated, (3) is technically and artistically effective and purposeful.

A substantial portion of the chapter was devoted to a discussion of guidelines for using oral interpretative reading, including the subjective and objective preparation for reading and the actual presentation of an oral reading. Distinctions were noted among the preparations for and presentations of several variants of prose and poetry. Reference was made to the role of the audience in oral reading and specific suggestions were offered for evaluating this speech form. The chapter closed with brief descriptions of representative classroom applications.

SELECTED READINGS

Textbooks specializing in the art of oral interpretation

Aggertt, Otis J., and Elbert R. Bowen. *Comunicative Reading,* 2nd ed. New York : The Macmillan Company, 1963.

Bacon, Wallace A. *The Art of Interpretation.* New York: Holt, Rinehart & Winston, Inc., 1966.

Grimes, Wilma H., and Alethea Smith Mattingly. *Interpretation: Writer, Reader, Audience.* San Francisco : Wadsworth Publishing Co., 1961.

Lee, Charlotte. *Oral Interpretation.* Boston : Houghton Mifflin Company, 1959.

Parrish, Wayland Maxfield. *Reading Aloud.* New York: The Ronald Press Company, 1941.

General speech textbooks

Robinson, Karl F., and Charlotte Lee. *Speech in Action.* New York : Scott, Foresman & Company, 1965. Part II : Interpretation, Chapters 1, 2, 3, 4, and 5. (An excellent high school speech textbook.)

Weaver, Andrew T., and Ordean G. Ness. *The Fundamentals and Forms of Speech.* New York : The Odyssey Press, Inc., 1957. Chapter 15 : "Oral Interpretation and Acting."

Essays of particular interest

Hargis, Clara A., and Donald B. Hargis. "High School Literature and Oral Interpretation." *The Speech Teacher,* II (September, 1953), 205–208.

Marcoux, J. Paul. "Current Trends for Literary Analysis for Oral Interpretation : An Overview." *The Speech Teacher,* XV (November, 1966), 324–27.

Mouat, Lawrence H. "The Question Method for Teaching Emphasis in Oral Reading." *Quarterly Journal of Speech,* XXXV (December, 1949), 485–88.

Robb, Mary Margaret. "Oral Interpretation and the Book Review." *The Speech Teacher,* V (November, 1956), 285–89.

Explication and criticism

Arms, George W., and Joseph M. Kuntz. *Poetry Explication,* rev. ed. Denver : Alan Swallow, 1962. (An extensive bibliography of explicative essays and other writings on the works of best known British and American poets.)

Gwynn, Frederick L., Ralph W. Condee, and Arthur O. Lewis, Jr. *The Case for Poetry—A Critical Anthology of Poems, Cases and Critiques.* Englewood Cliffs, N.J.; Prentice-Hall, Inc., 1965.

APPLICATION

PART **IV** *oral communication in the classroom*

12 *english*

Frequently, speech as *method* and speech as *object* of instruction and learning become as one, or at least they become complementary within a given subject field. This is especially true in English. In many high schools throughout the country, the English program assumes responsibility for basic instruction in speaking and listening, as well as its share of integrated instruction in these skills. In such cases, the program usually assumes one or more of the following patterns: (1) Designated speech-listening units at various points in the entire English sequence; (2) Assigned semesters or portions thereof to basic speech-listening; (3) Coordinated teaching of all language arts— speaking, writing, listening, reading—in a unified manner throughout the English program. Any of the foregoing plans may be accompanied by supplementary elective classes in speech or drama, cocurricular speech-drama activities, and by provision for the speech and acoustically handicapped.

It is neither necessary nor appropriate that we discuss the relative merits of the foregoing plans nor to argue the case for "basic speech instruction in separate speech classes." What we believe to be important, however, is that any plan of basic speech instruction, regardless of its administrative arrangement, should provide direct instruction and practice in the fundamentals of speaking and listening; be taught by competent speech-drama-English trained teachers; and be made an integral part of the educational experience of all high school pupils. The crucial ingredient in any field of learning, including speech education, is as always, *the quality of instruction.*

Certainly there are valid reasons for combining the teaching of the communicative arts in some type of unified program. All involve the common element of language; all are concerned with improving verbal communication. Both listening and reading are receptive, interpretative, linguistic functions. Speaking and writing are coordinate, expressive functions, which as Bryant reminds us, "depend for their efficiency and grace—that is, for their practicality—on many of the same accomplishments and acquirements in knowledge and experience, in methods of thought and of composition, in linguistic equipment and acuity."[1] Representative Yearbooks of the National Council of Teachers of English, as well as current textbooks in the methods of teaching English, accord high priority to the teaching of oral communication in the education of youth. Several call attention to the need for speech preparation of English teachers.[2] Some offer commendable general treatments of speech methodology for English teachers.[3]

Suffice it to say that English teachers have been and continue to be involved in teaching oral communication, either as an essential strand of the content of their subject or as means of teaching other integral parts of the English spectrum, including written composition and literature. And while the focus of this textbook follows the "oral-communication-as-a-medium-of-learning" theme, readers who find themselves charged with the task of teaching speech units or entire courses of speech fundamentals should have no difficulty in adapting substantial segments of this and other chapters to their particular needs. We are not suggesting, however, that this text or any single volume devoted to speech methodology constitutes an acceptable substitute for a program in speech pedagogy.

---

[1] Donald C. Bryant, "Critical Responsibilities of the Speech-English Program," *The Speech Teacher,* X (November, 1961), 276–82.

[2] See, for example: *The Education of Teachers of English,* 1963; and *The English Language Arts in the Secondary School,* 1956, National Council of Teachers of English (New York: Appleton-Century-Crofts).

[3] Consult, for instance, Walter Loban, and others, *Teaching Language and Literature* (New York: Harcourt, Brace & World, Inc., 1961).

SCOPE OF ENGLISH INSTRUCTION

One of the often repeated reasons for assigning the teaching of speech-listening fundamentals to separate classes in speech or to designated locations in the English program, is that besides permitting appropriate concentration on teaching speech skills, this practice reduces to more manageable proportions the range of material to be covered in the remainder of the English curriculum. Most certainly the gamut of responsibilities which the average English teacher faces is both diffuse and complex. The following POINT OF VIEW *for the language arts course of study* in a large metropolitan school system, quoted here in abridged form, suggests the scope of a typical high school English curriculum.

POINT OF VIEW

The aim of the Language Arts Program is literacy. The Language Arts are concerned with receiving, considering, and expressing thought. They are concerned, also, with attitudes, appreciations, and habits of studying, thinking, and acting. . . .

The Language Arts deal with ideas and critical thinking which are the products of observation, experience, and reading; with the development of sensitivity and creativity in the use of language; and with the total effect of literature upon the development of character. The Language Arts Program consists of communication: the receiving and expression of thought, and of composition: the composing of speech and writing. . . .

The skills taught in Language Arts classes are those needed for gaining, organizing, and expressing thought. They include reading comprehension and speed, note-taking, manuscript and letter forms, grammar, usage, punctuation, spelling, pronunciation, enunciation, sentence structure, vocabulary building, phonics, word analysis, dictionary use, library use, and outlining.

The Language Arts Program has two primary goals: knowledge of important content and development of language skills. Content and skills are equally important in composition and communication. Both must be taught and both must move along together.[4]

---

[4] *A Guide to the Teaching of the Language Arts in the Senior High School*, p. 5. Reprinted by permission of Seattle Public Schools, Seattle, Washington.

As a former high school English teacher, this author can attest to the formidability of the English teacher's task. Many school systems find that some type of division of labor is both necessary and prudent for meeting the various instructional responsibilities of the English language arts program. This can and should be done without sacrificing the interrelation of the various strands of the program.

SPECIAL PROBLEMS IN TEACHING ENGLISH

In addition to the problem of sheer bulk of content to be covered, English instruction must deal effectively with other challenges, most of which are common to all fields of learning but may appear for different reasons in English classes. We refer particularly to the problems of *individual differences, motivation, retention,* and *application.* What are some of the factors which make these problems somewhat unique in English?

Individual differences

Language ability varies profoundly from individual to individual. First of all, the span of mental abilities in a given classroom will account for some of the variations in language potential of pupils. In addition, since language is learned largely by imitation and influenced by the diversity of the learner's experience, it reflects the nature and symbolic pattern of the individual's customary environment. Before the child enters school, this environment is the home. Thereafter, it may be a combination of the child's home and peer group. The range of speech-language maturities spawned by these diverse environments is astonishing. Small wonder that teachers find communication in their classrooms difficult at best and the task of language improvement frustrating.

Motivation

"Probably in no other field," says Guth, "is joyless learning, or learning against the grain, as self-defeating as in language and literature."[5] Too frequently, we fear, the learning which takes place

---

[5] Hans Guth, *English Today and Tomorrow* (Englewood Cliffs, N.J.: Prentice-Hall, Inc., 1964), p. 312.

in English classes is joyless and routine; more pain than pleasure; more rhyme than reason. Is it not ironic that the functions which most distinguish man from the lower animals should offer so little appeal to many high school pupils? We believe there are reasons for this student apathy and frequent hostility. Possibly it is due in part to the belief that averageness, mediocrity of language facility, will suffice for daily needs. Possibly it is due in part to becoming surfeited with English instruction: no other subject receives so much continuous and repeated instructional attention from kindergarten through high school. Possibly we language teachers have not always recognized the need for creativity, for prescriptive instruction, for less learning *about* and more learning *with* language activities. If we are to avoid the pitfalls to learning in English classes, experiences must somehow engender a vital interest in language as a key to personal growth and self-realization. Although most of us may succeed in causing our pupils to fulfill their assignments of the moment, unless we also help them to like the thing learned better because of the experience or have a fuller appreciation of it because of the learning activity, somehow we have slighted the task.

Retention

As noted in other contexts of this work, retention is directly related to motivation and the impact of initial learning. When the instruction has become routine, repetitious, or divorced from meaningful application, learning is apt to be short lived or totally obstructed. However, there is yet another equally cogent, though somewhat less obvious, reason for failure to retain language learning. We refer to the conflicting stimuli in the language environments of youth. To explain : useful as dictionaries may be, some word meanings are personal, they differ from individual to individual. Moreover, usage standards vary from group to group. The pupil is in school for only six hours each day and no more than one of these in an English class. This limited exposure to standard language patterns may fail to compete successfully with the pressures of substandard patterns of the pupil's other daily environments. When the standards of competing environments are at variance, the more compelling environment will doubtless prevail, or the countereffects of the environments may lead to confusion, in which case learning is likely to be impeded and retention shortened.

Application

Closely related to the problem of retention is the application of learning. Obviously what is not retained cannot be applied; conversely, unless something is quickly and continuously applied in one's behavior or is well conceptualized it will soon be forgotten. We have an uneasy feeling that too much of what we have attempted to teach in our English classes has been approached as rote learning and therefore frequently fails to become an integral part of the learner's thinking and social behavior. We agree wholeheartedly with Loban, Ryan, and Squire[6] that language must be approached as *dynamic process.* Pupils must experience language as adventure in communication. They must learn how language works in human relations; they must discover for themselves how control of language is a first step to control of self and effective relations with others. And they must realize that the task of gaining language control is a lifetime job. We must teach for use, for application, if classroom language learning is to be applied in daily living. Fortunately certain trends in the teaching of English, we believe, can be expected to reduce some of these problems.

TRENDS IN TEACHING ENGLISH

Guth identifies four major movements currently affecting the teaching of English. The first of these is *the study of linguistics and its effect on the teaching of grammar,* an influence, which, according to Guth, "will cause school grammar to be more authentically English; and it will be more concrete, and to that extent more teachable, than it used to be."[7] A second movement is *the effort to modify the conventional schoolroom attitude toward usage,* in which the tendency is to move from *right* and *wrong* to *standard* and *nonstandard.* The emphasis here is on *appropriateness* rather than *correctness* as the criterion of "good English." A third movement currently affecting the teaching of English is that of *semantics and an emphasis on the responsible use of language in everyday life.* The study of semantics more than any other influence has helped us to understand how language works: to appreciate the important relations between word and referent, between

---

[6] Loban, *op. cit.,* Chap. I "Language as Dynamic Process."

[7] Guth, *op. cit.,* p. 13.

language and the world around us. Guth captures the essence of language in action:

> Language is always more than a code for the transmission of data. It is a complex, and often dangerously misleading, instrument of human relations. . . . Far from merely passing on a message, it betrays the speaker—his attitudes, backgrounds, ambitions, hopes, and fears. Far from merely describing reality, it sets up the terms and categories according to which we interpret—and shape—reality. On the one hand, it is a source of power, enabling us to impose our wills on others through the magic of words. On the other hand, it hems us in and limits us, until we become the prisoners of our own terms and slogans.[8]

The fourth movement influencing the teaching of English, according to Guth, is *a shift from the study of a literary work by emphasis on the author, his times, sources, to emphasis upon close reading of the text itself.* This influence owes its origin chiefly to the so-called "new criticism" which tends to center greater attention on close textual analysis but with full regard for the wholeness of the literary object.

The foregoing influences doubtless have helped humanize the teaching and learning of English, have brought it closer to the lives of pupils, have helped to vitalize the subject and make it more appealing to youth. Creative teachers have discovered innumerable other ways to make the study of English language a pleasant and profitable experience for the learner and a source of rich satisfaction for themselves. Among these approaches is the effective use of speech-listening activities as instruments of learning, as well as legitimate objects of instruction.

RECIPROCAL RELATIONS OF ORAL COMMUNICATION AND THE TEACHING OF ENGLISH

In Chapter Six we touched on some of the reciprocal relations of oral communication and English. We emphasized in particular the special contribution of English to oral language facility. We mentioned the special virtues of writing as preparation for speaking and con-

---

[8] *Ibid.*, pp. 16-17.

versely the value of speaking, particularly discussion, as preparation for writing. We also spoke of the instrumental values of oral interpretative reading and dramatics in vitalizing the study of literature. We noted the rich reservoir of man's experience and wisdom preserved in the literature of the ages—fertile sources of material for exciting, profitable speech activities. In the following section we shall illustrate more specifically some of the strategies for combining listening and speaking with English in ways that have been found to vitalize the learning of English and thus foster growth in verbal communication abilities.

SUGGESTIVE STRATEGIES FOR TEACHING ENGLISH

I. Speech as an integral object of instruction and learning in the English program

As previously suggested in this chapter, in many high schools it is considered advantageous to provide *basic instruction in speech* by making it an integral part of the English program. The following plan illustrates one way of teaching selected speech fundamentals in a designated unit of one semester of the high school English program.[9]

I.A. "The Jig-Saw Plan."

Description: This plan, when carried out to completion, calls for a series of short ($1\frac{1}{2}$–2 minute) one-point talks culminating in a longer multi-point speech. Each of the short assignments, oral paragraphs, emphasizes one speech delivery objective and one idea-support element. Normally the beginning sentence of the paragraph indicates the topic, belief, or assumption to be developed. Such topic sentences as: "Consider with me for a moment the complexity of a blade of grass;" or "We are being buried by our man-made air pollution;" or "If we like music, we might find something to like in poetry" are illustrative.

---

[9] Developed by J. Norman Cromarty, teacher of English and speech, Seattle Public Schools, presented here with his permission. See also "The Speech to Persuade," *The Speech Teacher,* XVII (March, 1968), 178.

SEQUENCE OF ASSIGNMENTS

Speaking Experience	*Delivery Objective*	*Means of Support or Development*
1.	Pause to secure audience attention before speaking; pause at conclusion	An appropriate quotation.
2.	Secure and maintain good audience contact; plus previous attention to pause.	An acceptable statistic.
3.	Reveal effective bodily response: appropriate gesture, facial response plus previously emphasized elements.	An analogy.
4.	Employ good vocal response: vocal vitality, variety; sincerity; plus previous factors.	An example or illustration
5.	Employ vivid, appropriate language; plus previous factors.	An example of an effective introduction for a talk.
6. (6–8 min).	A well-planned talk embodying all factors emphasized in the one to two-minute oral paragraph talks.	

The foregoing plan can be adapted in a number of ways. For example, the entire sequence may be carried out as a unit, or any one of its individual assignments may be employed singly in answer to a particular need. The plan has much to commend it: it is manageable and teachable. With preparation and presentation times reduced and major attention given to no more than one or two new items in each assignment, achievement is brought more readily within reach of all pupils. Moreover, for practical application, the one-point talk has far greater currency than the multi-point speech.

Preparation: To insure adequate pupil preparation and profitable use of the plan, the teacher must explain the purpose and nature of the entire sequence and of each individual talk. He should emphasize *clear thinking*, with delivery and idea-support factors as means to this end. He should teach pupils how to test evidence: to determine the validity of a statistic, to know and to apply tests of opinion, analogy, and illustration. *Pupils must earn the right to speak:* to select a worthwhile subject, to prepare well, and to speak effectively and responsibly.

I.B. "Team Learning."

After students have received basic instruction and have had some experience presenting ideas, concepts, or convictions in an orderly, logical fashion, they should have opportunity to perfect their skills and refine their techniques. One method of providing such opportunity is through the use of *Team-* or *Group-Learning.*

Procedure: Instead of having all pupils present short talks to the entire class, divide class into two-member teams or groups of three. Locate groups in various parts of the room or in small practice rooms if available. Then have each pupil present his talk to the other member for evaluation. Have pupils keep a diary of their experiences. If conditions permit, use tape recorders to assist in evaluating both talks and listener responses.

I.C. "The Library-Classroom Plan."[10]

In teaching speech fundamentals, when it is not essential that every pupil be present in the classroom to hear every speech, arrange with the school librarian to allow pupils to spend two class periods weekly in the library on research and preparation for the subsequent assignment.

Expect that the pupil will come to the classroom two days of the week (in addition, of course, to the one in which he himself is to speak) so that he may: (1) learn from the criticism and suggestions made in class, and (2) help to provide a suitable audience for the speakers of the day. To permit appropriate scheduling, allow each pupil to choose in advance the two days he will spend his class hour in the library.

I.D. "The Speech Emphasis Semester Plan."

In many high schools one semester in the English program is designated for primary emphasis upon speech fundamentals. While this arrangement provides for the basic speech instruction of all pupils, it does not reduce the need for advanced classes in speech, drama, and debate; nor does it lessen the need for some continuing attention to speech education in the remaining semesters of the English program.

The "Speech Semester Plan" is likely to stress a combination of not more than three or four of the following instructional areas: Listening, Short Talk, Discussion, Oral Interpretation of Literature, Parliamen-

---

[10] Adapted from procedures developed and used successfully in Kent-Meridian High School, State of Washington.

tary Procedure, and perhaps auxiliary units in voice, articulation and bodily action.

Important as it is to view speech as an *object of learning*, it is essential that we return to the main current of this work: Oral communication as a *medium of learning*.

II. Speech as a medium of learning in English classes

Throughout the English program, whether the emphasis at a given point is on speech improvement or on some other area of language study, we find speaking, listening, reading, and writing functioning interrelatedly. Improvement in one language element may thus be facilitated and reinforced by appropriate application of the related elements. It should be remembered, however, that merely juxtaposing related language functions does not necessarily result in desirable learning. Obviously thought and care must be given to proper timing, to selecting the activity, and to guiding the learning processes.

The following strategies suggest some of the ways in which the English teacher may employ oral activities as media of learning in English education.

II.A. Speech an Aid on Teaching Language Fundamentals.

By definition, English classes are engaged in the study of a language, its nature and its uses in intrapersonal and interpersonal communication. While all classes, regardless of their content, are concerned with and require the use of language for their successful functioning, English, drama, and speech classes *are* language classes. Their prime responsibility is to guide pupils toward more effective, more responsible, and more appreciative use of language as a communicative medium.

Donald Bryant appropriately reminds us that "talk or written discourse is first and foremost a tissue of words." He insists that it matters a great deal how something is said:

> That how a thing is said, in fact, is an important part of what is said; that the selection and management of language—including the utterance of it—make the final meaning of the message; that they incarnate the thought and the intention; that they give form and ultimate significance to what is transmitted and received.[11]

---

[11] Bryant, *op. cit.*

II.A.1. Teaching the strengths and limitations of language in conveying a percept.

Procedure: Sketch or arrange geometric figures on a field in some such fashion as shown in the design below; place the sheet with the design on a lectern or desk out of view of the class. Have the class attempt to reproduce the design with paper and pencil from directions given orally by one of their members as he faces the design. Allow ten minutes, then compare responses with original design. Have class draw inferences from the experiment. Follow with another design; have the pupil proceed with the description but this time allow the speaker to supplement oral symbols with gestures. Allow ten minutes; compare responses and have class draw relevant conclusions. Finally, have pupil describe a third design, but this time allow members of class to ask questions as the description proceeds.

From the experience, pupils should more fully appreciate oral communication pitfalls, the need for clarity, discreet choice of words, mutual orientation, value of visual cues, and the importance of feedback and readjustment in securing effective communication.

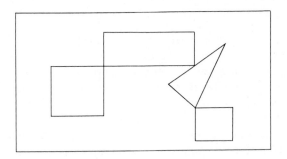

PLANE FIGURES ON A FIELD.

II.A.2. Teaching awareness of and skill in use of the abstraction process.

When we use words to represent things and various levels of classification of things, we engage in the process of *abstracting*. Hayakawa states that "learning language is not simply a matter of learning words; it is a matter of correctly relating our words to the things and happenings for which they stand."[12] Thus when attempting to define some-

---

[12] S. I. Hayakawa, *Language in Thought and Action,* 2nd. ed. (New York: Harcourt, Brace & World, Inc., 1964), p. 178.

thing, one would do well when possible to approach the task operationally : i.e., by indicating what one must do or observe "to bring the thing defined or its effects within the range of one's experience." This is precisely what the able speaker and the skillful teacher do almost intuitively. Broad statements are brought to focus, generalizations made meaningful through use of specific examples and illustrative experiences. And by reversing the direction of abstracting, arrays of detail are led to meaning when their import is capped with an appropriate generalization.

Procedure: Help pupils to become better communicators through intelligent, dexterous use of the so-called abstraction ladder, learning to move freely, consciously, effectively up and down the "ladder" as the situation demands. To communicate well, one must know when and how to offer experiential detail and when and how to tie the details together into larger wholes in the form of generalizations, principles or inferences. Hayakawa puts it neatly:

> The interesting writer, the informative speaker, the accurate thinker, and the sane individual, operate on all levels of the abstraction ladder, moving quickly and gracefully and in orderly fashion from higher to lower, from lower to higher—with minds as lithe and deft and beautiful as monkeys in a tree.[13]

EXERCISES

After a lecture or teacher-led discussion on the "abstraction process and the semantic ladder," have pupils engage in such exercises as the following:

1. As suggested by Hayakawa, "Starting with one at the lowest level of abstraction, arrange the following statements in order of increasing abstraction :
   a. I like motoring better than flying.
   b. I like Ford cars.
   c. I like American cars better than English cars.
   d. I like my Fairlane four-door sedan.
   e. I like travel."

---

[13] *Ibid.,* p. 190.

2. Transpose to lower abstraction levels, if warranted, such statements as :
   a. A Scout is trustworthy and loyal.
   b. They gave their lives in defense of Democracy.
   c. Short story: "Algy saw a bear. The bear saw Algy. The bear was bulgy. The bulge was Algy."
   d. I believe in freedom of speech.
   e. "And Brutus was an honorable man."
3. After being presented with a series of related specific statements, offer an oral statement of a higher abstraction level categorizing or generalizing the series of statements.
4. Present a short talk in which the object is to define a term or concept, such as *freedom, romanticism, transcendentalism, manifest destiny, cubism, counterpoint, or condensation.*

   Apply abstraction ladder. For example, after an appropriate introduction, offer a short paragraph in which the term is defined in a general way. Follow this paragraph with specific examples, an operational illustration or other appropriate lower level abstraction. Or reverse the order in offering a series of specific close-to-the-referent details followed by a capsulizing general definition or description.

II.A.3. Teaching the difference between fact and opinion.

Procedure: Using such topics as school spirit, civil rights, personality, air travel, hippies, have a number of pupils each express one *fact* concerning the item. Record responses on chalkboard without comment. Then have a number of pupils each express one *opinion* concerning the items; record responses on chalkboard in adjacent column. Compare and discuss characteristics of facts and opinions. Check lists for improperly entered items. Discuss tests and the usefulness of opinions in discourse.

II.A.4. Stimulating interest in writing.

Procedure: When students seem to have difficulty getting started with writing on a given subject, either because of lack of interest or having nothing to say, writing can be stimulated (ideas brought to focus and thinking clarified) through teacher-led exploratory discussion.

Similarly the teacher's oral reading of poetry followed by summarizing the essentials of the model can be an effective introduction to writing poetry. It is doubtful whether either rhythm or sensitivity to mood in the writing of poetry can be taught successfully without the aid of oral reading.

II.A.5. Teaching sentence sense.

Procedure: Dictate or have a pupil dictate sentences for class writing. Stress oral punctuation: use of pause, vocal emphasis, phrasing. Teach the functional nature of written punctuation.

II.A.6. Teaching language style.

Procedure: Dictate or have a pupil dictate sentences for class speaking. Assign planned listening to a series of prescriptively selected tapes in the listening laboratory. Examples: idea development, imagery, sentence structure, figures of speech.

II.A.7. Fostering objectivity.

Procedure: Have pupils present orally the basic issues of a controversial problem. Challenge: the speaker must maintain objectivity throughout and not betray either by word or manner his personal view or bias on the matter.

II.A.8. Viewing English as a living, growing language.

Procedure: Assign a series of short talks or have a symposium on "Our Language Family Tree" or "How to Make a Language." Include reference to Anglo-Saxon origins, Latin-Greek derivatives, mythology, loan words, name words, etc. Show how word meanings change.

II.A.9 Teaching structure.

Procedure: Assign short projects in expressing ideas vividly and grammatically. Have pupils orally create different sentences patterned after the basic structure furnished in models provided by the teacher. Wolfe suggests a number of variants of this exercise of which the following is illustrative for use with an advanced class:

> *Pattern: A past participle following the subject.*
> The lazy afternoon, bathed in a soft warmth of a reluctant sun, held a hint of a winter's coming chill.
> —Ruth Firor

Assignment: Describe an afternoon, a morning, a house, a yard. In your imitation of the pattern, try for personifying words such as lazy and reluctant.

Example: The raw December air, showered with gusts of swirling snow, swept down the lonely alley.[14]

II.B. Oral Approaches to the Study of Literature.

All speech forms discussed in Part Three of this volume may be used with profit in the study of literature. However, we customarily think of oral interpretation and variants of dramatization as *naturals,* virtually made-to-order media. Literature designed to be heard, such as poetry, drama, and certain prose works, obviously should receive some form of oral treatment. Guidelines suggested in chapters Nine, Ten, and Eleven of Part Three are intended to provide direction in the use of these speech activities.

II.B.1. Discovering the richness of literature through interpretative speech arts.

Although reading aloud and dramatization are standard classroom procedures of long standing, too frequently the readings and dramatizations are uninspired and perfunctory. The result may be comic relief, but scarcely a useful educational experience. Careful selection of material, thorough preparation, and sincere desire to bring the literature to living experience, however, can yield rich dividends in enjoyment, appreciation, and effective learning. Let us review merely a few of the possibilities for applying interpretative speech arts.

a. *Reading aloud for fuller understanding and enjoyment.* Use oral reading as either the means of studying and analyzing a literary object or as the culmination of its analysis. Vary the approaches through readings by the teacher, by pupils, guest artists, professional recordings, and by attending reader's theater productions. Plan group reading programs. If their quality is good, share programs with audiences beyond the classroom.

b. *Informal dramatization.* Have pupils dramatize scenes from favorite short stories, narrative poems, balalds, and selected passages from novels and biographies.

---

[14] Don M. Wolfe, *Creative Ways to Teach English* (New York: The Odyssey Press, Inc., 1958), p. 348.

c. *Semiformal dramatization.* Have pupils transcribe a short story into play form. Have them write original skits, scenes, and plays from germinal ideas drawn from controversial issues, news items, special events, and holidays.

d. *Role-playing.* Invite pupils to reenact a scene from a story by altering one or two of the variables in the situation. Emphasize value judgment and the problem of *choice*.

e. *Formal drama.* Have pupils act out with books in hand or with memorized lines one-act plays or scenes from longer dramas. Shakespeare can come to meaning through scene reading or acting, particularly when the teacher is a convincing reader or actor and participates with his pupils in selected scenes. Playing and replaying may bring to light many interesting, if diverse, interpretations of a scene or characters.

f. *Live or recorded drama.* Play recordings of standard plays. Discuss key elements. Attend professional or well-played amateur productions. Have pupils view motion pictures or video tapes of standard plays. Determine objectives for viewing; discuss after viewing.

II.B.2. Other oral approaches to the study of literature.

Should the teacher wish to approach a literary object primarily as a problem in the study of values, character delineation, or writing technique, he may wish to use variants of teacher-led discussion or small group student-led discussion.

II.B.2.a. Approaching literature through variable group learning and team teaching.[15]

Following is one method of grouping students for instruction, other than on the basis of ability, and employing a teaching team. Jody Nyquist, under whose direction the plan was developed, cautions that understanding the concept of the program requires our presupposing:

1. That the material which is to be presented has been researched and discussed and that the necessity of its presentation has been agreed upon by all members of the team;

2. That the students and teachers involved are in a "block-of-time," single-discipline program so that approximately one hundred students and four teachers are available during the same period each day;

---

[15] Developed and used with notable success in Shorecrest High School, Shoreline Public Schools, State of Washington; see Jody L. Nyquist, "Grouping Other Than Ability," *English Journal*, LVII (December, 1968), 1340–44.

3. That facilities can be organized to house the groups as explained; and

4. That all members of the team are willing to try new ideas.[16]

The plan calls for the creation of four different size-groups: LARGE GROUP (one hundred students and one teacher) where through lectures, movies, guest speakers, and similar activities, pupils receive background information on the units being studied. INTERMEDIATE GROUPS (approximately twenty-five pupils with one teacher) which provide opportunity for teacher-led discussions on themes, characters, and symbols in novels and short stories, as well as offer settings for tests and other standard classroom procedures. SEMINAR GROUPS (sixteen pupils with one teacher), in which half of the entire group, or fifty students, are subdivided into three approximately equal groups each with one teacher "for more closely directed work such as the explication of poetry." The fourth teacher meets with the remaining fifty students in a lecture situation. The following day, the two halves switch activities so that all pupils receive approximately equal learning experiences. SMALL GROUP (five to eight members): Whereas learning in the first three groups is teacher-led, the SMALL GROUP calls for student-led activity. This size-group lends itself particularly well to "literary discussions, analysis of each other's papers, and reviewing for tests." Obviously, best results from small groups obtain when students have previously received instruction in the discussion process and teachers provide insightful supervision.

Teachers who have employed the variable grouping plan praise its usefulness in promoting critical thinking, intragroup communication, as well as the pupils' interest in and understanding of the object being studied. The variety of learning experiences and groupings appears to satisfy a considerable range of individual pupil needs and seems to stimulate more general pupil involvement than is usually found in traditional classroom procedures.

The following outline adapted from the Shorecrest Plan suggests one of the possibilities for approaching the concept of *Puritanism*. On subsequent days, the classes take up the study of selections concerning Puritanism, including *The Scarlet Letter* and *The Crucible*.

---

[16] Quoted from Nyquist, "Grouping Other Than Ability," p. 1340.

PURITANISM

Materials	Groupings		
	Large—100-120 students.	*Intermediate*—25-30 students.	*Small*—5-8 students.
Works of representative Puritan writers.	*Procedure:* Lecture. *Topics:* Background of period, issues, biographical sketches of representative authors. (See Chapter 11.)	*Procedure:* Teacher-led discussion. *Emphasis:* Exploration—points of view and philosophies expressed in various selections. (See Chapter 8.)	*Procedure:* Pupil-led discussion. *Emphasis:* Evaluative thinking. Example: Are "Nature" and "Freedom of the Will" typical of Puritan ideas and attitudes mentioned in the opening lecture? *Patterns:* 1. Establish or obtain criteria for approaching question. 2. Discover facts and judge item on each criterion. 3. Draw conclusions from evidence presented. 4. Be prepared to share essence of conclusions with class members when intermediate section reconvenes. (See Chapter 8.)

LITERATURE COMES TO LIFE.
(Courtesy of Shoreline Public Schools, suburban Seattle.)

II.B.2.b. Approaching the study of poetry through teacher-led discussion.

Many teachers successfully employ some variant of teacher-led discussion in the study of poetry. Frequently, however, such approaches are allowed to become highly structured, with the result that the literary object becomes nothing more than an object, whereas it should be permitted to come to life, to represent living experience. We wish pupils to enjoy good literature; we want them to make books their friends, to continue to broaden their reading throughout life.

II.B.2.b.1. The following is one method[17] of employing teacher-led and subsequent panel discussions in the study of poetry. Through adroit and provocative questioning in a permissive atmosphere, the teacher is able to avoid the dead-ends which often paralyze such discussions and to guide the pupils toward the full measure of a poem.

---

[17] Described by Ellen McComb Smith, successful classroom teacher and Chairman of the Department of English, Roosevelt High School, Seattle.

With the appreciation of literature as the general goal, the teacher leads his pupils toward comprehension of particular poems which they have discovered, toward greater skill in communicating the joy of discovery, and toward an openness of thinking and expression regarding poetry in general and specific poems in particular.

The teacher may initiate the unit with a brief informal discussion on "the world of poetry," encouraging students to express their ideas about poetry: reasons for enjoying or rejecting or being indifferent toward it. In all events he should take stock of his pupils' poetic knowledge and attitudes. He might invite them to join in a voyage of discovery—discovering the message, the beauty, and the art of poetry. He could suggest that it may be fruitful for groups of students to work together in cooperative ventures of discovery. The teacher should be prepared to suggest a number of topics or poets suitable for group study: Such topics as Modern Man in Conflict, War, Death, Humor, Nature, Love, and the Search for Values are illustrative. Representative poets may be selected for study on bases of style, period, country. The

SMALL GROUPS ENHANCE CREATIVE THINKING.
(*Courtesy of Shoreline Public Schools.*)

teacher and class may prefer to approach the group project with a common theme, such as Love. On the day appointed a particular group will present its findings to the class, with one member of the group offering an appropriate introduction; each member will then read his selection and offer extemporaneously what he has discovered in the poem: what his study of the poem and the poet has added to his understanding of literature and particularly his appreciation of poetry or this poem. Copies of the students' written preparation, together with the group plan of presentation, are handed to the teacher prior to the actual oral presentation. Other teachers may prefer to employ a more typical panel study of a topic or a given poem, with all members participating in discovering and communicating an interpretation and analysis of the work for the benefit of the remainder of the class. In either case, before students are expected to carry out such a project, the teacher should lead them toward a method of analysis and preparation by taking the class through an actual "study" of a poem. The following poem by Stephen Spender is particularly appropriate.

I THINK CONTINUALLY OF THOSE WHO WERE TRULY GREAT

I think continually of those who were truly great.
Who, from the womb, remembered the soul's history
Through corridors of light where the hours are suns,
Endless and singing. Whose lovely ambition
Was that their lips, still touched with fire,
Should tell of the Spirit, clothed from head to foot in song.
And who hoarded from the Spring branches
The desires falling across their bodies like blossoms.

What is precious is never to forget
The essential delight of the blood drawn from ageless springs
Breaking through rocks in worlds before our earth.
Never to deny its pleasure in the morning simple light
Nor its grave evening demand for love.
Never to allow gradually the traffic to smother
With noise and fog and the flowering of the Spirit.

Near the snow, near the sun, in the highest fields,
See how these names are fêted by the waving grass
And by the streamers of white cloud
And whispers of wind in the listening sky.

The names of those who in their lives fought for life,
Who wore at their hearts the fire's centre.
Born of the sun they travelled a short while towards the sun,
And left the vivid air signed with their honour.[18]

Stephen Spender

It is suggested that the teacher read the poem aloud to the entire class. Following the reading, there may be a moment when no word is spoken. When the spell is broken, the teacher should ask for reactions: general at first; then more specific. Did you like it? Why? (Suggest tentativeness here.) What mood did it create in you? Then inquire as to the overall meaning: clues from specific lines, from the title, from major words of emphasis. Help pupils to draw analogies to other poems or writings which they may have read. If possible, draw all students into the discussion by adapting questions to the level of each pupil's competence.

Observe that this poem may be an excellent opening for a unit on biography or nonfiction. With this in mind, it would be appropriate to ask pupils to search for a single line which could serve as a thesis: ask whether there are reminders about other ages, the truly great who have lived. Ask also whether there are allusions to the little people, the unsung heroes who "know what life is all about."

Back to the study of the poem itself, to illustrate our point on questioning: Ask what the poem has to say about modern life. (Example: "Never to allow gradually the traffic to smother/With noise and fog the flowering of the spirit.") Ask about the reference to time or timelessness of eternity. (Example: "Soul's history," "in worlds before our earth," "hours are suns endless and singing.") In addition to the meaning, call attention to the techniques which the poet uses to accomplish his purposes. (Example: Note intensity of images: snow, ageless springs, light, sun, fire, air, sky.) Observe references to nature and elemental, simple living things. (Examples: "hoarded from the Spring branches/The desires falling across their bodies like blossoms." "Breaking through rocks in worlds before our earth." "in

---

[18] Reprinted by permission of Random House, Inc., from *Selected Poems* by Stephen Spender, copyright 1934 and renewed 1962 by Stephen Spender.

the morning simple light") Note lines which show celebration of life and joy. (Examples: "essential delight of the blood" "their lips, still touched with fire,/Should tell of the Spirit clothed from head to foot in song.")

As the students warm to the challenge of a lyrical, beautiful poem, many more ideas are likely to appear than the teacher has planned. If this doesn't happen, possibly the pupils are not as involved as they should be. With this class-wide preliminary study of a poem, students are then urged to move into their individual and group studies of other poems. With this type of poem as a standard, students are not likely to choose such works as "Trees" and "Little Boy Blue" for study and presentation.

In essence, we have suggested that through skillful planning and questioning, without coercion or intimidation, the teacher lays the groundwork for students' thoughtful approach to the reading of poetry, and then guides his class toward a fuller realization of the meanings and beauty of verse through oral reading, teacher-led discussion, and finally, small group discussions in the form of symposia or panels.

II.B.2.b.2. In a similar fashion, Loban, and others,[19] suggests the use of teacher-led or simultaneous small-group discussion in a "comparative approach" to teaching *values*. For example, discussion may center around the comparable and contrasting approaches to the parallel themes of *courage* and *personal sacrifice* in such works as *Giants in the Earth* and *A Furrow Deep and True;* or it may involve a comparison of the poetic treatments of a given subject, such as a portrait of Lincoln, as presented by Whitman, Markham, and Lindsey.

II.B.2.c. Communicating mood as an aid to understanding a poem.

Select a poem rich in imagery and illustrative of mood or a series of related or contrasting moods. See, for example such poems as "Silence" by Edgar Lee Masters, "Grass" by Sandburg; Shakespeare's "Fortune and Men's Eyes" and "The Negro Speaks of Rivers" by Langston Hughes.

Design a simple "semantic differential" along the following lines.

---

[19] Loban, and others, *op. cit.*, pp. 612–13.

*Place a check at a point on the continuum of each pair of descriptive terms
which most accurately describes feelings induced by the poem:*

elevated_____	_____	_____	_____dejected
enlightened _____	_____	_____	_____confused
repelled _____	_____	_____	_____attracted
sad _____	_____	_____	_____happy
interested _____	_____	_____	_____indifferent
pleased _____	_____	_____	_____displeased
bored _____	_____	_____	_____stimulated

etc.

Have pupils read the selection silently. Then ask them to indicate
their responses to the selection on the differential chart. Now, read the
selection to the class or have an able student read it aloud. Have class
members enter their responses on a second differential chart. Ask pupils
to compare their two charts; have groups of pupils compare their
responses. Discuss "findings." Finally, disclose on chalkboard or with
use of overhead projector or handout, a copy of your own "differential"
prepared as part of your study of the selection, and which presumably
suggests how you as a communicator felt about the material. Discuss,
emphasizing factors which may have helped or hindered in
communicating the intended feeling or mood.

II.B.2.d. Adapting the short talk to the book report.

The oral book report, while widely used, often proves to be something less than interesting, if not self-defeating. When treated routinely
or primarily as a check on students' reading, the oral book report
seldom contributes to good habits of communication or to the pupils'
interest in reading.

Wolfe[20] offers an engaging idea for the first book report of the
year. He suggests beginning the assignment with some such opener
as the following:

> Boys and girls, we have an official book list, and we
> are going to have book reports. But I have not read all
> the books on this list; I can hear reports intelligently only

---

[20] Wolfe, *op. cit.*, p. 301.

on those books that I have read. For our first report, then, I ask you to choose from among the books I have listed in the mimeographed sheet I just passed around. The first book report may sound peculiar to you. I do not ask you to read the whole book or even a certain number of pages. What I do ask is that you read until you come across a *scene,* a dramatic situation which you think would make this class eager to read the book. Then I should like you to tell the story of that one scene to the class.

The idea is to make that one scene very real by building it up with word pictures—sights, sounds, movements, and colors.

Professor Wolfe then recommends that the teacher present an example of such an oral report, confining the presentation to two minutes, a limit he imposes upon pupil reports.

This type of "book report" is challenging, concise, manageable. By concentrating on a single incident the speaker is more likely to engage his listeners' interest. By making the assignment short and oral, the class can acquaint themselves with several books in one series of reports. And by confirming the report to a dramatic situation, the experience can be engaging to the audience and satisfying to the teller. For many pupils, such experiences are the means of engendering a sincere and abiding interest in books and reading.

SUMMARY

The present chapter has suggested some of the special challenges of teaching English; it has pointed out the interdependence of English as a subject and speech as process. The chapter identifies the duality of "speech in English classes": i.e., speech as an *object* of instruction and learning and speech as a *means* of instruction and learning. It has offered a number of practicable suggestions for implementing both functions. These applications, while empirically sound, are far from exhaustive in scope. At best they are intended to provide the touch-stones with which the creative teacher may kindle his own imaginative resources to meet the needs of his individual classes in his particular school.

SELECTED READINGS

Bryant, Donald C. "Critical Responsibilities of the Speech-English Program." *The Speech Teacher,* X (November, 1961), 276–82.

The English Language Arts in the Secondary School. Commission on the English Curriculum, NCTE. New York : Appleton-Century-Crofts, 1956. Chapter 7 "Developing Competence in Speaking."

Guth, Hans. *English Today and Tomorrow.* Englewood Cliffs, N.J.: Prentice-Hall, Inc., 1964.

Grommon, Alfred H., ed. *The Education of Teachers of English.* Commission of the English Curriculum of the NCTE. New York: Appleton-Century-Crofts, 1963. Chapter 5 "The Academic Preparation of the Teacher of English for the Secondary School."

Hook, J. N. *The Teaching of High School English,* 2nd ed. New York : The Ronald Press Company, 1959.

Loban, Walter, Margaret Ryan, and James R. Squire. *Teaching Language and Literature.* New York: Harcourt, Brace & World, Inc., 1961.

13 *social studies*

Two major considerations make the teaching of social studies a matter of special interest and relevance to the purposes of this textbook. The first of these is the growth of problem-inquiry method of teaching and learning; the second, closely related to the first, is the functional combining of content and method in the processes of instruction.

Of course, it would be inaccurate and unfair to assert that only since Sputnik have social studies and social science teachers been concerned with the nature and solution of problems of human relations instead of facts, dates, places, people, events: knowledge *about* history, economics, geography, and government. Long before the so-called nuclear age, teachers of social studies asserted that knowledge of the record of man's efforts to solve his problems and of the sciences which treat with these efforts should greatly assist one in behaving in more personally satisfying and socially productive ways.[1]

Describing "the pulse of the sixties," in the *Thirty Third Yearbook* of the National Association of Social Studies, Carpenter[2] notes four significant characteristics of the times: (1) the *population explosion* with its attendant circumstance of rapid social change; (2) the *knowl-*

---

[1] See, for example: Fremont P. Wirth, "Objectives for Social Studies," *Eighth Yearbook* (National Council for the Social Studies, 1937).

Note also the following themes and points of view regarding the teaching of social studies as expressed in representative NCSS Yearbooks prior to 1945: *Education Against Propaganda* (1937); *Education for Democratic Living* (1938); *Citizens for a New World* (1943); *Adapting Instructions in the Social Studies to Individual Differences* (1944); *Teaching Critical Thinking in the Social Studies* (1942).

[2] Helen M. Carpenter, ed., *Skill Development in Social Studies: Thirty-Third Yearbook of the National Council of Social Studies* (Washington D.C., 1963), Chapter 1.

edge explosion—the probable doubling of our total knowledge with each succeeding decade of the century; (3) *fear*—the anxieties stemming from the uncertainties of a quarter century of cold war; and (4) the *confusion of values,* including the religious, the social, and the effect of cross currents that challenge the democratic tradition.

Teachers of social studies today must cope with these problems realistically, objectively, and effectively. The aforementioned *Yearbook* declares "the supreme challenge of the social studies teacher to be that of discovering how the functioning of the democratic citizenry can be reconciled with the realities of government and society today."[3] Leaders in the field of social studies are convinced this view calls for a more direct, functional, experimental approach to the teaching of such subjects than has commonly been the case in previous decades—in short, a "new social studies."

And while this *new social studies* subscribes to the traditional objectives of the field, its methods for reaching these objectives are new—at least their emphasis is said to be new. Massialas and Cox inform us that:

> Social studies today incorporates more concepts and data from the social sciences and fewer from history; it attempts to introduce interdisciplinary methods for the study of society; it stresses the analytical rather than the descriptive; and it shows concern for the problems of the individual as well as society. The curriculum is organized to emphasize the principles that explain human interaction and institutional development. And there is a growing trust in the student's ability to order his own learning.[4]

From the standpoint of procedure, the *method of inquiry,* they insist, is "the only appropriate and productive approach to social studies teaching." Today's social studies, then, have become more concerned with learning by experiencing, through intellectual, social, and physical involvement in tasks dealing with the fundamental problems of human relations.

We find, therefore, that today's teaching of social studies, which owes much to the thinking of John Dewey, is largely problem-

---

[3] *Ibid.,* p. 13.

[4] Byron G. Massialas and C. Benjamin Cox, *Inquiry in Social Studies* (New York: McGraw-Hill Book Company, 1966), *Preface.*

centered—inquiry- and discovery-motivated. Such emphasis has brought the development of certain fundamental skills into strategic focus. For example, as suggested by Jarolimek, instruction in social studies must give attention to skills that not only deal with these subjects as a field of study, but with human relations. He lists (1) work-study skills, (2) thinking skills, (3) group process skills, and (4) social living skills. Observing that all tend to be intellectual rather than motor in nature, Jarolimek asserts that "these skills are the tools which the learner employs in his pursuit of conceptional learning in the social studies."[5]

The implications of this emphasis on skills are especially relevant for oral communication, particularly problem-solving, exploratory, and evaluative applications of *discussion* as well as other forms of speaking which encourage youth to engage in meaningful and personalized experience with the problems of human relations. This chapter, therefore, attempts to provide the secondary social studies teacher with a rationale and some helpful guidelines for selecting and using speech activities strategically and effectively as channels and techniques of learning. In so doing it notes the reciprocal relations of social studies and oral communication; calls attention to some of the special instructional challenges which the teacher of social studies frequently encounters; and finally, offers a number of examples illustrating the use and guidance of speech activities as media of learning in the social studies classroom.

RECIPROCAL RELATIONS OF ORAL COMMUNICATION AND SOCIAL STUDIES

It is not at all surprising that the processes of oral communication figure prominently in the teaching of social studies. Deemed fundamental to effective living in a democracy, effective speaking and listening are viewed quite properly as worthy objectives and methods of learning in the social studies program. In fact, in this view of social studies, as suggested earlier, the fundamental methods and content are fused into a unified whole. Both speech education and social studies are concerned with human relations and the forces which facilitate or

---

[5] John Jarolimek, *Social Studies in Elementary Education*, 3rd. ed. (New York: The Macmillan Company, 1967), p. 32.

hamper social integration. Both are dedicated to preparing pupils "to act with cooperation and mutual consent in a more peaceful, prospering world." Since effective communication is one of the desired skill objectives of social studies, no serious objection can be raised to the time expended in teaching or reviewing the speech fundamentals essential to productive speech work in the social studies classroom. As suggested in Chapter Eight, this reciprocal relationship is particularly significant and meaningful when viewed operationally in problem solving group discussion. As observed earlier, "discussion is democracy in action": In the classroom it can become a tentative proving ground for many of the tenets of democratic society. Such experiences, hopefully, can minimize some of the apathy or resistence many pupils feel toward social studies, frequently associated with conventional teacher-centered classroom procedures. While speaking-listening activities are indeed prime instruments of learning and instruction in social studies classrooms, it is also evident that the social studies can contribute much to the speech education program of secondary education. This they do by offering an appropriate setting, an intellectual and social climate, and problem topics for the application of speech learning begun in basic speech classes.

Constructively viewed and creatively managed, the integration of speech and social studies proves to be a most productive union, particularly so as a means of coping with some of the persistent instructional challenges of social studies.

CHALLENGES OF TEACHING SOCIAL STUDIES

Motivation

It is a commonplace that teachers are constantly seeking methods and procedures for stimulating pupils toward self-initiation and enjoyment of learning. Social studies teachers are no exception. Indeed such teachers are aware that the study of history, for example, because of its temporal and geographic remoteness frequently holds little or no interest or meaning for many students. Of necessity, social studies must make considerable use of vicarious learning. For most pupils it is only by extending their imagination that they can sense something of the excitement and the hazards of life in colonial America, gain some impression of the customs and culture of Finland, the horrors of war in Vietnam, the functioning of Congress; or develop a meaningful concept of the abstraction: *Gross National Product.*

While it is necessary to engage the imagination in much of the study of history, as well as other social studies, modern methods of teaching can bridge some of these limitations by simulating reality through such methods as pictorial or other graphic devices, role-playing, various speech projects, and excursions to relevant centers of interest. Speech activities rightly selected and guided can do much to make vicarious experience come alive and thus generate conditions essential to effective learning.

Conceptualization

Closely akin to motivation is the challenge of *conceptualization* and the forming of *generalizations*—the essences of cognition and the ordering of knowledge. So important is the matter of concept-building that some authorities hold that "one of the most productive ways to develop the substantive content of social studies is to organize it around concepts and generalizations."[6]

Employed with sensitivity to the abstraction process, speech can become a highly useful means of developing accurate and vivid concepts; carelessly or glibly used, speech activities may result in little more than static—mere verbalism without meaningful referents.

Application and utilization

Still another challenge is helping pupils to incorporate the knowledge of social studies into personal behavior and to apply their learning to make the world more intelligible and one's place in it more meaningful. As noted in Chapter Six, we believe speech activities have much to offer in meeting the challenges of *application.*

---

[6] Massialas and Cox, *op. cit.,* p. 45.

See also S. P. McCutchen, "A Guide to Content in the Social Studies," *Social Educator,* XX (May, 1956), 211-14, for a statement of major goals of society as suggested by the Committee on Concepts and Values of the NCSS.

Retention

The problem of fostering effective retention of learning has always been a particular concern of teachers, including, of course, those in charge of social studies. Research[7] has shown that after a year's lapse, high school pupils are likely to retain about twenty-five per cent of what they had known at the end of the semester in which it was taught. We also know that the mode of initial learning, its thoroughness and frequency of renewal and reinforcement largely determine the extent of retention. It is significant that such studies find that attitudes, methods of problem-solving, skills—intellectual as well as motor—are among the most permanent outcomes of education. It would seem to follow that association of basic information of a subject field with skill-learning can be expected to promote general retention of social studies learning.

Guiding speech-listening activities

While admitting the educational value of speech-listening activities in the classroom, many social studies teachers are reluctant to attempt such procedures as discussion, dramatization, or student reports. Yet, in this area of instruction, as in the others, good communication of clearly shaped ideas is the *sine qua non* of learning. One cannot be said to have learned anything until he can handle it symbolically, until he can make it known to others. This textbook is based upon that simple premise.

* * *

We have reviewed some of the characteristics of what has been described as "the new social studies"; particularly significant is the shift in methodological emphasis from information-giving, memory-testing, teacher-centered procedures to inquiry-oriented, problem-solving student-centered activities. This emphasis relies heavily upon oral communication for its implementation. Indeed it has greatly expanded the opportunities for the use of speaking and listening as media of learning and has perforce made them legitimate objects of instruction in the social studies. In this connection, we have noted the

---

[7] See, for example, "Retention and Forgetting" in current works on educational psychology.

reciprocal relations of social studies and speech education with their common objective: *the study and improvement of human relations.* Finally, we have called attention to several pedagogical problems which challenge the creative resources of many social studies teachers, including motivation, conceptualization, application, and retention, as well as guiding classroom speech activities.

Viewed semantically, our discussion thus far in the present chapter has been largely *about* the teaching of social studies and *about* the role of oral communication in them. Although the observations and generalizations here advanced are soundly based on theory and classroom observation, their practical significance and meaning must be rediscovered and realized by each individual classroom teacher through personal experience with relevant teaching procedures. The following section, therefore, seeks to make this possible by suggesting some representative experiential strategies for using and guiding speech in a variety of social studies contexts. Perhaps their most useful function will be providing social studies teachers with springboards from which to launch their own more interesting and creative teaching procedures.

A SPECIAL REPORT BRINGS HUMAN INTEREST
INFORMATION.
(*Courtesy of Shoreline Public Schools.*)

A PANEL DISCUSSION CAN STIMULATE LEARNING.
(Courtesy of Seattle Public Schools.)

ILLUSTRATIVE STRATEGIES FOR USING SPEECH
IN THE TEACHING OF SOCIAL STUDIES

I. Seeing Speech-Listening Activities as Integral to a Unit in United States History. Unit—The Emergence of an Egalitarian Society (1829-1850),[8] c—3 weeks.

   A. *Contents:*

Concepts.	*Unit Description.*
1. The differences between egalitarian and status societies.	1. Cultural Growth (c—4 days). a. The impact of the frontier on the American society.

---

[8] Subject matter for this Unit has been adapted from *United States History Curriculum Guide,* and is reprinted by permission of Seattle Public Schools, Seattle, Washington.

Concepts.	*Unit Description.*
2. The consequences of accepting the egalitarian creed.	b. Religious readjustments. c. Reform and reformers. d. The nativist movement. e. Romanticism and transcendentalism in literature.

2. Jacksonianism.
   a. The growth of the "common man" concept.
   b. Economic philosophy and its effects.
   c. The reemergence of the two-party system.
   d. Historical interpretations.

3. Indian Policies to the Civil War.
   a. The Indian seen as a barbarian.
   b. The Indian seen as "the noble redman."
   c. Red Americans' views of the white Americans.
   d. U.S. governmental policies, colonial to the Civil War.

4. Manifest Destiny.
   a. How expansionists justify their ideas.
   b. Opposition to expansion.
   c. Results of expansion.

Unit Description.

1.) The annexation of Texas.
2.) War with Mexico.
3.) Acquisition of California.

d. Historical interpretations.

B. *Illustrative Questions for Study of Part I,* **Cultural Growth** *(abridged):*

1. Did the American utopian communities of the nineteenth century resemble at all the examples of world communism today? Why did they fail? Do their failures relate to the modern scene? Why, or why not?

2. Did various groups of whites differ in Southern society? How might this affect a possible civil war of the future?

3. Was early nineteenth-century America basically idealistic or materialistic? What indications are there?

4. Is it to the interest or disadvantage of the rich to educate the poor?

5. What relationship did the cotton gin, the sewing machine, and the McCormick reaper have to the Civil War?

6. If the Northern and Southern economies were dependent upon one another, why did the sections grow apart?

7. Did transcendentalism conflict or coincide with American values and concepts? Is there any movement today similar to transcendentalism?

8. What traits of the frontier still exist in the American character? What traits have disappeared? What has been the impact of the changes?

9. The South accused the North of hypocrisy regarding slavery. What was the basis of the criticism? Was it justified? Does this relate in any way to modern society?

10. If you had lived in the early nineteenth century, with your present economic and social background, which of the reform movements would you likely have joined? Which would you have resisted? Give reasons.

C. *Illustrative Speech Procedures Applied to Selected Questions Relating to **Cultural Growth:***

1. *Teacher-led discussion:* Portrait of Early Nineteenth-Century America (first day). Introduction: "A recent best-seller is Steinbeck's *America and Americans* in which the author paints a most interesting portrait of present-day America with its paradoxes of beauty and ugliness, its idealism and its crass materialism." (Read a few well-chosen passages.) Then proceed with such questions as:

    a. What key features of *America and Americans* do you think Steinbeck would choose to relate if he should write of America of the early nineteenth century?
    b. Where did those Americans live?
    c. How were they employed?
    d. Who were the Americans? Where did they come from?
    e. What significance did national origin have?
    f. What were their motivations? Were they primarily idealistic? Evidence. Materialistic? Evidence.
    g. Were they much different from Americans today? Elaborate.

    From this discussion suggest those who are interested may wish to play John Steinbeck for a day by sketching a verbal portrait of Americans : Early Nineteenth Century. (Give extra credit.)

2. *Lecture:* (Selected) Reform Movements of the Period (second day). Identify the *movements; compare goals, techniques, achievements,* and *effects.* Relate to spirit of Jacksonian age. *Stress listening: Main points and concepts.*

3. *Simultaneous Group Discussions* (third day). (Assigned at least one day in advance.)

    Procedure: Pose six or seven questions and have class settle on four. Assign class members to groups, if possible on basis of pupil preference. Appoint leaders. Supply each group with minimal guide questions. Notify groups that approximately fifteen minutes before period closing time, a spokesman from each group will be expected to report the major conclusions of his group. Assign area locations for each group. They begin their project.

Possible issues, together with suggested guide questions:

a. If the Northern and Southern economies were dependent upon one another, why did the sections grow apart?

(Primarily
fact-oriented)

    1. What were the natures of the two economies?
    2. In what ways were they interdependent?
    3. What led to the sections growing apart?
    4. What conclusions can be drawn from these events?

b. Was the South justified in accusing the North of hypocrisy regarding slavery?

(Analytical)

    1. What was the basis of this criticism?
    2. How justifiable was the accusation?
    3. Do you see any parallels in present day white America's views of American Negroes?
    4. What factors have helped and are helping to shape white Americans' views of American Negroes?

c. Can society hold inventors accountable for their inventions?

(Value judgment)

    1. What relation, if any, did the cotton gin, the sewing machine, and the reaper have with starting the Civil War? Determining its conclusion?
    2. To what extent should inventors accept moral responsibility for their inventions?

d. You have had some introduction to the philosophy of transcendentalism in your study of American literature.

(Relating history
and literature)

    1. What were its origins? Its major tenets?
    2. In what ways was its influence felt? With what success? How related to general American values of early nineteenth century?
    3. Who were some of its most influential exponents? How did they express their views?
    4. Does the movement have any present-day counterparts? Explain.

4. *Symposium:* Catching the Spirit of the Times (fourth day). (Assigned at least three days in advance.)

Plan a symposium with the following figures represented :
   a. A leading orator of the times.
   b. A novelist.
   c. A poet.
   d. A journalist.
   e. An historian.

Allot each speaker five minutes in which he may "speak for" his historical counterpart, by quoting from a speech, reading from a novel, a poem, an editorial or feature article, or historial account.

The object : to view the times as did those who lived them or those who have carefully researched the period.

*   *   *

While the foregoing activities are suggested as a sequence covering four days, the teacher may wish to select only one or two procedures or extend any combination of them over a longer period.

II. Capturing the Sense of Strategic Events Remote in Time and Place Through the Media of Sight and Sound.[9]

   A. At appropriate junctures in the course present selections from *You Are There* series.
   B. Play selected passages from *I Can Hear It Now*.
   C. Play taped speeches, interviews, broadcasts of debates, special events.

Objectives: Illumination of history. Training in effective observing and listening.

In all cases, there should be a preliminary briefing to help prepare pupils for the experience; e.g., cover the background, principal figures, issues at stake. Each special feature should be followed by appropriate discussion of information gained and possible inferences to be drawn from the experience.

III. Viewing Speech (oratory) in the Service of Man and Country.

At appropriate points in the study of any given unit arrange to have interested pupils do research on present excerpts from, dramatizations of, or reports on great speeches on important issues. Stress the role speech has played in shaping the history of a people. While many important speeches are available on tape or disc recordings, those of

---

[9] Consult local and state repositories of appropriate tapes and films.

another era will have to be studied in their written forms. The analysis questions given in Chapter Eleven should be used in helping pupils to prepare their material for interpreting speeches or making reports on speeches. Simulated debates may be arranged. The following list suggests something of the scope of possible speech resources.

VITAL ISSUES AND REPRESENTATIVE SPEAKERS

Issues	*Speakers*
1. Federalism and State Sovereignty.	Calhoun, Hamilton, Jefferson, Webster.
2. Manifest Destiny and Imperialism.	Calhoun, Polk, Albert Beveridge, Bryan, T. Roosevelt, Carl Schurz.
3. Slavery.	Wendell Phillips, William L. Garrison, Robert Toombs, Robert B. Rhett, William Yancey, Lincoln, Douglas.
4. Agrarian Problems.	Ben Tillman, Jerry Simpson, Mary Elizabeth Lease, Ignatius Donnelly, William J. Bryan.
5. Labor and Growth of Labor Unions.	Wendell Phillips, Eugene V. Debs, William Green, J. L. Lewis, Walter Reuther.
6. Trusts, Combines, and the Public Interest.	Woodrow Wilson, T. Roosevelt.
7. Right of Dissent and the American Ideal.	Robert Ingersoll, Oliver W. Holmes, Jr., Norman Thomas.
8. America in the Role of World Leader.	Herbert Hoover, William H. Taft, Vandenburg, Burton K. Wheeler, Wendell Willkie, F. D. Roosevelt, J. F. Kennedy.
9. Social Reforms: Woman Suffrage, Health, Fair Employment Desegregation, etc.	F. D. Roosevelt, J. F. Kennedy, Susan B. Anthony, Martin Luther King.
10. The United Nations: Credits and Debits.	H. C. Lodge, Jr., Adlai Stevenson, Mrs. Eleanor Roosevelt, U Thant, Harry Truman.

Anthologies of famous speeches:

Harding, S. B. *Selected Orations Illustrating American History.* New York: The Macmillan Company, 1909.

Johnston, Alexander. *American Orations.* 4 vols. New York: G. P. Putnam's Sons, 1896–97.

Parrish, W. M., and Marie Hockmuth. *American Speeches.* New York: Longmans, Green & Co. Ltd., 1954.

Wrage, E. M., and B. Baskerville. *Contemporary Forum* (1962) and *American Forum* (1960). New York: Harper & Row, Publishers.

Capp, Glenn. *Famous Speeches in American History.* Indianapolis: The Bobbs-Merrill Co. Inc., 1963.

For the current scene, see *Vital Speeches of the Day, Congressional Record,* etc.

IV. Using Speech-Listening Activities to Experience the Legislative Process: *Parliamentary Procedure.*

For many people, certainly for most high school pupils, the functions of government are, at best, remote and obscure; at worst, painfully boring. Yet few would deny the importance of government in human affairs. One's well-being, whether economic, social, or personal, is intimately related to the affairs of government, local, state, and national. If government is to continue in the service of the people, the people must understand its ways and play an active, constructive role in its operation.

Many social studies teachers have found that a simulated legislative body is an effective method of teaching the functions and responsibilities of government. Schools offering only one class in U.S. Government may adopt a unicameral congress; those with two or more may designate one as a senate, the other as a house of representatives.

Lay a foundation for the project through lecture, class discussion, directed reading, and, if at all possible, a visit to the State Legislature when it is in session. A lecture by a local Congressman or viewing a film, such as "How a Law is Passed" may add much to pupil understanding. With this background, students should then be helped to organize the class into a legislative body and to formulate and adopt the necessary rules (Constitution, or By-laws) to govern their procedure. The following suggestions may prove useful in formulating such rules:[10]

---

[10] These suggestions have been adapted from materials developed and used with notable success by Elmon Ousley, Bellevue Public Schools, State of Washington. They are reproduced here with his permission.

A. Members should represent various states or regions.
B. Elected officials should include a President, a Clerk, a Sergeant-at Arms, and a Timekeeper. These officers should be rotated during the session to permit the widest possible sharing of experience.
C. The session of the congress shall be that time allotted to the unit on the Legislative Branch of Government (2-3 weeks).
D. Each class meeting will constitute a meeting of congress.
E. Organization of the congress should provide for basic standing committees : e.g., Rules and Credentials, Ways and Means, Agriculture, Education, Labor, Public Welfare, Armed Services. All members of the congress will serve on one of these committees. In some instances, it may be preferable to dispense with individual committees and assign each bill to "Committee of the Whole" for study.
F. Each member or combination of two members of congress shall prepare and introduce a bill (legislative proposal) in proper form, which will be filed with and numbered by the Clerk.
G. Since the classroom congress is fundamentally a laboratory learning experience, the need for rules of operation is obvious, but the opportunity for exercise of critical thinking and development of sound judgment should be guaranteed: Pupils can be helped to recognize the wisdom of taking no action that is contrary to the rules of a higher body (the school). This limitation need not abrogate their freedom to make suggestions to higher authorities.
H. It is advisable to formulate and administer an oath. The following is suggested : "I do affirm that I will execute faithfully the duties as a member of the —— Congress, and I will do all in my power to promote the best interests of this organization."
I. Parliamentary Authority. The rules governing the legislature of the state in which the school is located may apply. Otherwise, use Robert's *Rules of Order,* Revised.
J. To initiate class organization, motions should be made to establish a student congress and to appoint a Constitution Committee.
K. The following Agenda is recommended for the opening meeting :
    1. Call to order.
    2. Roll call of the Congress Membership.
    3. Oath to the membership.

4. Adoption of the Constitution and/or By-laws.
5. Election of officers.
6. Message from the Chief Executive (teacher).
7. Disposition of business presented in the message of the Chief Executive.
8. Appointment of Standing Committees.
9. Call for new legislation to be placed in the Secretary-Clerk's hopper.
10. Special Order.
11. Announcements.
12. Adjournment.

L. All subsequent meetings may be guided by the following Agenda :
1. Call to order.
2. Roll call of the Congress Membership.
3. Oath to the new members.
4. Message from the Chief Executive.
5. Disposition of business presented in the message of the Chief Executive.
6. Call for new legislation to be placed in the Secretary-Clerk's hopper.
7. First reading and reference of bills and resolutions.
8. Special Order.
9. Consideration of the calendar.
10. Announcements.
11. Adjournment.

M. Legislative procedure: *Introducing Legislation.*

A Congressman wishing to introduce a bill or resolution shall place it in the Secretary-Clerk's hopper and that officer will have the legislation numbered and printed (duplicated).

Prior to the reading of the proposed legislation, copies of the bill or resolution will be supplied to each member of the Congress.

Under the regular meeting agenda "First reading and reference of bills and resolutions," the author of the proposal shall be recognized by the presiding officer and will be given the floor to read the proposed legislation to the membership. The President will then assign the proposal to the appropriate standing Committee or the "Committee of the Whole" for study.

The legislation will be considered in regular order of its number in agenda item number nine (9) "Consideration of the Calendar."

Any bill or resolution may be considered under agenda item number eight (8) "Special Order" if approved by a 2/3 vote of the Congress.

N. Legislative procedure: *Considering Legislation.*

When legislation is presented under agenda item number nine (9), "Consideration of the Calendar," it shall be read by the author, or if he is absent the President may request the Secretary-Clerk to read the proposal. After the second reading it should be moved that the legislation be adopted.

If the proposed legislation receives a second, the author shall be given the first opportunity to discuss the proposal. At the conclusion of the supporting arguments of the author or in any case at (the designated time) the legislation is open to further discussion and amendment from the floor.

No member may speak more than (the designated time) on any one bill or amendment and may not speak more than once on a motion before the house until all other members who have not spoken have had a chance to speak. The author of the proposal may have extended time approved by a majority of the members voting.

O. Legislative Procedure: *Voting on Legislation.*

Decisions on all bills and resolutions, and all amendments to bills and resolutions shall be determined by a vote of the members of the Congress. The President will determine the method of voting.

P. Evaluation:

One class period should be set aside at the conclusion of the session to evaluate the experience. A test may be given; however, some teachers believe that the legislative experience constitutes a sufficient test and indication of student comprehension of the process.

V. Using Speech-Listening Activities to Teach the Judicial Process in Government: *Simulated Court Trial.*[11]

After reading about and discussing the fundamentals of the judicial system, students should have the opportunity to observe the legal process in an actual courtroom. Provided thus with essential background information, they will find it especially rewarding to plan and hold their own court of law. The following suggestions are offered as guides for visiting courts of law and staging simulated trials.

[11] The authors are indebted to John R. Miles, history teacher, Snohomish High School, State of Washington, for suggestions on Simulated Court Procedure.

A. Visiting a Court of Law.
   1. Make arrangements with the Court Clerk to receive copies of the court calendar.
   2. Select a case which appears to hold promise of good learning experience and seems likely to be completed in one day. A lawsuit is generally preferable.
   3. Make all arrangements for the visit.
   4. Brief the class on general procedures to be followed and what especially to look for.
   5. If possible, observe a one-day case and depart immediately after the case is sent to the jury or before the judge renders his verdict.
   6. On following day, divide class into three juries, each to discuss the case and present its verdict. Compare reports with actual verdict reached in the courtroom.
   7. Discuss the day's observations.

B. Staging a Simulated Trial.
   1. Select a case, preferably one based on fact. The following instance based on an actual 1947 Wisconsin case is a good example :

   A motorist was driving on a country road. A farm extended along both sides of the roadway, and the owner of the farm had opened the gates on each side to allow a herd of cattle to cross over to the barn.

   Either because his mind was on other things or because he was going too fast, the motorist struck one of the cows and knocked it cold. He asked a man standing beside the road to go up to the farmhouse and summon the cow's owner. The innocent bystander went on his errand and then returned to the scene of the accident.

   Just at that moment the cow came to and decided to get out of there in a hurry. In her rush, she bowled over, trampled and severely injured the innocent bystander. He promptly sued the motorist for his injuries.[12]

   (Actual decision in foregoing case : The motorist had to pay for the bystander's injuries. It was the court's view that, since the motorist had been found negligent, he could be held responsible for injuries or damages that resulted from his negligence in a natural sequence. It was natural, in the opinion of the court, for the cow to

---

[12] From *You Be the Judge,* Ashley Halsy, Jr.,ed. (New York: A. S. Barnes & Co., Inc., 1952).

decamp in a hurry when she regained her senses, and the motorist could be held responsible for the wreckage she might leave in the path of her flight.)

2. Select principals and members of the staff, including a judge, a clerk, a bailiff, a jury, four attorneys : two for the plaintiff and two for the defendant.
3. Allow two days for each side to prepare its case.
4. Allow one (not more than two) class periods for presentation of cases and cross examinations.
5. Devote one class period to jury deliberation and verdict, followed by general discussion and evaluation of the project.

VI. Gaining Knowledge of a Social Science Procedure : *Informal Dramatization.*

As suggested earlier, one of the conditions which make the teaching of social studies a matter of special interest and relevance to this textbook is the functional combining of content and method in the process of instruction. In the following activity we have a good example of how pupils may gain knowledge of a social science procedure while becoming better informed on a social issue.

Classes in contemporary problems offer excellent opportunities for carrying out community opinion surveys on important issues of the day. To help pupils prepare for these home calls, have groups play scenes involving a team of interviewers and a husband and wife as interviewees. Instruct interviewees to respond in ways they think appropriate for such a situation. Have interviewers experiment with different modes of introducing, conducting, and concluding the interview. Have entire class participate in a discussion of the dramatizations. Summarize key points to be remembered in carrying out the survey. Following the field interviews, evaluate the dramatized scenes in terms of their usefulness in preparing students for the field work.

VII. Promoting Clear Thinking in Dealing with Social Problems : *Defining Terms in Discussion.*

Essential to both the aims of social studies and the requirements of effective communication is clear thinking. We have already alluded to several channels through which this ability may be cultivated, problem-solving discussion among others. Integral to thinking and communication is one's use of symbols. One important determinant of successful communication is the degree to which participants agree upon the meaning of fundamental terms incident to the discussion. The following dialogue, drawn from Massialas and Cox, illustrates one group's effort to arrive at a meaning of the word *environment* as it was used to relate to early colonial settlements in America.

Teacher: I think you have a problem on your hands here. Who sees a logical way out of it? Now, as I interpret it, Clara Sue was attempting to say that environment is a very broad concept. The people along with the climate, the land, the minerals, the buildings, and the production of the people become the environment. And if you have a brother and sister, these people are part of this environment.

Clara: Isn't that true?

Teacher: Now, that is certainly one kind of definition. But over on this side, George says that environment, as he has been thinking about it, is principally climate and land.

George: I did not say it was principally climate and land. I said that I do not think that that would affect that type of environment where you would have just the physical environment. What she was talking about would not affect the physical environment.

Teacher: Well, that could be. I would not argue with that. What are you thinking of, Clara? What happens within this family to change the environment?

Clara: I do not know. Anything could happen, I guess.

Teacher: What?

Clara: Anything could happen. But I thought environment was everything about you. But, I was not thinking of physical environment. I do not know.

Teacher: Let us determine some kind of meaning here. I do not think we are going to have any luck at all in this enterprise until we do.

Steve: Well, I want to go back to the colonists.

Teacher: All right.

Steve: I think it definitely meant a change in physical environment, meaning a change in the land and climate and possibly also the people in the colony and other things like this. I think it is the second thing.

> *Teacher:* The second thing being what?
> *Steve:* Things other than just the land, the climate, the people—ideas, and all this.
> *Teacher:* Here is a new dimension. The ideas which the society holds comprise a part of the environment.[13]

VIII. Additional Ideas for Employing Speech-Listening Activities as Media of Learning in the Social Studies.

   A. History.
      1. "States' Rights"—A simulated constitutional convention.
      2. Statesmen—Moving picture : "Abe Lincoln in Illinois."
   B. Contemporary Problems and World Affairs.
      1. Issues of the day—Planned radio listening or TV viewing.
      2. Social techniques—Lecture on methodologies of the social scientist—Guest Sociologist.
      3. Nations as Neighbors—Model U.N.
   C. Economics—Consumer Games.
   D. Government.
      1. "Lobbying in the Legislative Process"—Informal Dramatization.
      2. "Meet Your Congressman"—Your Congressman addresses the class or student body, or he holds a "press conference" for students.
   E. Personal Development Class—developing one's sense of value (integrity, responsibility, self-image) through role-playing or a case study method.

SUMMARY

In the beginning sections of this chapter we called particular attention to some of the important developments in today's teaching of social studies, including the emphasis upon inquiry-oriented, problem-solving, student-centered activities, with their substantial dependence upon oral communication as a principal instrument of learning. We noted some of the pedagogical challenges in teaching the social studies, such as problems of motivation, conceptualization, application, and retention.

---

[13] Massialas and Cox, *op. cit.,* pp. 130-31.

In the second half of the chapter we have presented some representative experiential strategies for using and guiding speech in the teaching of social studies. All the given examples are tested procedures and when properly used have been found to be effective means of achieving the purposes of social studies, chief among which is the study and improvement of human relations. Rightly used, the methods have demonstrated their usefulness in improving pupil motivation and in helping the learner to form meaningful self and social concepts. Properly selected and applied, the activities foster pupil involvement and help to create an atmosphere of reality in the classroom. In so doing, the experiences can be expected to secure meaningful application and retention of learning.

The illustrations included here are meant to be only suggestive. They do not begin to encompass the host of possibilities for using speech activities as instruments of learning. The creative teacher may wish to consider them largely as points of departure from which he may develop his own more specifically prescriptive activities.

SELECTED READINGS

Fenton, Edwin. *The New Social Studies*. New York: Holt, Rinehart & Winston, Inc., 1966. See especially Chapter 7 (John Dewey, "Reflective Thinking," and Jerome Bruner, "The Act of Discovery"), as well as several subsequent chapters devoted to applying the methods of inquiry and discovery to teaching social studies.

High, James. *Teaching Secondary School Social Studies*. New York: John Wiley & Sons, Inc., 1962.

Jarolimek, John. *Social Studies in Elementary Education,* 3rd ed. New York: The Macmillan Company, 1967.

Massialas, Byron G., and C. Benjamin Cox. *Inquiry in Social Studies*. New York: McGraw-Hill Book Company, 1966.

Wesley, Edgar B., and Stanley P. Wronski. *Teaching Social Studies in High Schools*. Boston: D. C. Heath & Company, 1964.

14 *mathematics and science*

The most tenuous relationship would appear to exist between oral communication and mathematics and the sciences. With the possible exception of the fine arts, no other areas appear to be more independent of oral communication. And yet, as is often the case, these very disciplines rely upon oral communication more than the others. While the physical activity involved in both the sciences and the fine arts would seem to be clear, precise and devoid of misunderstanding, the processes involved in arriving at the final products are shared and understood only through oral discourse. The technical steps necessary for the solution of a complex mathematical problem, while they can be listed and explained in writing, are best understood as a consequence of open discussion. Mathematician George Polya believes that "typical problems, which indicate a useful pattern, are solved in class discussion led by the instructor." It is this discussion which ". . . leads to recognizing and formulating the pattern involved."[1] Polya goes on to emphasize the importance of class discussions in learning mathematics either in the form of small buzz groups or a careful "Socratic dialogue" led by a capable and sensitive instructor.[2]

The same question of relationship arises at the suggestion that biology, chemistry, or physiology can be learned more easily and

---

[1] G. Polya, *Mathematical Discovery*, 2 Vols. (New York: John Wiley & Sons, Inc., 1965) p. 210.

[2] *Ibid.*, pp. 106–107; 211.

more effectively through the use of oral communication. What, in fact, are the common objectives of oral communication and the sciences?

Most obvious is the prime objective of every discipline taught in today's schools: *to aid in the fuller development of a civil and functioning human being.* A knowledge of the basic concepts which constitute the more regular and precise dimensions of his environment will help the individual to relate effectively. But this knowledge must first be acquired before it is tested and applied. To date, the most immediate, personal, and valuable method of doing these things is oral communication. It renders the information intelligible because it draws upon the experience and training of another *human being* whose flexibility and adaptability can be exercised in the oral process whenever a problem of understanding occurs.

Less obvious, but related to the prime objective shared by sciences and oral communication, is that of sharpening the *integrative* abilities of the individual. Students soon learn that things exist without their own personal perception of them and that this is true in both the microworld and the macrouniverse. But it does appear to take time for them to learn that the *relationships* among these things do *not* exist except by virtue of their articulation of those relationships in the form of prose, poetry, or arithmetical formulas. Both areas, in other words, foster the development of the student's observation-centered reasoning which Dewey identified as the true foundation of education.[3]

Finally, both oral communication and the sciences move toward the end of producing an individual who is more sensitive as he is more orderly in the use of the images drawn from his newly acquired sensitivities. Each area depends upon adequate analysis but moves toward synthesis and action. For mathematician Polya, good pedagogy in mathematics should recognize that: "... mathematical thinking is not purely 'formal'; it is not concerned only with axioms, definitions . . . , but many other things belong to it; generalizing from observed cases, inductive arguments, arguments from analogy. . . ."[4] And, as a beginning point, the mathematician should restrict himself to a limited "region of search"[5] much in the same way the good communicator limits himself to a specific commonplace or locus for his arguments. It is precisely this process which is at the heart of

---

[3] Charles Brauner, *American Educational Theory* (Englewood Cliffs, N.J.: Prentice-Hall, Inc., 1964), pp. 200, 222–23.

[4] Polya, *op. cit.,* pp. 100–101.

[5] Karl Duncker, "On Problem Solving," *Psychological Monographs,* LVIII (1945), 75.

Alfred North Whitehead's redefinition of Hegel's dialectic method which he feels to be applicable to good education. Instead of Hegel's thesis, antithesis, and synthesis, Whitehead suggests, in his well-known article, *The Rhythm of Education*,[6] that the stages ought to be called Romance, Prescision, and Generalization. In the Romantic stage, according to Whitehead, the individual is searching, toying, becoming acquainted and being sustained by the novelty of first exposure. During this time symbolic exploration is the rule and systematic procedures should not intrude themselves; nomenclature and basic identity prevail and, most often, in the form of internal or external "talking it out." The Precision stage is characterized by "exactness of formulation" and systematic procedures of exploration tend to be more than *ad hoc* occurrences. At this point, the individual student applies his more systematic and precise approach to the relationships he has uncovered in the nature, and to the scope and direction of his communication; he is involved with the grammar of language as he is with the grammar of science. The final stage of Generalization, or synthesis, is "a return to romanticism with the added advantage of classified ideas and relevant technique." The disciplines of mathematics, sciences, and speech share in the common responsibility of helping the individual student to master each of these important stages in the experience of learning.

SPECIAL PROBLEMS

In mathematics, as in the sciences, the problems of insuring purposeful *activity, motivation,* and *sequence* remain among the most perplexing to the experienced as to the inexperienced teacher. Polya reaffirms the role of the Socratic dialogue in the teaching of mathematics and goes on to note that, should time pressures restrict the employment of this form of teaching, only that form which lets the *student discover for himself as much as feasible* should be subsituted.[7] Active participation in *all phases* of the learning process is a difficult goal for the teachers of mathematics and science to achieve with any degree of

---

[6] Alfred North Whitehead, *The Aims of Education and Other Essays* (New York: The Free Press, 1967), pp. 17–19.

[7] Polya, II, *op. cit.*, pp. 104–107.

regularity. While the students are, obviously, always engaged in the solution of problems in these areas, it is seldom that they are afforded the opportunity (or challenge) to share in the responsibility of *formulating* the problems. Moreover, most problems assigned the students are solved in virtual isolation. It is a rare class that permits and provides for a joint experience in progressing through the various stages of analysis. Exercises suggested in most high school texts on mathematics and sciences are largely individual rather than group, and focus more upon competitive rather than cooperative activity in the solutions desired. While there is a need for providing ample opportunity for private solutions, the common problem of bringing reality to the systems of symbolization demanded by the nature of the exercises in these more specialized fields seems to argue for the help of "group communion"; personal confusions, misunderstandings, and doubts are very often dissipated through the very act of public confession. At the very least, a youngster confused by abstract symbols and complex relationships will think less harshly of himself and his ability if he hears similar confusions in the minds of his colleagues.

Motivational problems confronted by teachers of the sciences and mathematics tend to differ enough from those facing their colleagues in other disciplines so as to make them appear special. In truth, the teacher in any of these areas must remain "a salesman"—in the better sense of the word; he most certainly must be able to persuade as he informs. Teachers of mathematics and most of the sciences inevitably face an attitudinal block which appears to be almost absent from the parade of difficulties encountered by their fellow teachers in most other disciplines. As recommended by a famous teacher of mathematics,

> It is your duty as a teacher, as a salesman of knowledge, to convince the student that mathematics *is* interesting, that the point just under discussion is interesting, that the problem he is supposed to do deserves his effort.
>
> Therefore, the teacher should pay attention to the choice, the formulation, and a suitable presentation of the problem he proposes. . . . If we wish to stimulate the student to a genuine effort, we must give him some reason to suspect that his task deserves his effort.
>
> The best motivation is the student's interest in his task. . . . Before the students do a problem let them *guess the result,* or a part of the result. The boy who expresses an opinion commits himself; his prestige and self-esteem

depend a little on the outcome, he is impatient to know whether his guess will turn out right or not, and so he will be actively interested in his task and in the work of the class—he will not fall asleep or misbehave.

In fact, in the work of the scientist, the guess almost always precedes the proof. Thus, in letting your students guess the result, you not only motivate them to work harder, but you teach them a desirable attitude of mind.[8]

Stressed in the foregoing suggestions was the role played by oral communication in securing, maintaining, and developing the interest of students who come to mathematics and science with indifference or, worse, definite opposition. By arranging for their oral participation (in the form of guesses, defenses, challenges, doubts), the concerned teacher can chart the hidden barriers to learning and can plan for their removal or neutralization.

Sequential experiences of instruction, irrespective of the field, are the ingredients which form the final internalized vision so indispensable to effective learning. Yet, "the trouble with the usual problem material of the high school textbooks is that they contain almost exclusively merely routine examples."[9] While these isolated and routine examples can be used in certain phases of the learning process, "they miss two important phases of learning : the exploratory phase and the phase of assimilation."[10] Unless exercises are constructed and presented with a certain sequence in mind, the learning experience of the individual student could very well suffer. While such a sequence can be worked into the written instructions accompanying the statement of the exercises, it would prove more effective if the students themselves were made to describe the relation of one problem to another. Such an oral commitment, as described earlier by Polya, would spur the motivation while providing the instructor with an "in progress" statement of the student's understanding. Occasionally, the sequential pattern could well be provided in the form of oral transitions by the teacher as the assignments are given. A few moments of description concerning the relation between problems and between individual problems *and between individual problems and the intended goal* is a very inexpensive price to pay for the eventual reward of learning. Such

---

[8] Polya, II, *Ibid.*, p. 105.

[9] Polya, II, *Ibid.*, p. 106.

[10] *Ibid.*

oral transitions act as timely and effective summaries for all students. but especially for those who may be bogged down by silent doubts and confusions.

RECIPROCAL RELATIONS

The contributions of mathematics and science to improvement in individual habits of oral communication seem quite apparent to most persons taking but a moment of reflection. The analytic approaches which characterize these areas form the very basis of effective oral interaction. As we have already contended, the effective speaker-listener is one who, constantly aware of the diverse elements of each oral interaction, works for a dynamic relationship among them. Such activity requires accurate observation, orderly dissection, valid inferences, and proper evaluation—all of which are habits already ingrained in the well-trained student of mathematics and science.

In similar fashion, oral communication contributes to the learning experiences of students involved with the concepts and appreciations of mathematics and science. As noted earlier, it has been argued by some teachers of mathematics that the discipline is learned most effectively when the *awareness* of the method (rather than the method itself) is the goal sought by both teacher and pupil. Just as an awareness of the method of writing will make one better able to avoid its weaknesses and capitalize on its strengths while one who can only employ the method is limited by his rote acquisition of certain movements, so one who has an awareness of a method in mathematics can do more than solve problems. His *sense* of methods enables him to understand each method and its strengths and weaknesses and, therefore, he is better able to apply the best one in any given situation. Under the name of the *New Math,* students have been encouraged to give public form to their private manipulation of symbols; they have been asked to make oral their silent understandings and doubts. This insistence upon oral description of a proposed plan or a *solution in the process of being shaped* helps the student as it aids the teacher; both can test the nature, scope, degree, and color of the plan or process as they determine the degree of the individual's commitment to that plan or process. While a student may retire to his desk to correct a miscalculation by silently repeating the process explained by the instructor, neither student nor instructor will actually *know* the degree of student misunderstanding. However, in the very act of explaining his understanding of the process involved in the solution of a given problem, the student and the instructor have available an instantaneous detector with which to define that understanding. Thus, in the speed, tone, direction, hesitations, use of qualifiers and imprecise words in his oral explanation, the student will reveal to himself and the teacher both the area and degree of confusion.

Reciprocally, effective oral communication aids the youngsters to understand some of the difficult aspects of mathematics and science. In the course of seeking a successful route to the solution of his problems, the student often verbalizes his proposals. To do so, he must employ the ordered pattern of his language; he must abide by the historical sequence of subject, predicate, and object if he is to make himself understood. Should he reveal regular and important inconsistencies in this order, he might well be indicating a confusion which goes beyond the solution to the mathematics problem he is working on. He might well be revealing a lack of sensitivity to *all* or *any* forms of order—linguistic, mathematical, physical, etc.

Inferential reasoning, whether in mathematics or science or philosophy, depends upon an *orderly* movement from certain isolates of information (fact, opinion, number) to newly formed patterns of knowledge. The validity or soundness of the new patterns is determined by the degree of precision in relating the isolates, and this is as true with words and numbers as it is with events, procedures, or movements. A student using *beside* to describe a relationship of one object resting *upon* another, is as deviant as one who notes that four persons can be served by three pieces of pie. The relationships of time, space, part-whole, cause-effect, effect-cause pertain as much to the "ordinary topics" of conversation as they do to the more specialized topics discussed in mathematics and the various sciences. Consistent weakness or the inability to portray these relationships properly in one area will hardly be absent in the other. Contradictions regularly revealed in the linguistic order will rarely disappear when that same person handles problems using mathematical order. No system of logic has yet managed to sustain a principle accepting the use of contradiction and the student properly educated to appreciate this weakness in one will find it easier to avoid this blunder in any other.[11]

---

[11] Anatol Rapoport, "Escape from Paradox," *Scientific American*, No. 217 (July, 1967), 50–56.

Finally, a sound appreciation of the relationships existing among oral symbols furnishes the student with a foundation upon which the teacher may build the similes, metaphors, and analogies needed to insure that student's understanding of numerical and scientific concepts. Just as two numbers out of a list of 100 cannot furnish the average of that list of 100, a teacher may point out, two individuals out of a class of 100 can hardly furnish a representative standard of behavior for the class. Just as we must begin our understanding of geometry, for example, with certain assumptions (axioms and postulates), so most human dialogue is founded in certain unstated but generally held "truths." And, conversely, just as misunderstandings in human communication *very* often occur as a result of different basic assumptions accepted by the communicants, so many conclusions in mathematics and science are erroneous because of faulty or unexamined assumptions. In mathematics as in communication, we must often return to the assumptions in order to clear up confusions and correct errors.

SUGGESTED STRATEGIES

Insofar as the previous discussion has demonstrated the interdependence of oral communication and the math-science portion of the curriculum, it would appear possible to detail a few exercises, methods, or forms designed to capitalize upon this reciprocal relationship.

Of all of the forms of oral communication, the *dialogue* (a modified discussion form) would seem to carry the most immediate benefits for effective instruction in the areas of mathematics and science. Some educators, in fact, hold that "... science itself is only arrested dialogue."[12]

In point of fact, the oral dialogue, as a tool of learning, carries the advantage mentioned earlier in that it furnishes an immediate measure of student understanding and conviction. The degree of this understanding and conviction is revealed by the speed, direction, tone, fluidity, number, and nature of qualifiers disclosed in the learner's responses. When this form is used to establish, develop, and relate

---

[12] Walter J. Ong, *The Barbarian Within* (New York: The Macmillan Company, 1962), p. 229.

conclusions, the assumptions and convictions used by the learner to undergird them are revealed quite clearly.

More than this, the process of systematically "talking about" an activity serves to add strength to the degree of understanding and to the process of recalling that same activity. This is especially true whenever the teacher insists that the individual students employ new oral patterns of explanation. The more ways the student uses to "talk about" a newly acquired activity, the greater the number of fine, intellectual hair-roots which push forth to surround and stabilize the images representing that activity.

From the standpoint of time alone, the dialogue—often cited as the key to the Socratic education—has proven its worth. A favorite device of educators, religionists, politicians, and general reformers, the dialogue (and its forerunner, dialectic) has been employed as a standard form by Plato, Cicero, Augustine, Wycliffe, More, Erasmus, Galileo, Berkeley, Hume, Milton, and others to good advantage. For each of these persons especially, the realization has been that this very ". . . work involves him in a constant interior dialogue with the past, the present, and the future."[13] Making it an exterior dialogue is a very easy and automatic next step for all sensitive and dedicated teachers, since it furnishes them with a tool whereby they can help others in the process of helping themselves. "The method," notes Richard McKeon, ". . . is adjusted to the character of the disputants no less than to the peculiarities of their subjects; and the solution of the problem, the clarification of the understanding, and the development of the argument are inseparable parts of one process."[14] Galileo's experiences led him to crystallize his appreciation of the dialogue form by commenting "you cannot teach a man anything; you can only help him to find it within himself."

But the dialogue, as a method of teaching, also holds the important benefit of *flexibility*. Free from rigid sequence or prior commitments, the properly employed dialogue allows a purposeful roaming among whatever subjects, moods, and time periods are defined as relevant by teacher or pupil. Since real dialogue amounts to "argument by analogy," the purposeful roaming enables a free and—more important —a *timely* use of similitudes, contrasts, and nuances of thought which

---

[13] *Ibid.*, p. 220.

[14] Richard McKeon, *Thought, Action and Passion* (Chicago: University of Chicago Press, 1954), p. 32.

prove to be especially suited to the time, place, and circumstance. Without benefit of the clash of dialogue within oneself or with another, the insight of vision identified as the end product of all learning experience is rarely realized. In the very form of the dialogue, in the act of "unfolding" the experiences which will lead to the personal vision of the learner, the spirit of the "truth" is revealed. Truth, whether political, religious, scientific, or social, is rarely thrust upon individuals and accepted by them. It must be revealed, in its own good time, as a part of the individual's very existence or it will be rejected. "Do not," advises Polya, "give away your whole secret at once—let the students guess before you tell it—let them find out by themselves as much as is feasible."[15] By the reciprocal contributions which it demands of its participants, the dialogue assures the cooperative quest which marks good learning. Ernst Cassirer observes that the true dialogue is "...a constant cooperation of the subjects in mutual interrogation and reply."[16] To the modern student who can find little immediate use for mathematics, for example, the teacher might well deliver short *talks* on the role of numbers in our every day living experiences. On the other hand, that same teacher might take the time to have the student draw it out for himself. For example:

> *Pupil:* I don't know why I have to learn all this stuff about numbers anyway. I'm not going to be a mathematician.
>
> *Teacher:* Is that the only person who has use for "numbers," John?
>
> *Pupil:* I don't know. I guess so.
>
> *Teacher:* Outside of this class, don't you ever use figures to help yourself in performing simple, everyday things?
>
> *Pupil:* I don't think so.
>
> *Teacher:* How long have you been studying about "numbers?"
>
> *Pupil:* Well, ever since grade school. It's about six years now.
>
> *Teacher:* And how many more years do you have in school?
>
> *Pupil:* Two, unless I go on to college.

---

15 Polya, II, *op. cit.*, p. 105.
16 Ernst Cassirer, *Essay on Man* (New Haven: Yale University Press, 1945), p. 5.

> *Teacher:* Well, you may not care to, of course. At your age . . . how old are you?
> *Pupil:* Seventeen.
> *Teacher:* . . . Yes, well . . . at your age other things take on more importance, but as you can see from our very short conversation, you had to rely on "just plain numbers" several times to answer my questions intelligently.

A similar dialogue might well be constructed to draw out the realization that science and superstition are incompatible, or to establish a wider appreciation and understanding of such a specialized topic as *vapor*. As a prelude to a study of the various elements by a low-level class of high school freshmen, something like the following might apply:

> *Teacher:* What was the result of my act just now?
> *Pupil:* When you boiled the water in the test-tube, steam came out of the bent tube which was sticking out of the cork blocking the mouth of the test tube.
> *Teacher:* What was left in the test tube?
> *Pupil:* Nothing but air.
> *Teacher:* What happened to the water?
> *Pupil:* It changed into steam and disappeared.
> *Teacher:* Are there any examples in your home of this thing happening?
> *Pupil:* When my mother boils water for cooking.
> *Teacher:* What makes the water boil?
> *Pupil:* Heat of the fire.
> *Teacher:* Does steam ever rise from the out-of-doors?
> *Pupil:* Yes, after a rain in the summertime from streets, fields, and sometimes from house tops.
> *Teacher:* Could vapor or steam exist in the air without our seeing it?
> *Pupil:* I don't know. I don't think so.
> *Teacher:* When your mother hangs wet clothes on the line and they dry, where does the water go?
> *Pupil:* Does it evaporate?
> *Teacher:* Perhaps. When you write with pen and ink and the ink soon dries, where does the water part of the mixture go?
> *Pupil:* Does it evaporate also?

> *Teacher:*   Yes, but you do not notice it evaporating. Sometimes we can see the moisture in the air and sometimes not, but a certain amount is always present. Thus, you can see fog, steam, breath on a cold day but you do not see the vapor when ink dries, perspiration dries, or when your breath is exhaled on warm days and so forth.

Also of value to the teacher in the sciences and mathematics is the *short* talk. As an assignment, it lends itself to any phase of the curriculum and at almost any point in the progress of the school year. At the outset, for example, the teacher in mathematics might well assign certain pupils the task of giving a three minute talk on:

1.   The relations between mathematics and language;
        (symbols, combinations, rules);
2.   The need to study mathematics at the high school level;
3.   The special contributions of certain important mathematicians;
4.   The explanation of certain propositions, theorems, etc.;
5.   The need for definitions in mathematics or science.

The science instructor could assign a short talk on such subjects as :

1.   Science and superstition must be enemies;
2.   Basic attitudes needed for scientific work;
3.   The need for order in the work of a scientist;
4.   Basic assumptions for science;
5.   Universal life functions.

As explained in Chapter Ten the short talk leads to independent study and demands the application of orderly habits of research, reflection, and expression. Moreover, properly employed, it introduces a very refreshing variety of class procedures. With more time available, the teacher might well make use of selected "student instructors" to offer variety and a special opportunity to certain individuals who demonstrate more than the average understanding of certain aspects of the subject. These students could be assigned limited topics three or four weeks before the date of presentation and, on that date, could actually "conduct the class" for fifteen minutes. Prior to the presentation, each student (seldom more than three or four) should be asked to report his progress to the teacher at various intervals. To keep the value of variety and to allow for enough time in which to "repair" the student efforts, the teacher should avoid scheduling more than one per period; two per week for two weeks should be considered maximum.

For small classes, honor groups, or advanced students, teachers in both areas could use a sequence of talks—by one or several speakers over a period of time—to provide an "in depth" study. For example, the following related topics could be presented over the span of a quarter or semester :

Individual	*Country—City*	*Contribution*
Two-Three minute talk including: birth, education, physical characteristics, occupation, death, etc.	*Two-Three* minute talk including: location, topography, economy, education, politics, etc., *at the time* of the life of the person noted in column 1.	*Three-Four* minute talk including the *major* contribution made by the person selected in Column 1 as related to the course; relevant details of the theory or program should be a part of the talk.
1. Aristotle	Athens, Greece 4th century B.C.	Classification System
2. Galileo Galilei	Florence, Italy 16th-17th century.	Falling Bodies
3. Euclid	Athens, Greece 4th century B.C.	Elementary Geometry
4. Albert Einstein	United States 20th century.	General Relativity
5. Leonardo Da Vinci	Florence, Italy 15th-16th century.	Human Anatomy

Obviously, short talks can be extended in time or redirected in focus. Longer talks, by students or teacher, permit more detailed examination of the topic involved. Such detail is most frequently provided by selected audio-visual material which lends itself to the special requirements of the subject areas. Charts, blackboards, and flannelboards easily serve the speaker involved in topics drawn from mathematics and science. But less familiar aids serve as well and, in some cases, even better. In mathematics as well as science, three-dimensional models are being used to increase understanding and strengthen retention. Students find it easier to conceptualize mathematical relationships, physical structures, and functional systems which are set before them in model form. Even more effective is the assignment which provides for student construction of such models.

In addition, the "prosections and dissections" common to the biological sciences actually help create the demonstration talks used in other subjects. In the broadest sense, for example, one can provide a "prosection" for a talk in mathematics by constructing a chart ("strip-tease," multi-section, flannelboard parts, etc.) which can be revealed step-by-step for maximum audience attention. This "prosection" (preconstructed analysis by one person for use by all) has the advantages of time, controlled attention, and guided development which its counterpart, the "dissection" does not. "Dissection" (on-the-spot analysis usually done by one or more persons) usually takes the form of an on-the-spot solution to a problem scribbled on blackboards or flip-charts in the presence of an audience. Instances of this sort do not provide for undivided attention, are wasteful of time

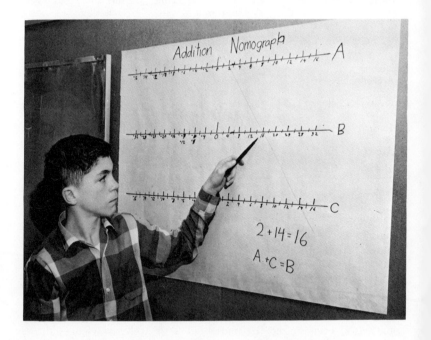

A PUPIL EXPLAINS A PRINCIPLE IN A MATHEMATICS
CLASS.
(*Courtesy of Shoreline Public Schools.*)

and, except for certain instances, do not lend themselves to a systematic progression of thought.

As noted previously, regardless of the time limit or the nature of the short talk, each student must have the benefit of a fair and honest criticism if his effort is to be worthwhile.

A more sophisticated version of the short talk which also promises to add variety to classroom procedures and experiences is the "modified symposium." Either as an oral examination, an introduction to the subject, or a concluding experience, this form carries all of the advantages of the short talk, some of the dialogue and a few of its own. Four or five students (rarely any more) should be selected to constitute a "panel" of speakers during part of each of ten periods—one period a week for ten weeks. In impromptu fashion (much in the spirit of the College Bowl), the students are asked to respond to a series of statements, questions, or problems. As a "team" the students can compare their efforts against those of succeeding teams; as individuals they can share in the responsibility of handling each item set out for response. The student efforts should be gauged individually as well as collectively immediately following the exercise. Individual criticisms should probably be given in written form while the more general comments about the actions of the team can be given orally so the other members of the class might profit.

If, for example, the class were involved in understanding the need for *definition* in mathematics or science, the following might illustrate a possibility for the panel:

1. What key words must be defined to bring meaning to each of the following statements :
   a. He is a qualified voter in a local election.
   b. He belongs to the United States of America.
   c. We have a place by the shore.
   d. Children are admitted without charge.
   e. Graduation from this university requires 180 units of credit.
   f. Only members of the White race are admitted here.
   g. John Jones is free at last.

2. Which word must be defined *first* in each of the following pairs?
   a. Car or Ford?
   b. Tool or shovel?
   c. Preposition or *before*?

   d. Novel or book?
   e. Primate or man?
   f. Touchdown or football?

On the other hand, if the matter of *assumptions* were under study in either of the disciplines mentioned earlier, these examples might hint at a possible approach:

1. What are the basic assumptions supporting each of the following :
   a. Since John is a good athlete, he will be popular.
   b. A soldier ran out of money and wrote home to his parents for more.
   c. Homer is quite old; he has gray hair.
   d. Fat Carol likes apple pie, so I'm going to avoid eating it.
   e. Brand X cigarettes must be best since they outsell all others.
   f. He's got to succeed, he is a graduate of Harvard.
   g. Candidate Boyd will make the finest president; he's the best looking.
   h. Dope addiction is not bad, the dope addicts say it is not.
   i. Professor Frisbee is a bad prof because my friend failed his course.
   j. Peter will have a successful life, he is a doctor.
   k. Elizabeth must know what she is talking about, she is a college graduate.

SUMMARY

No educational discipline is a separate and autonomous process unrelated to the act of oral communication and to the society of which it is a part. This is true of the study of mathematics as it is of physics, chemistry, biology, and the other sciences. Always at the point of acquiring, testing, and applying information and concepts in each of these fields, the individual student returns to make use of the process which lies at the root of his humanness—speech. If, as learner or teacher, the individual makes greater and more effective use of the various forms of oral communication, he improves the chances of creating a meaningful learning experience. Only oral communication, effectively utilized, can teach and test by immediate application; only oral communication can make private confusions public as it makes public concepts private awarenesses.

SELECTED READINGS

Beveridge, W. I. B. *The Art of Scientific Investigation.* New York: Random House, Inc., 1960.

Gordon, W. J. J. *Synetics.* New York: Harper & Row, Publishers, 1961.

McDonald, D. C., and Martin, R. B. "Word Association Training and Creativity." *Psychological Reports,* XX (1967), 319–22.

Ogilvy, G. S. "Higher Mathematics at Lower Levels." *The Key Reporter,* XXV (Winter, 1959–60), 2–3, 7.

Polya, G. *Mathematical Discovery.* New York: John Wiley & Sons, Inc., 1965. Volumes I, II.

Raths, L. E., and others. *Teaching for Thinking: Theory and Applications.* Columbus: Charles E. Merrill Books, Inc., 1967.

Shepard, G. "Language Is the Key to Science Learning." *The Instructor,* LXXVII (January, 1967), 675.

Walkup, L. E. "Creativity in Science Through Visualization." *Journal of Creative Behavior,* I (July, 1967), 283–90.

15 *the fine and applied arts*

At the beginning of human history man's sensitivities, insights, and judgments depended upon nothing more but the spoken word for their creation and perpetuation. Myths, legends, and folktales were the vehicles, and universal experiences the stuff of social education designed to perpetuate a sense of right and wrong, of the true and the erroneous. Soon visual representations were conceived to record the multi-dimensional experiences important to the group, tribe, race, or society and, heretofore, portrayed through speech. The literary culture developed first as a shadow of the preliterary era, then as a competitor, and finally as an innovator. In each phase, in each area, the developing culture depended upon oral communication, reflected it or used it as a tool in its continuing metamorphosis. The qualities taught by effective oral communication were those used and portrayed by the visual arts—order, balance, tone, harmony, rhythm, and unity.

From the earliest times, the fine and applied arts have been an integral part of the education of the liberal man, as have been the communicative arts. In ancient Greece, one was not considered a man until he was proficient in speech, music, and gymnastics. In the *Republic* Plato considered true melody to be composed of words, melodic intervals, and rhythm; but harmony and rhythm must follow the words. Greek dramatists in 400 B.C. were poets as well as composers and relied heavily on the *chorus* which united the symbolisms of dancing, tone, and word through the common rhythms.

Through the ages, the concern of *prosody* has been the unification of the arts of music and speech. The various meters and rhythms of speech help to inculcate an *appreciation,* at least, of the pleasant and effective aspects of *all* harmonious movement in sound, line, color, feeling, and thought. Counterpoint in music is antithesis in speech; meiosis or understatement in speech is the *chiaroscuro* (light and shade) of painting; the juxtaposition of certain colors which result in a new color has its similar result in the *oxymoron* used in communication;[1] parallel development of major structures in architecture finds its counterpart in the parallel construction of major points in a communication designed for strength and impact; the normal bodily action accompanying speech is mirrored and exaggerated in the pantomime of drama; the relationships developed among the discrete units of a mosaic are like those composed for the words of an operative sentence.

RECIPROCAL RELATIONS

Orderly movement of parts toward a complete and harmonious whole is a related concern of music, drama, home economics, industrial arts, speech, painting, architecture, and sculpture. Balance (proportion and detail), rhythm, lights, and shadows appreciated in one of the arts will, if not transferred directly, increase the likelihood of appreciation and understanding in the others. Very often the reflections of major moods and concepts of an era can be traced in the contemporaneous efforts of the divers artists of that period. William Fleming, introducing his work entitled *Art and Ideas,* makes the point in this fashion:

> Whether the artist be reformer or conformer, revolutionist or evolutionist, prophet of things to come or nostalgic dreamer of past golden ages, his contemporary society and its ideas is his point of departure. Techniques by which artists—whether architect, sculptor, painter, writer, or musician—produce their works will always differ radically. However, the end result of their labors, springing as it does from the same social source and in turn addressed to it,

---

[1] A figure of speech which juxtaposes two contradictory words whose meanings combine to produce a new third meaning: arrogant humility, cruel-kindness, luxurious poverty, illiterate literacy.

must have a certain unity. When these aesthetic phenomena are viewed as an interrelated whole, it begins to be possible to speak of a *style,* which might be defined as a synthesis of the outgrowth of man's changing ideas *as expressed in the symbolic language of the arts and consisting of certain features shared by them all.*[2]

Any listing of common goals or objectives shared by these arts must include the conception and expression of certain of the "shadow" aspects of life for their perpetuation. Giving body and shape to *relationships* is as much the concern of the speaker who creates conclusions and moods with words, as it is of the painter who does so with line, form, and color; or the home economist who does it with organic ingredients; while the media vary from artist to artist, the need for an harmonious and balanced use of these ingredients does not. Each individual functions to record feelings, to give structure, refinement, and direction to his inner life through one or the other of the arts.

Moreover, all arts share in the common objective of producing an object, movement, or event which reflects an *aesthetic judgment.* The score, speech, painting, dance, or structure which is judged effective must demonstrate some orderly arrangement of its parts and reflect some feeling, tone, or mood. To reach his goal, whatever his field, the educated individual learns to draw from the related and complementary arts to feel what he knows and to know what he feels. Intuition, insight, reflection, and knowledge are the common parts of the purposeful behavior peculiar to each art. Developed by work in one or the other of these areas, these factors become viable parts of any of the other areas to which the individual turns his attention and they contribute to the development of a critical sense of beauty. The individual possessing these attributes is equally at home with visual symbols, tones, physical constructs, or shapes since he realizes the importance of a subjective balance of body and spirit, of action and intellect.

To this discussion of reciprocity between oral communication and the arts must be added the kindred spirit of *creativity.* As a musical composer creates a unique composition by using commonly shared notes, so a communicator employs conventional words and actions to create a unique message. Lewis E. Walkup, writing in the *Journal of*

---

[2] *Art and Ideas* (Syracuse, 1955), p. x (Italics ours).

Creative Behavior, maintains that "creative behavior appears to depend on the degree to which images can be manipulated and . . . the degree to which one can sense the properties of the newly created results."[3] Whether to science or the arts, a *spirit* of creativity is brought by an individual carefully educated to the true nature of oral communication and sufficiently practiced in its efficient use. But just as everyone who speaks or writes does not become an Adlai Stevenson or a T. S. Eliot, so everyone who paints is not a Michelangelo or a Frederic Remington. Nevertheless, for having shared some of the joys and traumas of creativity, the nonmasters can console themselves with a sense or spirit of creation which enhances their understanding and appreciation of the miracles wrought in other fields as well. There is born a sensitivity for the *whole*—whether it be a sentence or speech, a painting or a dance. And, more than this, there is born a sense of *empathy*.

Empathy is largely the product of the kinesthetic sense; it stems from the same sense which enables the average person to know where and how his limbs are placed without looking at them. As a consequence of this ability, man has an unusual facility for imitation; he is easily drawn into mimicking the behavior (and feelings) he sees in others. Yawning, giggling, crying, laughing in response to the same action in others is the simplest example of empathic activity. In more sophisticated instances, the overt action being witnessed may be abbreviated as it is imitated (stifling a yawn by keeping the lips tightly closed, etc.), but the accompanying emotion will not. In either instance, the human observer tends to become a direct part of the activity or mood he witnesses if enough elements of the activity or mood are recognized by him. Thus, the degree of empathic response is generally greater when people witness a dying scene in a dramatic production than when they see that same scene portrayed in an oil painting. More communion is experienced by one listening to Edward Kennedy eulogizing his assassinated brother, Robert, than by listening to an operatic rendition of Othello; more in being an ear-witness to a neighborhood quarrel than in listening to a Senate debate. But regardless of the variance in degree of experience, empathy developed and refined through training in drama or painting or sculpture reflects itself in the ordinary experiences of everyday communication and vice versa. Empathy, that bodily state which permits

---

[3] "Creativity in Science Through Visualization," I (July, 1967), 283–90.

the individual to be momentarily oblivious to all but the thing he contemplates, is the true common denominator of the arts. Today, as in the time of Socrates, the indispensability of the mind-body combination is obvious in the act of producing a speech, dance, painting, sculpture, building, or musical score. The strength of the arts rests in their ability to reduce the number of persons for whom an artistic act is received as the product of either the mind or the body.

SPECIAL PROBLEMS

In the fine and applied arts, most teachers experience some special problems with motivation, conceptualization, application, and retention. While these may not be problems peculiar to teachers in these areas, they do have certain thorny ramifications which are different enough to demand a few moments of extra attention.

Motivation usually derives from the magnetism created when an individual's needs are placed in the vicinity of an attainable satisfaction. A student is motivated to do better work when he perceives that the improved work insures his continued participation on the football team; and that very participation satisfies his need for excitement, competition, physical contact, reward, etc. Yet this realization, the actual perception of the bond between the need and the possible satisfaction must often be drawn to the attention of a person by another. As noted in Chapter One, the image of one's environment is actually more important than the environment itself since this image can be reworked much more easily than its physical counterpart. A good teacher provides or helps the student provide for himself new images; he is instrumental in helping the student to see relationships between needs and satisfaction. The popular notion of *interest* is actually rooted in this bond between need and satisfaction. It is that bond which answers such questions as "Why should I study music?" "What can I get from learning about poetry?" "What is there of value in the study of painting?"

One step in providing a recognition of the bond between need and satisfaction (of providing answers to the question of interest), is a review of the importance of oral communication to the life of each student. Once they have refreshed their appreciation of *its* value, similarities and analogies can be drawn with each of the arts being studied. If, for example, because of its symbolization, oral communication is recognized as of utmost importance in freeing the individual from the weight or confusion or infection of his innermost thoughts and feelings, then music can be shown to do something of the same thing. The following poem can be made to apply to either:

PLEAS

Stir my nerves
With rhythms pure
Which harmony propounds.

Work my mind
Profound and bright
With color, depth and mounds.

Clean my soul
With gentle tongue
In scratchless verbs and nouns.

Build my love
In moments new
When tenderness abounds.

Give me life
By careful thoughts
Put into special sounds.

Dominic A. LaRusso

Other similarities can be drawn to the commonly shared materials, approaches, forms, and outcomes. But it must be done *with* the students. While part of it can be done via lecture, the major portion of the realization should derive from student conclusions—even if guided, directed, and encouraged by teacher action. Unless the heat and energy of participation are used, the inner flames of motivation will seldom be ignited.

This is also true in the area of conceptualization. Here, the efforts expended to motivate the students might well die. Unless fed with the fuel of new and exciting visions, the flame kindled by the heat of original participation will be snuffed out. Having once convinced himself that there *is* some worth to the study of the arts, the student expects to be rewarded with regular bits of tangible evidence. If, instead, he continually runs into abstractions which cannot be crystallized, concepts which he finds difficult to visualize, his adolescent motivation will be sapped. While it is inconceivable to expect to provide each abstraction of feeling, thought, or mood with a sensory counterpart, it is reasonable to assume that the teacher will help the student form an atmosphere which will help rather than hinder the development of an "inner vision." This atmosphere is best realized through the use of oral similes, metaphors, and analogies. For instance, composition, or the end result of perfect balance between proportion and detail, can be understood much more easily in painting when it is made analogous to that in a play, a building, a speech, or a dialogue. In each case, successful composition depends upon the force of some dominant factor (character, idea, figure, color, or theme) supported and defined by carefully related minor factors. Christ in Da Vinci's *Last Supper, Macbeth,* the dome of St. Peter's cathedral in the Vatican City, the idea of dedication in John Kennedy's inaugural speech all are made dominant by the interplay of minor but contributing figures, characters, structures, or ideas. There must be harmony of relation between the parts and a unity which defines the whole toward one clear purpose. Still another instance of difficulty is the principle of chiaroscuro (light and shadow) applied to painting. For some reason, young people have difficulty in accepting the absoluteness of the proportional relationship between light and shade. Many times, this principle can be made more meaningful by comparison with the same need revealed in communication. Any speech—formal or informal—composed only of assertion or propositions is considered by most listeners as too harsh to be acceptable. Without the occasional but necessary opinion, testimony or example, without the "softening" influence of the supporting material, the *whole* of the composition is not made apparent and the persuasive force is dissipated. Paintings composed only of highlights show themselves as flat, harsh, unidimensional creations much like those of the early Egyptians. On the other hand, a communication which has supporting material, such as humor, which stands out more than the assertion or main proposition is as poorly composed as a portrait with nose, chin, forehead, and lips as bright as the sides of the face or the neck. Thus, whatever the artistic endeavor, a proper blending of highlights and shadows is indispensable to a meaningful and effective whole.

Another special problem area usually encountered by teachers of the fine and applied arts is in student application and retention of the principles and appreciations most recently acquired. In point of fact, application and retention are part of the final process in learning; application affects retention as retention determines the success of application. Regardless of which half of the problem is being considered, the truth of the observations in Chapter One holds: in proportion as the individual is involved in the discovery and acquisition of the experience to be learned, they will be retained and applied effectively. This thought is affirmed by Dr. Bernard Z. Friedlander of the Mental Development Center, Western Reserve University. Writing in the *Harvard Educational Review* he declares:

> . . . Teaching by means of discoveries involves the student as an active participant in his own instruction. He cannot be a discoverer and at the same time be a passive observer. Because of his own participation in developing what is revealed or resolved in the discovery process we expect that the student will retain his new knowledge more completely than he would retain a system of facts and ideas imposed upon him from the outside.[4]

And the most efficient method of securing student involvement, as discussed earlier, is the symbolic exploration, organization, and evaluation made possible by oral communication. "The narrative of teaching," writes Jerome S. Bruner, "is of the order of the conversation. The next move in the development of competence is the internalization of the narrative and its 'rules of generation' so that the child is now capable of running off the narrative on his own."[5] Through dialogue, short talks, student discussions, and the like, students can help construct the cognitive processes which will make the material to be learned more durable and easily retrieved for application.

---

[4] "Concepts, Curiosity, and Discovery," XXXV (Winter, 1965), 18–38.
[5] "Act of Discovery," *Harvard Educational Review*, XXXI (Winter, 1961), 21–32.

SUGGESTED STRATEGIES FOR TEACHING THE FINE
AND APPLIED ARTS

The principle of involvment in learning is as applicable to the teacher as it is to the pupils being taught. The following material suggests ways in which the foregoing discussion can be implemented. But to make it meaningful, the teacher ought to "talk them through" with others and to talk about them with the students.

Most relevant and easily applied to the problems of learning encountered in the fields of fine and applied arts are the forms of oral communication referred to as: short talk, panel discussions, oral interpretation, and the dialogue.

The short talk, as explained more thoroughly in Chapter Eleven, can be used in the discovery phase of the youngster's learning. At the beginning of the term, for example, to spark motivation and enhance conceptualization students might well be assigned the task of discovering the significant relationships among each of the items in the following groups and presenting the discoveries in a series of talks scheduled throughout the quarter or semester :

Artist	*City—Country*	*Concept*
Michelangelo Buonarroti	Florence, Italy, 16th century	Florentine School of Painting
Ludwig van Beethoven	Vienna, 18th-19th century	Symphonic Composition
Salvador Dali	Spain, 20th century	Surrealism
Frank Lloyd Wright	America, 20th century	Functional Architecture
Diego Rivera	Mexico, 19th-20th century	Mural Forms in Painting

Each of the three talks offered by the student should be thoroughly researched and organized carefully enough to be presented in two or three minutes before classmates. At the discretion of the teacher, one of the talks might be extended to four minutes. It is advisable to have these presented *as part* of several periods over a long period of time rather than as a unit. If two are presented every other day for fifteen days, student interest in each of them would probably be maintained at a fairly high level. Overwhelmed by six or seven speakers a day for a week, most students of high school age will become bored—at the least. More important, the spread suggested above insures a longer exposure for both student speakers and student listeners. Research can be made more rewarding, material learned better, and discussions more sparkling if students have more than a two- or three-day association with this phase of their experience in the arts. Talks on the individual artists might be structured so as to include information on birth, education, physical characteristics, occupational experiences, death; those on the country should be made to cover such items as location, topography, economy, education, politics *at the time of the artist's affiliation with it;* those on the concepts should strive to present something of the history, details of the concept, metamorphosis, and present stage. Truly, *all* details of the sort suggested above cannot and should not be included in the short talks designed for a two or three minute period. Nevertheless, in that same period, if properly organized, most of the suggested topics can be touched upon with the bulk of the time reserved for those which are the most pertinent. Also, the short talk might well be used for reports on local developments in the arts. Critiques of plays, concerts, art exhibits, pageants all lend themselves to this form of oral communication as do descriptions, reports and evaluations of local artists, directors, or musicians.

Most obviously, the short talk can be used as explanations or demonstrations pertinent to the area of study. Thus, a student may give a talk on constructing a mosaic, preparing food for quick-freezing, composing a Japanese haiku poem, organizing a fashion show, or constructing wrought iron structures. In such cases, the student truly demonstrates the role of oral communication in his personal learning experience. While not as directly profitable, short talks by special resource persons do contribute to student learning. A noted local chef on food preparation, a successful landscape designer on care of shrubs and flowers, a dancing expert on the use of rhythmics, all help bring vitality and new information to the students' learning endeavors. Finally, the short talk is admirable for testing purposes—either alone or in conjunction with a written or performing experience. Explanations of principles, exemplification of theories, implementation of procedures, or symbolic application can all be evaluated through the use of the short talk. A student offering a talk on the artistic bonds between Russell Conwell's *Acres of Diamonds* speech, the cathedral in Milan, Italy, Joyce Kilmer's poem, *Trees,* and Da Vinci's painting of John the Baptist will surely reveal the nature and scope of his

COMMENTARY BRINGS AN ESSENTIAL DIMENSION TO
THE VISUAL IMAGE.
(*Courtesy of Shoreline Public Schools.*)

insight and understanding.[6] Regardless of the time allowance or the nature of the talk, it is imperative that the instructor present the student with a fair and honest criticism. To do anything else would be to make the student experience practically worthless.

Panel Discussions and Symposia can also be employed to good effect by the teachers of fine and applied arts. Many of the topics suggested for the short talks could be approached through various discussion forms. Assuming four student panelists, the topic could be

---

[6] Similar "discovery" exercises which can easily be created by each teacher should include examples from various fields in order to extend student appreciation of the universal nature of many of the principles learned. Thus, the following might also serve: (1) Vachel Lindsay's poem, *Congo, The Song of the Volga Boatman*, the Tahitian sword dance, the Guggenheim Art Museum, Lincoln's Gettysburg Address; (2) the poem *Finnegan's Wake*, Rodin's *Gates of Hell*, Debussy's musical composition *Sounds and Perfumes on the Evening Air*, Salvador Dali's surrealistic paintings.

"The Life and Times of Michelangelo Buonarroti" or any artist, composer, architect, or director. Panels or symposia of this sort could be assigned to cover almost every phase of the semester's work and carefully rotated so as to include every student at least once. Moreover, such discussions serve extremely well as either introductory or culminating experiences for any given unit of study; they insure student participation, provide variety to classroom procedures, and furnish the teacher with another opportunity to evaluate the progress of teaching as well as of student learning. But the panel also operates well with such less structured topics as: "What contributions can the various arts make to the progress of the world?" "How best may beautiful experiences be shared?" "How do harmony, rhythm, and balance apply to the arts?" "What constitutes good behavior?" "How does the family unit contribute to world harmony?" "how best may *maturity* be reached?"

Small group discussions, although more informal than the panel, work exceptionally well for exciting ideas and initiating intellectual activity which may be along more imaginative lines than those provoked by the panel. In the heat of easy and more fluid interaction, an avalanche of ideas for a fashion show, money-raising projects, new approaches to child-raising and the like would not be unusual. Certainly such activity is well suited for the imaginative tasks of creating new menus, recipes, tools, procedures, and forms suited to one or the other of the fine and applied arts.

The *oral interpretation* of literature has a part in the education of young persons involved in learning the arts. As a solitary exercise, much like the short talk, this form can spark motivation, enhance conceptualization and insure application and retention because it has its life in student involvement. Readings from primary sources such as letters, autobiographies, notebooks, and formal documents bring an air of reality to the study of artisans of other times and other places. To hear a description of Leonardo Da Vinci's doubts as written by him in his notebooks gives them more probative force than when described in paraphrase by another writer or a teacher; details of a musical score are more easily understood when offered by the composer than by another party; and a dancer's exhilaration during certain performances can best be rendered in his own words, however halting. A student searching out such material is aided as much by the process of search as he is by the flavor and feeling offered by the content. But, even more, he benefits from the experience of *creating* his own artistic composition from the bits and pieces he selects out of the original works. Just as he must learn to unify his own words and phrases to create a whole, he must exert something beyond mere selection to complete a total, meaningful experience in the time allotted. He learns that what is omitted may be more essential than what is retained; that reorganization is even more difficult than organization; that the total artistic experience is captured neither in the words nor the final product of the artist; that the agony and the ecstasy of artistic effort is usually deeper and higher than most persons imagine.

As a group exercise, oral interpretation can also contribute to the learning experiences of young high school students. In some ways, group experience is even better suited to this age than is the solitary exercise. In groups of four, six, eight, or ten the students can be made to discover, create, and apply certain principles or appreciations. One example which has a successful history of use is often referred to as the *group poetry* experience. In a class of thirty, five students may be assigned to one of six groups and each group is assigned a different theme (War, Love, Law, Society, Art, Harmony, Unity, etc.). Each group member writes five different phrases or sentences on the assigned theme; the sentences of each member must be produced independently of the other members. The group members then get together to compose a unified poem from the individual efforts making certain *not to alter any sentence, even if there are duplications*. Finally, each group is allowed time to offer a *group* recital of their composition. The composition and the individual assignments for the final choral effort must remain a group effort. As with all other student activity, the teacher must give the students (here in the form of a group appraisal) constructive and fair criticisms. The benefits of this exercise, beyond those mentioned for the solitary oral interpretation experience, are closely related to the objectives of a course in the arts. Most obvious is the benefit of experiencing something of the pain of creation. By active involvement, the student gathers a greater sensitivity for the exercise of his imagination and his sense of order; he is in a better position to appreciate the interrelation of unbridled imagination and necessary arrangement; he finds it easier to recognize the artistic possibilites in his fellows. Here is a sample of a poem as might be composed by many people.

TIME

it is a face glowing   (*Men*)
it is a soul mending   (*Women*)
it is a flower growing   (*Single Woman*)
     nothing—everything   (*All Voices*)
   everything—nothing
   everywhere—nowhere
     nowhere—everywhere
the clock measures it   (*Men*)
the earth feels it
God controls it
     nothing—everything
   everything—nothing   (*All Voices*)
   everywhere—nowhere
    nowhere—everywhere
       it is a world.   (*Single Woman*)

SUMMARY

The fine arts and communication share in and are supported by a common spirit, purpose, tools, and outcomes. The same spirit motivates the student to crystallize his concepts and moods through some conventional symbolic process of line, form, color, tone, or action. He uses any or all of these in the struggle to make public what has been private, to organize the formless and give substance to his innermost shadows. Certain sounds can move us as readily as a certain pattern of color or a cluster of bodily actions, and the training designed to increase the discrimination between sound values and patterns can be made to help increase the sensitivity to varying values among patterns of color or action or forms.

The mark of a man's character and personality is shown as much by the products of his communicative artistry as by those fashioned in other areas of the fine and applied arts. The most rewarding and enduring learning will ensue from the careful integration of oral communication and the other artistic experiences.

SELECTED READINGS

Bruner, J. S. "The Act of Discovery." *Harvard Educational Review,* XXXI (Winter, 1961), 21–32.

Burke, Kenneth. *A Rhetoric of Motives.* New York: George Braziller, Inc., 1955.

Coon, Beulah I. *Home Economics Instruction in the Secondary Schools.* Washington, D.C.: The Center for Applied Research in Education, Inc., 1964. Chap. 5 "Applying Principles of Learning in Home Economics Instruction."

Fleming, William. *Art and Ideas.* New York: Holt, Rinehart & Winston, Inc., 1955.

Friedlander, B. Z. "A Psychologist's Second Thoughts on Concepts, Curiosity, and Discovery in Teaching and Learning." *Harvard Educational Review,* XXXV (Winter, 1965), 18–38.

Giedon, Siegfried. *Space, Time and Architecture.* Cambridge : Harvard University Press, 1941.

Hall, Olive A., and Beatrice Paolucci. *Teaching Home Economics.* New York : John Wiley & Sons, Inc., 1961. Chap. 8 "Determining Learning Experiences."

Holt, Elizabeth Gilmore, ed. *Literary Sources of Art History.* Princeton: Princeton University Press, 1947.

Kneller, George F. *The Art and Science of Creativity.* New York: Holt, Rinehart & Winston, Inc., 1965.

Vasari, Giorgio. *Lives of the Most Eminent Painters, Sculptors and Architects.* Trans. Mrs. Jonathan Foster. London : Bohn, 1859.

APPENDICES

APPENDICES

A securing optimum interest and skill

Interest and intelligibility are intrinsic to effective communication. These qualities should emerge from well-chosen subjects, wisely selected speech activities, and thoroughly prepared presentations: matters which have received attention in the main body of this volume. Frequently, however, additional measures must be taken to secure optimal interest and clarity in classroom speaking. For this reason it is appropriate to append some additional information for coping with communication problems arising from limitations in the manner of speaking. We shall limit our attention to voice, articulation, pronunciation, bodily response, and the use of audio-visual supplements to speech.

VOICE, ARTICULATION, AND PRONUNCIATION

Effective communication requires that the oral symbols used in speaking clearly express what the speaker *has in mind* and what he *means by what he says*. To accomplish this, the processes of voice, articulation, and pronunciation, among others, must be carried out efficiently, accurately, and easily.

Voice

The term *voice* refers to the sound which is initiated in the larynx through vibration of the vocal folds and modulated and reinforced by the resonators of the throat, mouth, nasal passages, and other cavities and bony structures of the head and thorax. Its variables include *loudness, pitch, duration,* and *quality,* all of which in various, if subtle, ways serve to reveal what the speaker means by what he says and which, at the same time, indicate something of the speaker's personality, his emotional state, and his environmental background.

Loudness is a psychological term denoting the strength or force of a tone. It can be measured in decibels. In a general way, loudness determines the audibility of speech, and is therefore crucial to speech intelligibility and effective communication. In addition, loudness, as a means of emphasis, plays an important role in revealing meanings. Like pitch change, loudness variations serve to differentiate major and subordinate idea relationships, and to indicate strength of feeling and attitude. Indeed, teachers discover that most high school pupils are prone to limit their vocal expressiveness to variations of loudness, the least subtle of the several modes of emphasis.

Problems of loudness (too loud, too soft, or inadequate variation) are usually of psychological rather than physical origin. Matters of fear, suspicion, doubt are more influential in determining vocal volume than is mere lack of breath control.

Skill in the use of force as a mode of emphasis, as in the case of other vocal variables, is largely dependent upon the speaker's sensitivity to the thought and emotional properties of the message, and upon his physical and psychological relationship with his listeners. In oral reading, for example, pupils can be helped to recognize clues which call for variations in loudness. In all types of speaking, pupils can be made aware of the need for modulating their voices in accordance with the size of audience and acoustical peculiarities of the room.

Pitch refers to the position of a tone on the musical scale. In communication, we are concerned with its general level and its degree of flexibility in response to thinking and feeling. Its most common limiting characteristics are lack of sufficient variation and presence of pitch pattern, sometimes observed as a sing-song melody in reading poetry, or an annunciatory style in oral reporting.

Rules governing pitch change are not very dependable. However, in American English speech a very common mode of emphasis is raising (or lowering) the pitch on key words or phrases, as shown in the following:

1. *I* am going to the city tomorrow. (Not someone else.)
2. I *am* going to the city tomorrow. (You can't prevent me.)
3. I am going to the *city* tomorrow. (Not the country.)
4. I am going to the city *tomorrow.* (Not today or next week.)

The foregoing illustrate the kind of pitch change usually described as *interval* or *step,* a clean jump from one level to another. Pitch can also be modulated by bending the continuous tone up or down, as in the examples:

1. Oh ⟋   (Is that so? I didn't know that.)
2. Oh ⟍   (What a shame.)
3. Oh ⟋⟍   (Now I see what you mean.)

Pitch monotony is usually due to such functional causes as habit, fear, and lack of mental discrimination and purposiveness. Thus, with proper motivation, it is nearly always possible to guide the individual toward more effective pitch variation. Pitch problems which do not yield to suggestion or thought stimulation are likely to be deep-seated in origin and may therefore require the attention of a speech therapist.

Duration refers to the temporal length of individual speech sounds, particularly vowels. This variable, together with *pause,* the interval between words and phrases, determines the rate at which one speaks and therefore to some extent the intelligibility of the message. Severely clipped sounds and ineffective phrasing and pausing can seriously interfere with communication. Similarly, drawled speech, though intelligible, may be so dull and lacking in continuity as to cause listeners to "tune out."

Let it be noted, however, that there is no such thing as *an* appropriate rate for all occasions and for all persons. *Rate is relative.* Intelligibility must be served. Some people with special articulatory skill and unusual coordination can speak quite intelligibly at speeds much greater than the average of 125 to 150 words per minute. Others, less skilled in speaking are scarcely intelligible at moderate rates. Then, too, the nature of the subject will dictate its rate: some require a slow rate; others, a moderate or fast rate. The nature and complexity of the subject, the emotional content of the material, the size of the audience, and the speaker's vocal skill: all should be considered in determining the appropriate rate of any given moment of speaking.

Quality, a resonance phenomenon, most characteristically distinguishes one voice from another. Although vocal qualities of members of a family and of people living in close association may bear notable similarity, an individual's vocal quality tends to be virtually as unique as his personality. This uniqueness is explained by the fact that the physical factors which affect resonance are conditioned by the unique physical and temperamental characteristics of each individual. No vocal element is as likely to reveal as well as quality the implied or connotative meanings of a speaker's language. In so doing, it contributes eloquently to the interest and intelligibility of oral messages.

Among high school boys and girls the most common faults of quality are likely to be tonal flatness, nasality, breathiness, hoarseness, and stridency. Flatness is usually a product of nonpurposive, unresponsive, uninspired speaking. Therefore, well-motivated speech assignments and thorough individual preparation can do much to help pupils eliminate flatness and develop full resonant voices. The classroom teacher would be wise to seek the assistance of a speech therapist in treatment of other problems of vocal quality.

Quality as a mode of emphasis is dependent primarily upon three important steps: sensing the emotional meaning of the material or message, giving oneself time to experience this feeling, and allowing this feeling to prevail at the moment of utterance. Obviously there is need for control and the exercise of good taste in expressing emotion in speaking. Professional actors and readers painstakingly strive to secure this control. In the classroom, however, the problem is more likely to be one of securing some measure of freedom in pupils' emotional response, some discernable evidence of feeling, mood, and purpose. Many pupils are reluctant to "let go" in their classroom vocal responses for fear of appearing silly, "hammy," or "square" to their peers. Here, as with other modes of emphasis, pupils must be helped to realize that their major purpose is effective communication: *how* one says something should accurately reveal *what one means.*

Articulation and pronunciation

Articulation refers to the process of forming and joining speech sounds or phonemes. It is concerned primarily with the distinctness and accuracy of vocal utterance. *Pronunciation,* though intimately related to articulation, has to do with the forming and joining of speech sounds in word and phrase patterns according to the conventions of a particular geographic region or ethnic-cultural group. Carrell and Tiffany remind us that

> A word is *mispronounced* if it contains one or more wrong sounds or if the correct word pattern is distorted by adding, omitting, or transposing sounds or by improper use of stress. A word is *misarticulated,* on the other hand, if the sounds it contains are not spoken with sufficient accuracy and precision.[1]

In America, as in all countries, numerous dialects are spoken. Phoneticians, however, have identified three principal dialect regions, which are designated as *Eastern American, Southern American,* and *General American.* While the regions are only roughly defined, Eastern American is characteristic of the speech heard in New England and New York City; Southern American is identified with the speech of the so-called deep South; and General American is spoken in the remaining states. Although more people speak General American than Southern or Eastern, this dialect should not be considered preferable to or better than the others. As we have said, effective communication requires that the message be intelligible and the manner of speaking free of conspicuous substandard usages within a general dialect.

Communicative speech

Communication is best served by (1) a voice which can be easily heard, which has an interesting and meaningful variety of pitch and loudness, and whose quality is basically pleasing; (2) an articulation characterized by distinctness and precision without affectation, together with an appropriate rate of utterance; and (3) a pronunciation which

---

[1] James A. Carrell and William R. Tiffany, *Phonetics: Theory and Application to Speech Improvement* (New York: McGraw-Hill Book Company 1960), p.4.

approximates the standards exemplified by most educated people in a given speech region. How then can the general classroom teacher help his pupils meet these three basic speech criteria?

Guidelines for effective voice, articulation and pronunciation

Basic Conditions

On the premise that one's manner of speaking at any point in time is conditioned by one's mental, emotional, and physical states, teachers should do all in their power to provide a classroom atmosphere that is intellectually stimulating and emotionally healthful. In other words, teachers should endeavor to provide conditions which contribute to pupils' sense of well-being and feeling of personal worth and achievement. They should encourage pupils to approach their speaking assignments with well-defined purposes and a listener-centered orientation. If teachers will strive at all times to engage well-motivated speaking experiences, see to it that speech preparations are thoughtfully and thoroughly carried out, and that honest efforts are made to communicate effectively with one's listeners, it is more than likely that most vocal weaknesses of functional origin commonly found among high school pupils will be largely eliminated. In essence: to obtain the best possible vocal responses from pupils, teachers must first give attention to the conditions which underlie or affect such responses. And while the vocal response is a product of certain physical processes, these processes are conditioned largely by thinking and emotion. The teacher's first concern, therefore, should be with stimulating the psychophysical causes of speech. This first step is basic and wholly practicable for classroom teachers, regardless of the depth of their speech sophistication.

Important as stimulating basic "causes of speech" may be to fostering good voice and articulation, it must not be forgotten that one's manner of speaking is also a product of imitation and conditioning. Speech reflects one's social environments, particularly those of the home and immediate peer groups. Even with excellent stimulation in the classroom, all too frequently pupils' voices fall short of effective communication requirements. Fortunately speech habits are learned; they are therefore amenable to guidance and retraining. And although the primary responsibility for teaching basic speech skills should rightly be lodged with speech and, in some cases, English classes, general classroom teachers share some of this responsibility if only to reinforce and further improve the good speech habits begun in speech classes. In any event, the classroom teacher will find it necessary, certainly advisable, to devote some attention to specific and direct guidance of his pupils' vocal skills.

Suggested Prescriptions.

A. *For securing better operation of the vocal mechanism:*
   1. Provide relaxation exercises,
   2. Teach voice hygiene : sensible care of the voice instrument,
   3. Lead pupils in lip and tongue flexibility exercises : jingles and tongue twisters,
   4. Provide ear-training exercises: listening to tape recordings to improve sensitivity to speech sounds, pitch variation, phrasing, and pausing.

B. *For developing appropriate loudness:*
   1. Emphasize audience-mindedness; discourage speaking as a performance,
   2. Use puppets, dramatization, and role-playing to reduce self-consciousness and fear and to promote objective projection,
   3. Use class leaders as volume monitors,
   4. Use tape recorder to compare student loudness levels.

C. *For securing pitch variety and expressiveness:*
   1. Help pupils to search for meanings; use question method to discover and emphasize important words,
   2. Show vocal effects of comparing and contrasting ideas: e.g., "Hoover was a *Republican,* but Franklin D. Roosevelt was a *Democrat,*"
   3. Employ role-playing to encourage freedom,
   4. Note how pitch varies when speaking with conviction : challenge the reticent pupil to support a conviction.

D. *For developing appropriate rate:*
   1. Teach the importance of phrasing and use of pause,[2]
   2. Give special attention to the general emotional adjustment of pupils who present rate problems,

---

[2] See Chapter 11 for additional discussion of this point.

3. In special cases, require pupils to speak at a rate that will permit the class to take notes,
4. Illustrate the relation between speaking rate and mood of subject, complexity of topic, and size of audience. Illustrate relation between rate and intelligibility.

E. *For improving vocal quality:*
   1. Encourage interested, purposive attitudes in pupils' speaking,
   2. In teaching poetry, seek out moods; help pupils to identify with these feelings in oral reading,
   3. Employ improvisations in which pupils will have opportunity to play roles suggesting various personalities, moods, and attitudes: e.g., a timid little man, a petulant lady, an angry father,
   4. Above all, teach pupils to develop conviction in speaking through thorough preparation and desire to communicate with one's listeners.

F. *For improving articulation and pronunciation:*
   1. Conduct an informal discussion on such topics as "Why people talk as they do," "Does good speech make a difference?" or "What is good speech?"
   2. Carry out some informal "experiments," such as:
      a. Having pupils observe and describe how different people talk; draw conclusions regarding possible relationship between manner of speaking, personality, interest, intelligibility,
      b. Having pupils listen to well known radio and TV announcers; draw conclusions regarding what constitutes *good diction.*
   3. After helping a pupil to recognize his articulation or pronunciation errors, assign a short talk in which he is to make a special effort to avoid committing his usual errors.
   4. Give particular attention to the pronunciation of words which are found in the "special vocabulary" of the subject being taught. For example, po/em (not pome), adj/ec/tive (not adjective), e/lec/tor/al college (not electorial college), gov/ern/ment (not govment), U/ni/ted States (not Nigh Stace), point (not pernt), etc.,
   5. In English classes, always give appropriate attention to correct pronunciation of words included in vocabulary improvement exercises,

6. Refer to correct pronunciation as a mark of the considerate, thoughtful speaker,
7. Have pupils review, if necessary, the interpretation of dictionary phonetic symbols.

In our effeorts to hely boys and girls speak better, we must maintain a sensible balance between content and form: between the *what* and the *how* of speaking. Patently, *what* one says is more important than *how* one says it. But, as Carrell and Tiffany point out, it is also evident "that there can be no fully effective communication through spoken language unless the manner of speaking gives force and impact to the thoughts and feelings that are to be conveyed."[3] Indeed, as we have stated earlier, in oral communication, voice and body action make thought and feeling manifest.

Speech is learned behavior; one's manner of speaking is learned mostly by imitation. Every classroom teacher who believes in the importance of oral communication in the teaching-learning process and who recognizes his role in his school's speech improvement program, will provide environments and experiences conducive to the development of good speech habits. In so doing he will make sure that his own speech is exemplary and he will not hesitate to call upon speech teachers or speech therapists for assistance in guiding speech activities in the classroom.

BODILY ACTION

The images of things experienced directly and indirectly appear preserved in the very musculature of man from a time prior to the creation of language, and are considered "instinctive" by some authorities. Purposeful use of posture, gesture, and movement of the human body is thought to antedate oral communication by at least a million years. Certainly, the evidence derived from the action and tradition of various tribes of Negritos, subcultures in Bali, and others in Africa appears to verify this belief. It can even be said that oral symbols used by most human cultures are but refined gestures of certain specialized body parts. Thus, while bodily actions exist as com-

---

[3] Carrell and Tiffany, *op. cit.*, p. 1.

municative elements in their own right, oral communication does not. Without bodily action, without the "refined gestures of certain specialized body parts," speech would be impossible. The dependent relationship binding audible and visible activities appears significant to the success of these oral encounters, regardless of the society.[4] It is not surprising, therefore, that from primitive times to our own day, it has been common for individuals to listen as *ear-witnesses* and *eye-witnesses* at one and the same time.

But attending to the symbols designed for the eye is not as easy as noting those offered to the ear. Most bodily actions have not been formally recognized and defined; there is no dictionary of visible symbols to which the speaker-listener may turn in moments of doubt or confusion. What exists is an informal albeit universal "feeling" about the meaning of certain demonstrated postures, gestures, and movements among most members of a given society. By virtue of continuous contact in a multiplicity of situations, most sensitive individuals are able to tap the common reservoir of meaning and to produce a high percentage of valid judgments based upon such meanings. The fundamental nature of these nonverbal actions carries the color of their motivation more than the words we use. Physical activity, as the *sine qua non* of all life, is tied more closely to the *real* internal world of the speaker-listener. When a listener is faced with the task of determining a speaker's intent from *his words* or *his actions,* he usually chooses the speaker's actions as a more accurate index. A speaker who says, "I am so sorry about your tragic loss," and accompanies that statement with a broad smile will be thought by the listener to be sarcastic or untruthful.

Since communion does not flow in a straight line from the conventional sounds of one individual to the mind of another, nonverbal action is used as a supplementary force. From time to time, as has already been said, there are periods of speaking-listening transactions during which the nonverbal activity is more evident than the verbal. When oral symbols are no longer clear and firm, the average speaker reaches out (many times unconsciously) to his treasury of more basic nonverbal activity. A shoulder pat often carries more meaning, with more strength, than an oral paragraph; a firm handclasp accompanied by direct eye contact speaks more eloquently than any collection of words.

---

[4] This relationship is dramatically described by Mary H. Kingsley, *Travels in West Africa* (1897), p. 504.

Posture should be thought of as the relative position of body parts which when controlled, alert, and balanced, enables the human being to engage in his social interactions with efficiency and ease. Most young adults have neither the knowledge nor the experience required to provide this efficiency, particularly in oral communication. The greatest service can be rendered by teachers who call attention to the role of good, functional posture without appearing to harp on the subject. Often this attention can be directed toward the positive by timely reference to the negative. Examples of poor posture which interfere with freedom of gesture or movement (slouched, twisted, off-balance stance, etc.) or which convey a message of indifference, rejection, doubt, and the like can motivate youngsters to adopt the opposite actions.

The following exercises are designed to produce an awareness of the role of posture and an appreciation of the more effective modes:

1. Divide the class into groups of six or less with each group member responsible for presenting to the entire group three postures depicting certain moods or thoughts. Group members are to guess what mood or thought is being represented. *No movement should be a part of the portrayals.*

2. Have the students assume the following positions (without movements as a part of the position once it is assumed) and have each guess the mood or thought being portrayed after having been in the position for a few moments :
    a. Seated position, chin cupped in both hands, elbows side by side and resting on the desk;
    b. Standing position, hands in pockets, shoulders slumped forward, weight mostly on one leg;
    c. Seated position, arms and legs crossed, leaning backward with most of the weight supported by the tailbone.

3. Have the students observe body postures in two extended discussions outside of class. The observer is *not* to be a direct member of the group, but is to note:
    a. Approximate distance between participants;
    b. Position of head, shoulders and trunk of each person in relation of their legs and feet (in the same line, opposite directions, etc.);
    c. Position of participants' bodies in relation to each other (both directed or away from each other, at right angles to each other, etc.).

Students should give an oral description of their observations (to permit use of accompanying bodily movement and their interpretations.

Gesture refers to the definite movement (or immobility) of the head, face, shoulders, trunk, arms, and hands during social interactions. Unfortunately, as a consequence of the indiscretions of some past teachers of oral communication, gesture has suffered from too much attention or purposeful ignorance. At either extreme, oral communication is made less effective and misunderstandings grow. Students should be guided toward the understanding that the matter of gesture in effective communication is something more than "that which is put into a talk." In much the same way one would pin a tail on a donkey during a parlor game. Gesture is truly a movement of *spirit* and becomes incarnate through bodily actions. As with our diction, gestures bear the traces of past efforts of our society and ourselves, and arise from sources buried within us. Improvement will occur when young people are told:

> ... work for spontaneity and avoid practicing specific motions for specific portions of your communication. In other words, while awkward and irrelevant gestures have often served to confuse or belie the meaning of your words, it does not follow that your communication will improve with improvement in and emphasis upon specific, standardized gestures. It will come, rather, from a specific endeavor on your part to (1) rid yourself of the attitude that gestures are "wrong," (2) practice for that freedom of action which is normal for you, and (3) work to refine those which are normal for you and yet are not distracting.[5]

Activities which help the students to achieve spontaneity, freedom, and effectiveness in gesture should be drawn from those similar to the following:

1. Students should be asked to compare the role of gestures revealed in the paintings of Michelangelo in the Sistine Chapel with those of any modern painter of their choice;

---

[5] Dominic A. LaRusso, "Visible Communication: Bodily Action," in *Basic Speech Improvement* by Horace C. Rahskopf (New York: Harper & Row, Publishers, 1965,) p. 228.

2. Have the students make a chart noting the frequency of gestures observed in two extended conversations: one between teen-agers and one between persons over fifty years of age;
3. Have the students participate in a conversation with at least three persons, *each of whom is blind-folded* throughout the course of the conversation. Have each then describe the difficulties which arose;
4. Divide the class into groups of five, insist on a rotating leadership, and have each group member respond to the gestures of the leader *with the opposite gesture as quickly as possible.* Thus, a smile from the leader should elicit a frown from the members, a nod should call forth a side-to-side head shake, etc. Later, a representative from each group may form a panel selected to respond to the signals of the teacher;
5. Have each student demonstrate (and feel) the difference between :
   a. Opening a stuck door vs. teasing out one colored thread from an intricate woven pattern;
   b. Forcing an oversized cork into the neck of a bottle vs. working a pipe cleaner into a pipe stem;
   c. Painting the siding of a house vs. painting in wrinkles on a portrait;
   d. Shooting a pistol, a rifle, a bow and arrow vs. tossing a discus, a javelin, a hammer-weight;
   e. Smelling a bouquet of gardenias, ginger, or lilacs vs. smelling rotten eggs, formaldehyde, or dirty sweat socks;
   f. Viewing a dim star emerging at dusk vs. reading fine print on a medicine label;
   g. Feeling a gentle summer rain falling on the face vs. a surprise dunk into a cold mountain stream;
   h. Gazing directly into sunlight reflected from the surface of a lake vs. walking into a darkened theater from broad daylight;
   i. Experiencing a good, full yawn vs. sucking on a lemon or persimmon.

Movement, a dynamic relationship of posture and gesture, is the most dramatic and forceful of bodily actions used in formal or informal communication efforts. To be effective, to act as an aid rather than a hindrance, movement should be positive, unambiguous, and coordinated. Whenever possible, the speaker-listener should move toward his counterpart rather than away and he should avoid movements which are at right angles to his companion's line of vision. Young adults are usually guilty of too much movement rather than too little, and, to make matters worse, most of the movement is random, uncoordinated, and inappropriate. While these conditions do pose problems and should be channeled as soon as possible, a more important problem is created by those youngsters who are restricted or inhibited. The former group can be easily directed toward refinement and discipline; the latter must be stimulated and motivated before refinement can occur. The following suggestions are offered with the more reserved students in mind, though all can profit from the exercises:

1. Have the students work for smoothness and rhythm as they alternate between extreme movements such as :
   a. Carrying a heavy suitcase from one side of the room to the other vs. carrying a large, empty cardboard box from one point to another;
   b. Sitting down in a plush, overstuffed chair vs. sitting on a footstool which is much too short and much too small;
   c. Walking along the water's edge during an incoming tide vs. walking along the edge of the street curbing;
   d. Walking through a brush-filled forest in search of a lost dog vs. walking to meet a friend within sight and already waiting;
   e. Moving to greet a stranger vs. moving to greet a friend who has been away a long time.
2. Have the students prepare three short talks related to the topic currently being studied. One talk is to be delivered from a sitting position; a second is to be delivered half from a sitting position and half from a standing position; the third talk is to be given from a standing position. Have the students record their reactions to each talk as listeners and speakers.

In retrospect, bodily action can be seen to be an important adjunct to the oral-aural characteristics of any speaking-listening encounter. In proportion as these actions are purposeful, economical, and appropriate they will enrich the communicative situation. And the enrichment will be shared by both speaker and listener in that these actions facilitate the communion being sought by each. As gestures of this type aid the speaker in developing deeper and more meaningful thoughts, they contribute to the listener's understanding of those thoughts by communicating the emphasis and mood behind them. In like manner, movements which are purposeful and appropriate stimulate listener empathy and result in a fluid and reciprocal interchange.

If nothing more, a study of bodily actions in ordinary oral communication will help build the students' sensitivity to nonverbal forms of communication and they will inevitably improve in their own use of such forms as aids to their total communicative efforts.

SELECTED READINGS

Allport, G.W., and P. Vernon. *Studies in Expressive Movement*. New York: The Macmillan Company, 1933.

Birdwhistell, Ray. "Background to Kinesics," *Etc.*, XIII (1955), 10–18.

Bolinger, D. L. "Visual Morphemes." *Language*, XXII (1946), 333–40.

Crichthy, MacDonald. *The Language of Gesture*. London: Edward Arnold (Publishers) Ltd., 1939.

Deutsch, F. "Analysis of Postural Behavior." *Psychoanalytic Quarterly*, XVI (1947), 195–213.

———. "Thus Speaks the Body, III. Analytic Posturology." *Psychoanalytic Quarterly*, XX (1951), 338–39.

Ekman, P. "Body Position, Facial Expression and Verbal Behavior During Interviews." *Journal of Abnormal and Social Psychology*, LXVIII (1964), 295–301.

Fromm, Eric. *The Forgotten Language*. New York: Holt, Rinehart & Winston, Inc., 1951.

Hall, E. T. *The Silent Language*. New York: Fawcett World Library, 1951.

———. *The Hidden Dimension*. New York: Doubleday & Company, Inc., 1966.

Ruesch, Jurgen, and Gregory Bateson. *Communication: The Social Matrix of Psychiatry*. New York: W. W. Norton & Company, Inc., 1951.

———, and Weldon Kees. *Nonverbal Communication*. Berkeley: University of California Press, 1956.

AUDIO-VISUAL MATERIAL

Selection and use

Without doubt, aside from failing to recognize the importance of adequate and timely audience analysis, the greatest single error in most teaching situations has to do with the *misuse and overuse of audio-visual aids.* Largely as a result of the influence of public relations and advertising "experts," a belief has evolved that aids insure learning or persuasion. *There is no objective evidence available to substantiate that assumption.* Audo-visual aids, as with medicines, are intended only as *supplements* to a more basic phenomenon. In the hands of a skilled physician, drugs are dispensed to enable the body to help itself. However, used inappropriately, they can damage both the short- and the long-range goals of the treatment. The *immediate* health of the patient may well be destroyed so that future therapy programs may also be undermined. In like manner, in the hands of an effective teacher, audio-visual material is used to strengthen the basic learning experience of the pupils. Used insensitively and indiscriminately, however, these aids can be rendered harmful to the immediate learning experience and to the students' over-all attitude toward his education. What evidence is available underscores the importance of *discretion* in the preparation and use of these aids. As has already been observed:

> A common and, by far, the most serious error in the use of visual material is the tendency to have it become the presentation. During these talks, the speaker has the dubious honor of serving as a glorified guide, shunted into the background on the false notion that "a picture is worth a thousand words." Were this true, of course, all education would devolve into a process of producing comic strips; all industry would operate with movies as chief instructors; all sales would be conducted by a reciprocal exchange of photographs. Only a moment's reflection is needed to highlight the fact that photographs do not always convey the same message to all viewers, that one skilled speaker drawing upon the resources of experience, training, and personality to meet the dynamic needs of a live audience is superior to volumes of photographs. Visual [and auditory] materials,

therefore, serving as merely supplementary aids to understanding and belief, are only as effective as the speaker who makes and employs them.[6]

Still, visual aids which are properly constructed and wisely employed do assist the teacher and the learner. As has been noted already, such aids tend to improve initial acquisition and retention of moods, attitudes, ideas, and understandings.[7] But they do so only when they are:

1. *Suggested by the message itself.* Most often, because of a misunderstanding of the nature of communication, poor audience analysis, or an overdeveloped case of stagefright, teachers feel the need to use audio-visual material "which can't do any harm," instead of material which is *especially constructed for their message and their audience.* What has been used by some instructors for some students is usually ineffective when used by and for others. Every aid introduced must be patently related to the subject matter, must be a direct, clear, and helpful interlude or it will serve only to distract the listener. This is true whether the visual aid is more complete than needed or so simple and obvious as to insult the intelligence of the pupils. Effective aids are those which are composed only *after* the talk has been completely and clearly organized and only for those sections of the talk which could prove confusing, ambiguous, or vague.

2. *Appropriate to the situation.* On the assumption that reasonable choices of audio-visual aids are made to effect a sustained change in the students, any audio-visual material should be constructed so that it is within the range of the students' experience. It should relate as well to the teacher's experience. Nothing is more damaging to a presentation than to have the teacher apologize for using an aid which is obviously unsuited either because it is more complicated than necessary for the student, or because the teacher does not really understand it or the role it is supposed to play. The teacher's confusion will rarely be conveyed as lucidity to his students regardless of the subject

---

[6] Dominic A. LaRusso, "Visible Communication: Bodily Action," in Horace G. Rahskopf, *Basic Speech Improvement* (New York: Harper & Row, Publishers, 1965), pp. 229–30.

[7] A. L. Long, "Recent Experimental Investigations Dealing with Effectiveness of Audio-Visual Modes of Presentation," *Educational Administration Supervision,* XXXI (February, 1945), 65–78.

area.[8] The material used must also be appropriate to the time and place. It ill behooves the teacher to use a tape recording which, because of bad acoustics or too much ambient noise, cannot be heard or understood. The feeling that "the pupils will at least get the flavor of the message," serves only to preserve the ego of a teacher who is made painfully aware of his bad choice. Neither is it advisable to make excessive use of cartoons when making presentations to the average high school audience. Insurmountable barriers are often created by a teacher who, by his manner, his message, and his material, often reflects a low opinion of student capabilities. When told that "Communication is an important consideration in periods of national emergency," intelligent youngsters do not need to have a picture of a telephone and a radio flashed on a screen to aid their comprehension or retention.

3. *Technically adequate.* "All time, money, and energy expended in the selection of supplementary material is rendered null and void unless the material can be easily seen or heard by the audience. Generally speaking, the *smallest* visual material of any value in the average classroom (20 feet × 40 feet) is $8\frac{1}{2}$ by 11 inches. This means, of course, that the main feature of the diagram, map, photograph, etc., must be of that size. It would not do, for example, to use an $8\frac{1}{2}$ × 11 inch map of the United States when the main feature of the visualization had to do with the peculiar size, shape, and location of the Cimarron River in Oklahoma. So, also, a speaker should avoid the use of auditory material which cannot be clarified or amplified to the degree necessary for easy assimilation by the audience. If ambient noise makes recognition and intelligibility of sound difficult, then that material ought not to be used no matter how pertinent or how much apology may be offered for it. Finally, shaky easels, poor blackboard lighting, noisy projectors, and other inadequate mechanical supports which transform good aids into unwelcome distractions should be avoided."[9]

4. *Properly employed.* The most effective aids are those which reflect care and concern for the needs of the audience as well as those demanded by the occasion and the speaker. Quite obviously, the best way of showing such care is to consider those needs in the preparation

---

[8] R. Likert, "A Neglected Factor in Communications," *Audio-Visual Communications Review*, II (Summer, 1954), 163–77.

[9] LaRusso, *op. cit.*, p. 231.

as well as the presentation of the audio-visual material. Planning should also provide for such physical and mechanical adjustments as are required to make certain the material performs its intended function. But even more important to the success of the learning experience, early planning should provide for the proper and timely introduction of the aids. The greatest benefit is derived when the aids are employed at the exact point in the discussion that made their use necessary. They should not, in other words, be displayed prior to their need in the *immediate* development of ideas. When they are introduced care should be taken to insure full and continuous view *by the audience* during the period of their relevancy. Nothing is more frustrating to the average student than a poorly positioned, ill-timed, or hastily revealed aid.

With these basic rules before him, the teacher has some assurance that audio-visual material will, indeed, prove an *aid* in his task of clarifying meaning and improving the understanding of his listeners. Nevertheless, something more should be understood about the selection and use of the various types of audio-visual material.

Just as careful language and pertinent examples are employed to make basic ideas more understandable and acceptable, audio-visual material should meet the criteria of purpose, economy, and propriety. However, supplementary or audio-visual aids demand more than one teacher's resources. During the organization of a class or course, for example, audio-visual aids may be prepared by persons other than the teacher and consequently, considerations of *time, money,* and *effort* must be added to the criteria of pertinency, clarity, and simplicity if audio-visual material is to be used advantageously.

5. *Properly timed.* There are two considerations here. *First,* effective preparation demands that the teacher maintain a sense of proportion to amount of time given over to the use of such aids. It must be remembered that these aids are only *supplements* to the basic presentation made by the instructor; as such, they ought to occupy not more than thirty to thirty-five per cent of the total time expended in a class session. *Second,* if professional artists or illustrators are needed in the production of these aids, some definite decision must be made on the amount of time which will be devoted to their creation. Most industrial illustrators confess that this is their greatest problem in the production of audio-visual aids. While they usually are given wide latitude in the use of money and material, little help is afforded by school officials and teachers who fail to appreciate (and make

allowances for) the amount of time involved in the creation and production of these materials. Not only is artistic temperament riled and professional efficiency curtailed, but the teacher is often unable to make use of these aids since they are unavailable or poorly executed because of inefficient scheduling. Difficulties are avoided and efficiency increased by an adequate consideration of the *time* factor.

6. *Properly budgeted.* Involved with the second instance of *time*—the time required to create and produce the material—is the matter of *money*. Again, many visual-aid coordinators and teachers encounter difficulties during the final stages of preparing a course simply because inadequate attention has been given to the costs of production and use. Elaborate audio-visual materials such as movies, slides, sand-tablets, and mock-ups necessarily drain the budget heavily. Others, dependent upon special equipment, will make additional demands which must be planned for at the outset of any school year or semester. Unless they are properly planned for, these aids will be hastily and poorly produced or will drain the budget allowances for other equally important areas. Finally, proper budgetary considerations during the initial stages of the program will help determine the number and nature of aids used.

7. *Properly produced.* Questions of *production* and *approval* must be settled early in the planning period to avoid waste of time, money, and effort. The teacher, with the advice and counsel of the coordinator, is the person best qualified to formulate the preliminary choices concerning nature and number of aids used. *However,* if professionally produced, only the illustrating staff can give an accurate estimate of labor and materials required for their production. As a result, after viewing the preliminary suggestion of the teacher and considering the suggestions and estimates of the illustrators, the *coordinator* should be in a position to make the final decision. Where this is not feasible, one person ought to be designated as final arbiter—preferably neither the teacher nor the artist for obvious reasons of personal involvement.

While it may be generally believed that one particular type of aid is uniformly superior to another, experimentation indicates that each has its peculiar advantages. One should maintain a flexible and *ever-questioning* attitude toward any audio-visual material since its efficiency varies with subject, speaker, audience, and occasion. Still, some of the demonstrated advantages and disadvantages ought to be known.

Mechanical aids

Of the mechanical aids *movies* are the most popular. Some of this popularity is probably due to: (1) ease of use; (2) economy of time; and (3) uniqueness of content and format. (They show things unavailable to the naked eye—growth phenomena, emergency procedures, disaster sequences, complex relations, inaccessible areas, etc.) Films also have a certain degree of flexibility in their use of sound, angles, motion, color, and music. However, films carry certain dangers which must be recognized by the teacher. Certainly, one great disadvantage is that any good film can become a vivid competitor to a mediocre speaker. It can also very easily become the dominating feature of any session or series of sessions. For this reason, films *must be carefully previewed* before their use so that their relevance to audience, message, time, and place can be properly evaluated. Every film should be properly introduced so that its relevance can be emphasized and the students' attention directed to the important factors to be remembered. Properly alerted auditors gain much more, for longer periods of time, than those who are merely exposed to the films. After the showing, some time should be allotted for discussion *unless the film is self-contained* or unless the feeling or attitude desired is generated by the film itself. In this case, if the film is so well prepared that it serves the teacher in the fullest possible way, then any comments afterward should be avoided lest they be construed as an attempt to "gild the lily."

Another basic disadvantage of films (added to the obvious one of high cost) is that it is inflexibly limited by *time*—in material and sequence. It is a self-contained unit which must be used as a whole or not at all. Of necessity, this factor must be among the more important criteria of selection for use in the ordinary schoolroom sessions.

This disadvantage is *not* shared by *slides*. In addition, slides have the advantages of: (1) ease of production; (2) ease of use; and (3) flexibility in the sequence and type of material. Properly prepared and employed, slides benefit the auditor in that they do help in directing and sustaining attention as they also increase the amount of material retained. Slides are best employed when they supplement the talk by making available charts, graphs, tables, maps, or pictures which would be awkward and unwieldly if used themselves. Further, slides are helpful when the speaker wishes unified attention which he can then direct to important or troublesome areas. This could not be done, for example, if each student were given a copy of the map of the

United States and then left to be distracted by his own interests while the teacher attempts to concentrate on the southwest region.

A major disadvantage of slides is that they seem to encourage misuse more than any other type of visual aid. Generally, the misuse is either in faulty production (too much text, too much color, too elementary in content) or in quantity (many, many, too many). An effective ratio of slides to total speaking time is a maximum of one to five; that is, one slide (*if needed*) for every five minutes of presentation. Whenever possible, *the slides should be shown when needed;* they should, in other words, be integrated into the talk rather than be set apart to be run all together for a block of "slide showing time." Equally important is the need for a careful numbering or other designation which will guarantee the planned sequence at the moment of presentation.

Projections (other than slides and films) carry the advantage of flexibility. Here we speak of such things as *opaque* and *overhead* or transparency projections. With either of these, the instructor is free to use more of an "on the spot" approach; that is, any suitable map, chart, picture, graph, diagram or the like found in an available text can be used *in its original form* (without the additional cost of constructing slides, special transparent copies, etc.) by the use of the opaque projector. In the case of transparency projection, the teacher is free to construct his charts, diagrams, and the like as he speaks—much the same as when using a blackboard. The chief benefit over the blackboard is that the speaker need not turn his back on the audience and, further, the view of the material is far better and more instantaneous than when placed on a blackboard. Finally, of course, projections are more flexible because, unlike films, they may be used in any sequence desired.

Still, one must be selective in the use of these projections for, as with other forms of audio-visual aids, they carry possibilities for misuse. Great restraint must be exercised in limiting the number of selections to be shown by opaque projector. Because of the danger of burning the material (since an intense light must be used to show it), a strong fan must be used to keep the heat to a minimum. As a consequence, opaque projectors are very noisy. Moreover, since most uses of opaque projections require a prolonged period of darkness, high school students especially are enticed toward distraction or activity under-cover of darkness which is not related to the subject under discussion.

With transparencies, one must be careful to avoid making the same errors mentioned in the discussion on slides (too much text, too much color, elementary content, and many, too many selections). Here, also, the effective teacher must shun the tendency to use *typewritten* selections since type does not carry the impact that printing does. Most typewritten materials are too light, too uniform, and too familiar in layout to impress most students. Once the slide or transparency has been deemed necessary and the most effective lay-out decided upon, the task of construction should be delegated to draftsmen or artists *under the supervision of the teacher or the coordinator*. If technical help is not available, then the typed materials may be used *if* they are kept *short, simple,* and wherever possible, in *outline form*.

Filmstrips should be used in accordance with the rules suggested for films, slides, and other projections since they carry the same advantages and disadvantages. Filmstrips, of course, may be used in conjunction with either live oral commentary or prepared recordings. In the latter instance, extra care must be taken to synchronize perfectly between the audio and visual materials or the speaker will find himself having to deal with laughter, disappointment, or indifference.

Recordings, as supplementary aids, have been very popular for some time. This is due, for the most part, to the availability of a wider range of materials which have been more faithfully reproduced. Recordings carry the advantages of: (1) ease of use; (2) some measure of flexibility; (3) familiarity (we listen more than we read); and (4) dramatization. Through the use of recordings (records or tape), the teacher brings to bear the force of the actualities related to the idea, action, or program under discussion. For example, in support of the major point on self-sacrifice, the speaker might well employ the words and voice of John Kennedy urging Americans to "ask not what your country can do for you but what you can do for your country." Obviously, by quoting Kennedy, the speaker may still use those thoughts to support his major point but he will have lost the added impact of the personality and the original mood.

Adherence to the general rules mentioned earlier (relevance appropriateness, technical adequacy, and proper conception) is as important a requirement in the use of recordings as it is for any visual material. Further, recordings must be previewed, introduced, and concluded by the speaker if they are to be of maximum benefit. During the preview, the speaker should be especially concerned that the quality of the reproduction be *under the same degree of amplification as would be required during the actual presentation*. What sounds adequate in one's office may very well prove inadequate when amplified to the degree necessary for comprehension in a large lecture hall. Finally, the speaker must always prepare a reserve written copy of the text in case he should have to quote if the phonograph breaks down.

Displays

As with mechanical aids, the various *displays* (maps, charts, models, etc.) must adhere to the general rules cited for audio-visual material. Moreover, certain basic considerations peculiar to this type of material must be a part of the over-all planning. Instructors must consider the impact of the nonverbal aspects of the displays as well as to that of the oral or written text. Obviously, unusual size, offensive color, confusing placement of labels, and poor sequence can be as harmful to printed material as to three-dimensional models. Each special type of display has its additional requirements for effective use.

Maps, whether of real or hypothetical places, have as their chief function the graphic representation of distance, direction, location, size, and the various relationships which exist between these factors. Recent developments in the form of overlays, color, and three-dimensional representations have increased the use of maps as visual supplements to a presentation. Proper use of maps requires extreme care in avoiding the dominance of size, color, or detail. The focus of attention should be *automatically* evident whenever a map is employed; if the educator has to spend extra time in directing (and maintaining) the auditors' attention, then the map is not suited to the presentation. Furthermore, if certain representations such as boundaries or rivers have to be explained away because the map is outdated by the facts, then it ought not to be used.

Charts, like many maps, are useful for their representation of simple relations and for their ability to provide total impressions. If they adhere to the general rules discussed earlier, and if they demonstrate simplicity and clarity above all, charts prove to be very effective supplements. Of all possible versions, the *striptease* chart carries the greatest impact since it has the advantage of controlling attention and providing a "joy of discovery" which remain important factors in productive communication. Charts of this type should be planned carefully enough to provide for a list (short phrases, properly designated by number, spacing, dots, coloring, etc.) which can be covered in such fashion as to permit individual revelation of each item. While large charts can be constructed, transparencies work better unless the group is small enough to permit the use of charts which are not larger than four feet by four feet. Anything larger introduces an element of distraction in the physical dexterity required of the instructor in pointing to items, stripping the covers from each item, etc.

For efficient representation of statistical relations and interpretations, *graphs* can hardly be surpassed. Each form of graph has its own chief strength in such presentations. For example, line graphs (those usually associated with showing company sales progress) are the most effective in showing the direction and scope of various trends. Here time continuity is an important factor and is usually charted against units such as number of incidents, percentages, etc. Along one axis (usually the horizontal) days, weeks, months, years, or decades are plotted while the other axis (usually the vertical) records the unit factors under consideration. The bar graph, on the other hand, can best demonstrate quantitative relations. Continuity of time is of secondary importance in such relationships. The number of lives lost in each of the major earthquakes during the last century would be shown in a bar graph which used the vertical axis to display total numbers and the horizontal to record the time and place of the disaster. The pie graph's major strength is that it focuses upon proportions. In one view (in a diagram shaped in the form of a circle cut up according to percentage units), the audience can be made to see how the various parts of a whole relate to the whole and to each other. When used with discretion, appropriate symbols, cartoons, and pictures serve to accentuate the relationships shown. For example, if the graph (in any of the forms mentioned) were concerned with student population at various colleges or in various disciplines, small proportional cut-outs of human figures would enhance the impression.

Writing boards are quite popular in industrial presentations. Flannel boards, flip charts, and magnetic boards are used much more widely than blackboards. Simplicity is a basic rule which cannot be ignored in the use of these materials. The advantage of the "unfolding" principle of learning is quite well demonstrated by the effective use of the various boards. The student is introduced to the information bit by bit in both oral and visual forms, at a speed which can be suited to his varying ability to comprehend. Important, also, is the flexibility of the boards. Concepts emerging from the discussion can be immediately visualized and developed as the occasion demands. To maintain these advantages, the speaker must make certain to avoid crowding, poor handwriting, excessive speed, dropping items (made of chalk, magnets, or flannel), leaving materials exposed beyond need, and other errors of this nature. He must also avoid the tendency to display the obvious or the insignificant merely because he feels "something must be shown."

Physical representations (models, displays, mock-ups, and the like) have the advantage of presenting a view of the concept or program which appeals to more than one sense. The three-dimensional view (aided on occasion by movement) helps maintain the students' interest. The realism of an actual satellite, a new math model, an Indian artifact, or a teaching machine arouses interest and provides an appreciation and understanding which verbal explanations cannot hope to do. Nevertheless, it must be remembered that the model is *merely an aid* and should be used for reasons other than interest.

The possibilities of audio-visual material as tools in the learning process have justifiably occupied entire textbooks. Here, only the most important aspects have been discussed. Complete understanding can come only through individual study and guided practice in the preparation and use of the broad types mentioned here. But it should be remembered that, insofar as they are partners in the teaching-learning experience, both teacher and pupil are encouraged to follow the suggestions for effective use of audio-visual material.

SELECTED READINGS

Haas, K. B., and H. Q. Packer. *Preparation and Use of Visual Aids.* Englewood Cliffs, N.J.: Prentice-Hall, Inc., 1950.

Jayne, C. D. "A Study of the Relations Between Teaching Procedures and Educational Outcomes." *Journal of Experimental Education,* XIV (1954), 101–34.

Likert, R. "A Neglected Factor in Communications." *Audio-Visual Communications Review,* II (Summer, 1954), 163–77.

Wittich, W. A., and F. Schuller. *Audio-Visual Materials: Their Nature and Use.* New York: Harper & Row, Publishers, 1953.

B *cooperating in speech and hearing therapy*

Although the incidence of speech and hearing disorders in high school populations is somewhat less than in comparable elementary school populations, the need for providing therapy and guidance for high school pupils with speech and hearing deficiencies is no less urgent. Many pupils with these disorders reach high school without having received any therapy whatever; others, even with the benefit of remedial treatment in grade school, have not succeeded in overcoming their problems. Still others may have developed a speech or hearing difficulty in early adolescence. While fewer than in the lower grades, speech and hearing problems among high school pupils are likely to be more complex, often more severe, and therefore more difficult to treat than those of younger children.

Many high schools provide the special services of a speech and hearing therapist. With or without the benefit of such trained personnel, the classroom teacher performs a major role in assisting the child with a speech or hearing disorder. However, under no circumstances should the classroom teacher, untrained in speech and hearing therapy, assume major responsibility for diagnosing or performing other specialized functions of a therapist. There are nevertheless important ways in which the teacher may and should participate effectively and confidently in speech and hearing therapy.

The following paragraphs, adapted from *A Guidebook for Teaching Speaking and Listening* (Washington State Speech Association, 1960), outline three significant and essential steps which a classroom teacher may take in assisting pupils with speech or hearing disorders. These steps include: *locating, assisting in diagnosis, and participating discreetly in actual remedial instruction.*

THE TEACHER'S ROLE IN SPEECH AND HEARING THERAPY[1]

1. The teacher should take steps *to locate* children with speech or hearing handicaps. In those schools served by resident or itinerant speech therapists, systematic surveys will normally be carried out. Schools without therapists must depend largely upon classroom teachers for locating these children. In both instances the teacher performs a valuable service. To help locate children with hearing or speech handicaps, the teacher must understand what to look for. In a general way, speech is defective when it deviates so far from the norm that it calls attention to itself, or when it seriously interferes with communication. The defect may be one involving articulation—the forming and joining of speech sounds; it may concern voice, such as serious problems of loudness, pitch, or quality; or the speech defect may be stuttering. These three constitute the most common types of speech disorders found in the classroom.

The classroom teacher must also learn to recognize and locate pupils with hearing losses. In addition to consulting the health records of his pupils for reports on hearing tests, the teacher should be alert to the common symptoms of hearing loss in his pupils, such as inattention, confusion, apparent straining to hear, failing to follow directions, etc.

The teacher should never assume that the pupil's speech or hearing problem is being cared for. He should call it to the attention of the therapist or school principal once a pupil demonstrates serious speech or hearing difficulty in class.

2. The teacher may assist *in securing a diagnosis* of the speech or hearing problem. Whether referral is made to a local speech therapist or to one of the various clinics available in nearby cities, colleges, or

---

[1] Reproduced here in abridged form by permission of the authors, John M. Palmer and Oliver W. Nelson, University of Washington.

universities, the teacher can furnish information which may prove invaluable in securing an appropriate diagnosis of the problem. To prepare himself to supply such information, the teacher should take especial care to observe the child—his personality, his social tendencies, his language, study habits, school attendance record, as well as the nature of his speech or hearing behavior.

3. The teacher should *participate in the program of treatment* and rehabilitation. Once a diagnosis of the speech or hearing problem and prescription for treatment have been secured from appropriate sources, the teacher is in a vital position to assist in the child's retraining program.

He should continue to furnish helpful information to the therapist regarding the child and his problem. But even more significant, he should learn from the therapist what he can and should do in the classroom to reinforce learning initiated by the therapist. He should guide the child along lines suggested by the therapist, and find ways of helping the child discover his rightful place in the peer group. In a general way, this assistance tends to fall into two major categories: (A) providing the appropriate psychological climate in the classroom, and (B) carrying out specific guidance practices.

A. Classroom atmosphere is a matter of special importance in the guidance of children with communication disorders. At this point let us reemphasize the need for establishing an air of friendliness in dealing with all pupils, exhibiting patience and objectivity in personal behavior, being genuinely interested in all pupils and their welfare, and showing sincere enthusiasm for the work at hand. Such a climate may also be developed by bringing other members of the class into the "program of treatment." Youngsters with normal speech and hearing need to develop some appreciation of the handicapped child and his problem. They should learn how to live with people less fortunate than themselves—how to respond to these people appropriately in and out of class.

B. The classroom teacher may carry out certain specific guidance practices for the handicapped child. For the hard of hearing pupil, such practices may include: (1) checking the hearing aid to be sure that it is both operative and operating during class; (2) speaking directly to the child, making sure that he understands directions; (3) seating him in the front of the room, preferably near windows so as to enable him better to see the faces of other class members; (4) checking on his vocabulary recognition; (5) reinforcing his therapy by expecting him to perform in class up to his recognized limits; (6) being tolerant of errors of understanding which are bound to appear.

For the pupil with a speech handicap similar measures may be taken. While the nature of the problem will dictate its own special remedial activities, certain general guidelines for classroom "therapy" may be suggested: (1) Provide the child with opportunity to practice what he has learned in the special speech lesson. (2) Reward the pupil's efforts, although in actual achievement he may be somewhat below the mark; always try to understand the pupil and his problem. Obviously, the speech therapist will offer specific remedial suggestions according to whether the problem is stuttering, faulty articulation, inadequate voice, or a problem of hearing. But fully as important for the teacher to know is that the corrective prescription will be governed by the over-all nature of the handicapped child. Thus it is essential that the teacher follow closely the agreed-upon plan of treatment prescribed for each individual child. (3) Encourage the child by commending him for meeting basic class assignments. Avoid such specific remarks as "Excellent, John, you didn't stutter once in your report today, did you?"; such comments, while seemingly constructive, actually are not since they suggest that, above all, it is most important that the child *avoid stuttering.*

SELECTED REFERENCES

Eisenson, Jon, and Mardel Ogilvie. *Speech Correction in the Schools,* 2nd ed. New York : The Macmillan Company, 1957.

Fairbanks, Grant. *Voice and Articulation Drillbook,* 2nd ed. New York: Harper & Row, Publishers, 1960.

Johnson, Wendell, Spencer F. Brown, James F. Curtis, Clarence W. Edney, and Jacqueline Keaster. *Speech Handicapped School Children,* 3rd ed. New York : Harper & Row, Publishers, 1967.

Van Riper, Charles W. *Speech Correction: Principles and Methods,* 4th ed. Englewood Cliffs, N. J. : Prentice-Hall, Inc., 1963.

C speech resources: anthologies, films, and recordings

ANTHOLOGIES

One-act plays

Deseo, Lydia G., and Hulda M. Phelps. *Looking at Life through Drama.* New York: The Abingdon Press, 1931.

Webber and Webster, eds. *Short Plays for Junior and Senior High School.* Boston: Houghton Mifflin Company.

Zachar, Irwin J., ed. *Plays as Experience,* rev. ed. New York: The Odyssey Press, Inc., 1962.

Poetry

Reeves, James, ed. *The Cassell Book of English Poetry.* London: Cassell & Co., Ltd., 1965.

Sitwell, Dame Edith, ed. *The Atlantic Book of British and American Poetry.* Boston: Little, Brown and Company, 1958.

Untermeyer, Louis, ed. *Modern American Poetry.* New York: Harcourt, Brace & World, Inc., 1950.

———————, and Carter Davidson. *Poetry, Its Appreciation and Enjoyment.* New York : Harcourt, Brace & World, Inc., 1934.

Van Doren, Mark. *Introduction to Poetry.* New York: Holt, Rinehart & Winston, Inc., 1951.

Short stories

Bullard, Catherine, and Julia Maus, eds. *Tall Tales and Short.* New York : Holt, Rinehart & Winston, Inc., 1938.

Fenton, Charles A., ed. *The Best Stories of World War II.* New York : The Viking Press, Inc., 1957.

Foley, Martha, ed. *The Best American Short Stories.* Boston : Houghton Mifflin Company, 1965.

Kelley, Robert F., ed. *The Sportsman's Anthology.* New York : Howell, Soskin and Co., 1944.

Linscott, Robert N., ed. *The Best American Humorous Short Stories.* New York : Random House, Inc., 1945.

FILMS*

Communication

	Length	*Source*
Communication: Story of Its Development	11 m	Coronet
Do Words Ever Fool You?	11 m	Coronet
Effective Listening	12 m	McGraw
Say What You Mean	20 m	McGraw
Why Do People Misunderstand Each Other?	30 m	NET

---

* *Key to sources of films:*

Coronet—Coronet Films, Coronet Building, Chicago, Illinois.

McGraw—McGraw-Hill Book Company, Text-Film Department, 330 West 42nd Street, New York, New York.

NET—NET Film Service, Audio - Visual Center, Indiana University, Bloomington, Ind.

YAF—Young America Films, Inc., 18 East 41st Street, New York, New York.

Discussion

Group Discussion	12 m	YAF
Judging Facts	11 m	Coronet
Let's Discuss It	9 m	McGraw

Short talks

Build Your Vocabulary	11 m	Coronet
Making Sense With Outlines	11 m	Coronet
Speech: Planning Your Talk	13 m	YAF
Using Visuals in Your Speech	14 m	YAF

Oral interpretation

Literature Appreciation: How to Read Essays	13-1/2 m	Coronet
Literature Appreciation: How to Read Plays	11 m	Coronet
Literature Appreciation: How to Read Poetry	11 m	Coronet

RECORDINGS

Consult catalogs of such distributors as :

Caedmon Sales Corporation, 227 Fifth Avenue, New York, New York.

Columbia Records, Educational Division, 779 Seventh Avenue, New York, New York.

Decca Distributing Corporation, 50 West 57th Street, New York, New York.

Encyclopaedia Britannica Films, 1144 Wilmette Avenue, Wilmette, Illinois.

National Council of Teachers of English, 704 South Sixth Street, Champaign, Illinois.

RCA Victor, Camden, New Jersey.

index

Abstracting, 35–36
Adolescence and adolescents
    as class members, 51–52
    general characteristics of, 45–46
    as individuals, 51, 129
    language characteristics of high
        school pupils, 48–50
    social organization of, 52
Aggertt, Otis, 186
Arnold, Carroll C., 109
Articulation, 291
Arts (fine and applied), 270–284
    reciprocal relations, 271–274
    special problems of, 274
    strategies for, 278–283
Aschner, M. J. McCue, 114
Atmosphere for learning, 63–64 (see
        also Climate, classroom)
Attitudes, 24–25
Audio-visual material, 302–312
    kinds, 307–312
Auer, J. Jeffrey, 97

Bales, Robert F., 40
Barr, A. S., 65, 67
Barriers, 33–42
Barzizza, 5
Bennett, Margaret E., 98
Bernstein, Basil, 36
Bining, Arthur C. and David H., 76
Biology, 19
Bodily action, 28, 37, 295–301
    gesture, 298
    movement, 299–300
    posture, 297
Borgatta, Edgar F., 40
Bowen, Elbert R., 186

Brauner, Charles, 254
Bruner, Jerome, 277
Bryant, Donald C., 204, 213

Carpenter, Helen M., 230
Carrell, James A., 291, 295
Cartwright, Dorwin, 100
Cassel, Russell N., 65
Cassirer, Ernst, 262
Catharsis, 20, 98
Chesler, Mark, 133
Clark, Richard W., 66, 68
Climate, classroom
    physical, 57–63
    psychological, 63–64
    teacher's role in determining, 64–68
Cognition, 16
Coleman, James S., 47
Communication (see also Oral Com-
        munication, Speaking and
        Listening)
    importance of, 4
    learning, 3–8
    mental health, 20
    models of, 8–10
    principles, 29–31
    religion, 22
    social reform, 21–22
Concept of environments, 6, 7, 8, 33
Cox, C. Benjamin, 231, 234, 250, 251
Creativity, 18, 19, 20, 31, 272
Criticism, 82–90
    defined, 83
    guidelines for effective speech
        criticism, 87–89
    methods of, 83–85

Cromarty, J. Norman, 210
Crowell, Laura I., 41, 66–67, 105, 108, 110

da Feltre, Vittorino, 5
Dale, Edgar, 169
Daydreaming, 7
Deseo, Lydia G., 127
Deutsch, Karl W., 6
Dewey, John, 21–22
    five steps of, 116
Dialogue, 261–264
Discussion, 93–121
    classroom application of, 115–120
    defined, 94
    form of speaking, 76
    guidelines for using, 101–115
    qualities of good discussion, 95–96
    topics, 101–103
    types of, as determined by
        leadership, 98–99, 107, 110–111
        purpose, 97–98
        time and place, 96–97
    values and limitations of, 99–100
Dramatization (drama, dramatics, creative drama, educational dramatics), 122–151 (*see also* Role-playing)
    classroom application of, 147–149
    defined, 123–125
    evaluating dramatics, 145–147
    guidelines for using, 126–132
        formal drama, 139–144
        informal drama, 128–132
        role-playing, 132–136
        semi-formal drama, 136–139
    guiding the audience, 144–145
    values and limitations of, 125–126
Duncker, Karl, 254
Dyce, J. R., 137

Education, theories of, 5–6
Empathy, 273–274
English, 203–229
    problems, 206–208
    reciprocal relations, 78, 209–210
    strategies for, 210–228
    trends in, 208–209
Environment, internal and external, 6, 7, 19, 30 (*see also* Climate)

Evaluation, 82–90
    defined, 83
    of discussion, 105–106, 109–112
    of formal dramatic activities, 145–147
    of oral reading, 193–196
    of short talks, 169–171
    of unit or procedure, 83–85
Evidence, tests of, 109–110, 170
Ewbank, H. L., 97
Extempore speaking (*see* Short talks)

Feedback, 37
Fessenden, Seth A., 53
Fest, Thorrell B., 93
Finkbeiner, Joy D., 38, 39
Fleming, William, 271–272
Fletcher, John Gould, 183
Fox, Robert, 133
Friedlander, Bernard, 277

Gesture, 28 (*see also* Bodily action)
Grimes, Wilma H., 176
Guth, Hans, 206, 208, 209

Haley, Jay D., 25
Halsey, Ashley, Jr., 248
Hance, Kenneth G., 94, 97
Hare, A. Paul, 40
Hargis, Clara A. and Donald B., 79
Harnack, R. Victor, 93
Hart, Frank W., 65
Hayakawa, S. I., 35–36, 214, 215
Hobbes, Thomas, 21
Hora, Thomas, 17
Hubbard, Eleanore, 125, 148

Images, 7, 8, 9, 17, 20

Jarolimek, John, 232
Jennings, Helen H., 54
Jesuits, 5
Johns, W. Lloyd, 65
Joyce, James, 19

Kerikas, E. J., 88
Kingsley, Mary H., 296

Language, 11, 27–28, 34, 36, 37, 41
LaRusso, Dominic A., 26, 30, 298,
    303, 304
Learning
  approaches to, 67
  climate for, 56, 70
  effectiveness, 70
  theories of, 3, 5, 6, 15, 17, 34, 52–62
Lee, Charlotte, 190
Lee, Irving J., 115
Lewis, Thomas R., 39
"Library-classroom Plan" (see
    Strategies in English)
Likert, R., 304
Lindgren, Henry C., vii, viii
Listening, 38–40, 192
  habits of, 39–40
Literature (see English, Oral inter-
    pretation)
Loban, Walter, 204, 208, 226
Long, A. L., 303

McBurney, James H., 94, 97, 166
McClendon, Jonathan C., 77
McCutchen, S. P., 234
McKeon, Richard, 261
Martin, Harold C., 17
Massialas, Byron G., 231, 234, 250,
    251
Mathematics, teaching, 19, 253–269
  New Math, 258
  problems of, 78, 255–258
  reciprocal relations, 258–260
  strategies for, 260–268
Mattingly, Althea, 176
Mead, George, vii, 17, 25
Metaphors, 19
Miles, John R., 247
Miller, George A., vii
Models of human communication, 8
Montessori, Maria, 5
Motivation
  in English, 206–207
  in fine arts, 274
  general, 117
  in mathematics and science, 256–
    258
  in social studies, 232–233

Movement, 28 (see also Bodily action)
Music, 19

Nelson, Oliver W., 75
Ness, Ordean, 175, 182, 189
Nichols, Ralph G., 38, 39
Nonverbal activity, 9 (see also Bodily
    action)
Nyquist, Jody L., 219, 220

Ong, Walter J., 260
Oral communication (see also Speak-
    ing-listening)
  components, 23–29
  importance in learning and teach-
    ing, 3–8
  principles, 29–31
Oral interpretation of literature, 174–
    200
  application of, 197–198
  defined, 175–176
  guidelines for using, 179–191
  reading poetry, 189
  reading prose, 186–189
  values and limitations, 176–179
Ousley, Elmon, 244
Outlines
  for guiding discussion, 105–106, 118
  for literary analysis, 181–182
  principles for constructing, 159
  for short talks, 158–167
  for speech content analysis, 187–
    188
Overstreet, Harry, 17, 18, 25

Palmer, John M., 314
Parliamentary procedure, 244–247
Payne, Stanley L., 114
Pestalozzi, 5
Phelps, Hulda M., 127
Poetry, 189–190, 196
Polya, G., 253, 254, 255, 257, 262
Port Royalists, 5
Posture, 28
Practice, 3
Pronunciation, 291
  guidelines, 292–295
Psychiatrists, 18
Public speaking, 152–153

Quintilian, 68, 79

Rahskopf, Horace G., 298, 303
Rapoport, Anatol, 259
Rationalization, 8
Reading, 38
Responsibility, social, 30, 31, 36, 72
Rhetoric, 152
Rhythm, 19, 29, 270
Richards, I. A., 33
Riesman, David, 7
Robinson, Karl F., 88
Roethlisberger, F. J., 20
Rogers, Carl R., 20, 25, 40
Role-playing, 132–136
Rousseau, Jean-Jacques, 5
Ryans, David G., 65

Sayers, Dorothy L., 17
Schneiders, A. A., 46
Schwartz, Alfred, 84
Self, 11, 17, 31
Shaftel, Fannie R. and George, 132, 133
Short talks, 152–173
    classroom application of, 171–173
    defined, 153–154
    guidelines for using, 156–169
    listener's role in, 169–171
    qualities of good talks, 154–155
    types, 153–154
    values and limitations of, 155–156
Silence, 22
Skinner, B. F., 5
Smith, Ellen McComb, 222
Social studies, 230–252
    challenges of, 233–237
    reciprocal relations, 232–233
    strategies for, 237–251
Society, 11
Socio-drama (*see* Role-playing)
Sociogram, 52–54
Sociometrics, 52–54
Speaking-listening, 14–31
    components of, 23–29
    principles, 29–31
    role of, 14–23
    values, 14, 16, 17, 19, 21, 22

Speech activities
    bases for selecting, 70–80
    learning situation, 74–75
    reciprocal relations with subject matter, 75–76
    requirements for wise use, 80–81
    student needs and abilities, 72–73
    time limits, 73–74
Spender, Stephen, 224–225
Spolin, Viola, 132
Stevens, Leonard A., 39
Still, Dana, 38
Strategies, for teaching
    arts (fine and applied), 278–283
    English, 210–228
    mathematics, 259–268
    social studies, 237–251
Symbolism, 190
Symbols, 7, 28, 33, 34, 249

Teacher as person-communicator-educator, 64–68
Theory, 3, 5
Therapy, speech and hearing, 313–316
Thought, 26, 37, 63
Tiedeman, Stuart, 84
Tiffany, William R., 291–295
Topics
    for discussions, 101–103
    for short talks, 156–157

Unfolding, 30
Units, use of discussion in planning, 117–119

Verbal, 35–38
Vives, Juan Luis, 5
Voice, 29, 37, 288–295
    duration, 289–290
    loudness, 288
    pitch, 288–289
    quality, 290

Wagner, Russell H., 109
Walkup, Lewis E., 272–273

Ward, Winifred, 124
Weaver, Andrew Thomas, 175, 182, 189
Weiss, M. Jerry, 125
Wesley, Edgar B., 76
Whitehead, Alfred North, 255
Wilson, Woodrow, 4

Winans, James, 167
Wirth, Fremont P., 230
Witty, Paul, 65
Wolfe, Don M., 218, 227, 228
Wood, Ben D., 65
Wrage, Ernest J., 166
Wronski, Stanley P., 76